Asian Americans On War & Peace

Edited by Russell C. Leong
Don T. Nakanishi

AMERICAN FARMER

JAPS OR HINDUS NOT WANTED

Anti-Alien Ass'n

UCLA Asian American Studies Center Press

Asian Americans
On War
& Peace

Russell C. Leong
Don T. Nakanishi
Editors

ucla asian
american
studies
center
press

The articles in *Asian Americans on War & Peace* were selected from
and originally published in *Amerasia Journal* 27:3/28:1 (2001-2002),
and are copyrighted by the UCLA Asian American Studies Center Press
with the exception of the following which are copyrighted by the authors: "The Hip Hop Generation Can Call for Peace," ©2002, Jeff Chang;
"Notes from a New York Diary," by ©2002, Jessica Hagedorn; and,
"Thinking through Internment: 12/7 and 9/11," ©2002, Jerry Kang.

Printed in the United States of America.

Library of Congress Control Number: 2002103948
ISBN 0-934052-36-0

EDITORS   Russell C. Leong
                    Don T. Nakanishi

                                        ɑs

                                        ucla asian
                                        american
                                        studies
                                        center
                                        press

DESIGN/PRODUCTION   Mary Uyematsu Kao
EDITORIAL ASSISTANT Stephen Lee

PUBLISHER   UCLA Asian American Studies Center Press

Frontcover photographs:
"American Farmer—Japs or Hindus Not Wanted," Phoenix, Arizona,
February 6, 1935, United Press International; Mother and brother of
Japanese American soldier, Colorado River Relocation Center, Poston,
Arizona, 1944. Photographer unknown/WRA. (*Executive Order 9066*, Maisie
and Richard Conrat (Los Angeles: UCLA Asian American Studies Center, 1992); and
Sikh candlelight vigil at Central Park, New York City, September 15,
2001. © 2001, Corky Lee. All rights reserved.

Backcover image:
"A Reflection of Faith." Amatulaah Almarwani, executive secretary of
the Islamic Society of San Francisco, September 21, 2001. Photograph by
Yuri Miyatake, *Nichi Bei Times*.

Table of Contents

iii. Geopolitics

iv. Peace

Photographers:

Corky Lee has been documenting Asian American history through photography for over forty years. Self-described as "just 'an ABC (American-Born Chinese) from NYC' with ordinary photographic skills but with perhaps extraordinary will." The Museum of Chinese in the Americas held an exhibit of his work in 2001, titled "Not on the Menu: From Asian/Pacific Islander Roots to American Reality." He was hired by *Amerasia Journal* to cover the lives of Asian Pacific Americans in New York City after 9/11.

Eric Chang practices medicine professionally, while his passion for photography gives us a window into the region that borders the war in Afghanistan. The photographs by Chang were taken while in Central Asia before and immediately after 9/11.

Mary Uyematsu Kao has been photographing the Asian American experience since the early 1970s. She is publications coordinator for UCLA Asian American Studies Center.

Note on photographs: The boundaries of war and peace, and the linkages between racism, and internment and civil liberties, are vividly captured by three images on the cover of this book. These images span more than sixty years of American history, from the days before World War II to the days immediately following the attack on the World Trade Center. The central image, "American Farmer: Japs or Hindus not Wanted," is a United Press photograph from February 6, 1935. Signs such as this were commonly posted on ranches and farms in the Phoenix, Arizona area. The second photograph, circa 1944, is of a Japanese American family in an U.S. wartime internment camp: a mother and the brother of a deceased Nisei soldier who fought for the United States. The photograph was taken in the Colorado River Relocation Center, Poston, Arizona. The third photograph, taken by Corky Lee, is a Sikh candlelight vigil at Central Park, New York City on September 15, 2001. The gathering drew approximately 2,500 people from New York and New Jersey. Together, these images—of a white farmer, of an interned Japanese American family, and of a Sikh immigrant—form an agonizing triptych. This triptych reveals the convergence of political forces, which link the events of 9/11 with the longer history of Asians and South Asians in the United States.

War and Peace:
When Past and Future Became the Now

Russell C. Leong and Don T. Nakanishi

Asian Americans on War and Peace is the first book to respond to the tragic world events of September 11, 2001 from Asian American perspectives, from the vantage points of those whose lives and communities in America have been forged both by war and by peace. We are at a moment in our history, according to Roshni Rustomji-Kerns, when "the past and the future became the now."

We have always written in this moment—in the wake of war-torn worlds, among ashes of smoking cities, under white banners of peace. Refugees from our history, we reach back to places we once called home. Cavite. Nagasaki. Hiroshima. Manzanar. Poston. Heart Mountain. Manila. Seoul. Saigon. Bach Mai. Haiphong. Phnom Penh. Basra. Baghdad. New York. Karachi. Kabul. Kandahar. Ramallah. Jenin. Jerusalem.

Twenty-four scholars, writers, activists, and legal scholars have written for this collection. This volume foregrounds the geopolitical crisis of the continuing violence in Afghanistan and the Middle East, and also provides vital documentation of the Asian American, South Asian, and Islamic presence in America in the days before, and following, 9/11.

Their words are in effect, words written in the midst of crisis. Their words are alternatives to the rhetoric uttered by presidents and generals, politicians and pundits living in the East and in the West. Together, their voices reveal how Asians, Asian Americans, South Asians, Arabs, and others view the future of the planet in relation to the events of both yesterday and today.

These essays were written immediately after the World Trade Center attack and during the U.S. bombing of Afghanistan. Although the post-Taliban interim government has now emerged, the U.S., Britain, France, Russia, and China continue their "anti-terrorist" activities, while India and Pakistan remain on uneasy terms. President Bush has declared a new alignment of an "axis of evil" involving Iran, Iraq, and North Korea. Domestically, anti-terrorism and surveillance laws (USA Patriot Act) are on the books, and an untold number of individuals remain detained by the FBI and the INS. The crisis of war and peace continues in the Middle East, as Israelis and Palestinians wage violence upon each other.

Asian Americans on War and Peace is divided into four sections.

I. Worlds of Crisis provides both domestic and global viewpoints on the crisis that crosses national boundaries. Veteran journalist Helen Zia examines the atmosphere of xenophobia and racial profiling against Asian Americans. In her essay, she analyzes the relationship of 9/11 to the campaign finance debacle of 1996-1999, the spy mongering years of 1999-2000, and the role of Asian Americans, "especially immigrants from China, India, and Pakistan," in the high tech industry. Novelist Jessica Hagedorn, in her "Notes from a New York Diary," provides insights into spiritual and material crisis. As a bystander at Ground Zero, Hagedorn juxtaposes the debris and human destruction of the World Trade Center to the Smokey Mountain refuse dump in the Philippines.

Roshni Rustomji-Kerns takes us on a journey—from her child-hood in Karachi in the 1940s to Lebanon, to living and teaching in Durham, Berkeley, and Sonoma. In her memoir, she links all the wars she has experienced in her life:

The next morning, the past and the future became the now. The "there" of the rumors of a savage war became the "here"of refugees. People, strangers, suddenly appeared, flooding the streets of Karachi.

In the next essay, Vijay Prashad of Trinity College delves into the machinations of U.S./European oil interests in the Gulf, the role of the CIA in maintaining Western interests in the Middle East, and the contradictions of global capitalism in the current crisis. Writer Amitava Kumar shares his poetic dispatches to America and to India, stating, "the twin towers were like alphabets linked to words like America and power and security. The towers were destroyed by men who fiendishly read that meaning in a clear way." Russell C. Leong, the editor of *Amerasia Journal*, in his poem, "Today," asks a difficult question: "But what if the enemy lurks within?"

II. Civil Liberties and Internment examines the premises behind the analogy of the terrorist attacks of 9/II/01, and the Pearl Harbor attack of 12/7/41 in connection to racial profiling and civil liberties today. Jerry Kang, a legal scholar at UCLA, draws parallels between the curtailments of civil liberties for newly interned Arab and South Asians with the internment of 120,000 Japanese Americans sixty years ago. Amplifying Kang's argument, Eric K. Yamamoto, of the William S. Richardson School of Law, University of Hawaii at Manoa, and Susan Kiyomi Serrano, of the Equal Justice Society at the same school, state that:

> national security crises coupled with racism or nativism and backed by the force of law generate deep and lasting social injustice. Court rulings, in particular, legitimize even extreme, albeit popular, governmental actions—in the 1940s, the internment. . .today, potentially, groundless detentions, secret trials and deportations and government racial profiling and harassment.

Writer Frank Chin, in his statement, denounces the Japanese American and Chinese American civic organizations—the JACL (Japanese American Citizens League) and the OCA (Organization of Chinese Americans) for not living up to their missions as "civil rights organizations" during moments of political crisis.

Two writers in their accounts further personify the crisis of racial profiling. Mustafa Bayoumi, of Brooklyn College, in his essay, "How does it feel to be a problem?" probes into the status of Arab Americans having "to contend with fitting their mixed hues into the primary colors of the state." He uncovers the complexity of what it means to be brown: from Syrian immigrants in 1909 to recent immigrants from the Middle East, Armenia, and Western Asia. Stephen Lee, who received his MA in Asian American Studies at UCLA, grew up in New Mexico. His personal account, "What Does

Danger Look Like?" explores the relationship of the World War II Santa Fe internment camp to current calls for the internment of civilians.

The work of poets rounds out this section: San Francisco poet laureate Janice Mirikitani recounts her experience of the Japanese American internment, of "Those camps containing the innocent. Children behind barbed wire." Chicago-based poet Ifti Nasim, in his poem, states: "I feel like Rosa Parks and there is no bus for me/ because I am not only two shades darker than an average white man/but I am also a Muslim."

III. Geopolitics considers the events before and after "9/11" from multiple historical, humanistic, and theoretical perspectives. An historian of modern Chinese political thought, Arif Dirlik in his essay, "Colonialism, Globalization, and Culture" critiques the ways in which colonialism, globalization, and modernity affect how Eastern and Western societies think about, and rationalize, their histories. Dirlik reminds us that "capitalism and colonialism also have histories, and that they may not have the same meaning, or the same consequences, at all times or places."

In a recent talk at Wayne State University, Grace Lee Boggs recounts her sixty years as a philosopher, activist, and theoretician. She states that "twenty-first century revolutionaries need new ideas and strategies for our anti-systemic struggles and academics also need new paradigms for their work." She points to Detroit as a model of hope and progress: "the destruction of the World Trade Center that had taken place in five seconds before the eyes of the whole world on September 11 has been taking place in slow motion over the last fifty years in Detroit, but. . .a new society is rising up from the ashes."

Vinay Lal, a UCLA historian specializing in South Asia, was in India during the 9/11 crisis, and reports on the crisis from the perspective of South Asian media, together with an examination of the ways in which Afghanistan, Pakistan, and India share an intertwined history. "Sandwiched between the Islamic and Indic worlds, Afghanistan has been seen as belonging to neither, and has suffered the fate of those who cannot be accommodated within the known categories," Lal states.

David Palumbo-Liu of Stanford University in his essay decries American-style "national identity thinking which targets ethnics, immigrants, diasporics." This dangerous and volatile trend, Palumbo-Liu contends, is premised upon the idea that the West represents "civilization" as we know it; and the enemy will be "non-civilized," e.g., exotic varieties of terrorists, Islamic fundamentalists, and U.S. minorities."

IV. Peace, the final section, contains essays which address peace-making—reasons to move toward peace, the problems involved, and the potential for creating a world different from the past hundred years of warfare. The section is followed by a chronology compiled by Stephen Lee of September 11 events in relation to hate crimes and community responses within the U.S.

James N. Yamazaki, a pediatrician, fought in the European Theater during World War II and was imprisoned by the Germans following the Battle of the Bulge. After the war, he joined the Atomic Bomb Casualty Commission and was sent to Japan to study the effects of nuclear radiation on child survivors in Hiroshima and Nagasaki. In his essay, he probes into the ethnical, technological, and human questions around September 11 in relation to the usage of nuclear weapons in the future. He states: "Neutralizing the threat of nuclear weapons and other weapons of mass destruction must be the primary objective of all people."

Jeff Chang, author of *Can't Stop, Won't Stop: A Political and Cultural History of the Hip-Hop Generation*, surveys the origins of hip-hop in the 1970s Jamaican music and culture of defiance. He contends that the hip-hop generation is in a unique position to understand wars of survival—cultural, political, and social—and thus can contribute to peace around this crisis.

Attorney Angela E. Oh, a member of the Los Angeles City Human Relations Commission and a Buddhist priest, puts forth "A Call to Humanity," asking us to embrace grief and sorrow as an extension of compassion. Vietnam War veteran and law activist Michael F. Yamamoto has "seen firsthand who dies in war, and it is the children, theirs and ours. . . . My experience with the 'official body count' is a pile of kids, too young to comprehend the political forces that have sacrificed their lives and too fully indoctrinated to turn back, wounded and dead before they can finish growing up." He, too, urges us to "bless the peacemakers," because he sees no other choice.

In the closing essay of this volume, Mari J. Matsuda raises the peace banner and challenges us anew. A professor of law at Georgetown Law School, Matsuda chooses to organize around peace, but

> not the idealized peace of the summer of love. No lilac in my hand this time. This is a cold, calculating peace activist. Someone out there wants to kill me, and I have to figure out how to save my own life out of the history I know and the tools I have. . . .

She continues: "Asian Americans know of mistakes made in the name of war. My grandmother waited behind barbed wire for her son to come home from World War II. Military necessity is never an excuse I can accept without question." Matsuda then calls upon us to action: "This time, march to save your own life. I call on Asian Americans to join the new peace movement."

For the past thirty years, the UCLA Asian American Studies Center through its Press and its scholarly journal, *Amerasia Journal*, from which a number of these articles originated, has been at the forefront of shaping the critical dialogue around Asians in the Americas in relation to war and peace. We join activists, students, and scholars throughout the world who continue to question both the ongoing crisis of the American presence in the Middle East, and the concurrent crisis of civil liberties and democracy in the United States.

RUSSELL C. LEONG is Editor of *Amerasia Journal* and Adjunct Professor of English at UCLA.

DON T. NAKANISHI is Director of the UCLA Asian American Studies Center and Professor of Education and Asian American Studies.

The former Hiroshima Prefectural Building for Promotion of Industry, which was preserved as the "Atomic Bomb Dome."
Both images at pegasus.phys.saga-u.ac.jp/peace

CIVILIZATION IS *SAMSARA* INSTITUTIONALIZED.

—ALBERT SAIJO

I. WORLDS OF CRISIS

Lin Meijuon, Chen Xian and Lin An Le (left to right) march alongside NAPS (National Association for Prevention of Starvation) handing out American flags printed by Oriental Art Printing Company, Chinatown, New York City, September 15, 2001.

©2001, Corky Lee

Chung toi di cac chua tai San
Diego de thap nen cau nguyen
cho Anh Chi Em tu nan tren
nuoc My

Sign on bus of Buddhist prayergivers: We are going to
all Buddhist Temples in San Diego to pray for all the
victims that were killed in the tragedy of terrorism in
the USA. (translation for Vietnamese)

Only two days after the horrific September 11 events, these organizers pulled together an impressive pan-Asian coalition to plan a press conference and a national candlelight vigil at the Japanese American National Memorial on the mall. The site memorial was built to commemorate Japanese American soldiers who fought and died for our country during World War II, as well as the Japanese American families who were interned in American concentration camps after Pearl Harbor. The organizers' purpose: to draw attention to the need for tolerance and restraint in the face of hate crimes and domestic terrorism against Arab, Muslim and South Asian Americans. Their remarkable efforts succeeded in garnering the attention of the national media, other civil rights groups, members of Congress, and even the White House.

This example stands in sharp contrast to those Asian Americans who might find solace in the false notion that yellow Americans won't be racially profiled—at least not right away. These folks must not have noticed how the news blared "SECOND PEARL HARBOR," a comparison that was thin on the facts but full of the venom reserved for especially evil enemies. Even as pundits grasped at the Pearl Harbor metaphor, their studied failure to name the architect of the World Trade Center was glaring. The acclaimed Minoru Yamasaki, a second-generation Japanese American, had designed many American architectural landmarks, and the World Trade Center was his crowning glory. Regarding this point, I am certain of two things: first, that every newsroom covering the continual imagery of the Twin Towers' destruction was aware that the towers were designed by Yamasaki. Second, I am certain that it was a deliberate decision not to mention this detail, lest the Asianness of the icons' creator detract from the theme of an America under kamikaze attack.

I arrived in Washington on the evening of September 10 to be part of a panel discussion at the Smithsonian on the occasion of a new exhibit, "On Gold Mountain," tracing the history of Chinese Americans. The Asian American exhibit and the panel discussion were evidence of historian Franklin Odo's efforts to keep Asian Americans in American history, to reclaim our "MIH" Missing-In-History past. On September 11, we were to discuss issues facing Chinese Americans.

There were certainly no shortage of topics—for example, the spy plane incident over China's Hainan island that occurred only five months earlier, disgorging a vile, subcortical anti-Chinese, anti-Asian racism that would have made the Exclusionists of the 1800s proud. Talk show hosts called for the internment of Chinese Americans and made on-air "ching-chong" calls to people with Chinese surnames, picked at random from phone books. The American Society of Newspaper Editors, whose members are the top editors of the nation's newspapers, hooted and howled at a yellow-face skit about the incident that was performed at their convention—and they refused to apologize even after one of their Chinese American interns called them on their racism.

But even before the spy plane incident, the Committee of 100 had conducted its landmark survey on American attitudes toward Chinese and Asian Americans. The results included these points:

- 34% of those polled believe Chinese Americans are more loyal to the People's Republic of China than to their country, the United States of America.
- 32% believe that Chinese Americans have too much influence on high technology.
- 42% believe that Chinese Americans are likely to pass U.S. secrets to China.
- 68% feel negative about Chinese Americans and Asian Americans.

The poll had some other "surprises." Pollsters Yankelovich and Co. asked two separate samples of Americans the same questions—one group was asked about *Chinese* Americans and the other about *Asian* Americans. There was no statistical difference in responses by the two samples. So here was hard evidence of the "racial lumping" that is so well-known to every Asian American kid who was ever called the slur of another Asian ethnicity.

Then there was the racial profiling of former Los Alamos nuclear scientist Wen Ho Lee. Though Dr. Lee was born and raised in Taiwan, his ethnicity was enough to make him the only person to be investigated as a suspected spy, even though there were dozens of other European Americans at Los Alamos who had the same access to nuclear information and to PRC scientists as Dr. Lee. The book I co-authored with Dr. Lee details how he was racially profiled by the U.S. government: when the FBI couldn't find any evidence of spying, they charged him instead with fifty-nine counts of "mishandling of classified information," including thirty life sentences, even though no one had ever been similarly charged for mishandling classified information. John Deutch, the former CIA director, had downloaded details of the CIA's international intelligence network, onto diskettes and his home com-

Youth Speak Out, September 22, 2001, New York University.
© 2001, Corky Lee

puter, which was linked to the Internet. He could not account for what happened to those diskettes. Deutch, a white male, received a mere slap on the wrist, and then a Presidential pardon; he is now teaching at MIT. In contrast, Wen Ho Lee spent nine months in solitary confinement, where he was held in chains and manacles under "pretrial detention." He was only released after he pled guilty to one of the counts against him; the government dropped the other fifty-eight charges. Unfortunately, there are many reports from other Asian American scientists who have also been racially profiled.

Looking forward, it seems clear that the chill over Asian Americans during the campaign finance headlines of 1996-99 and the spy mongering years of 1999-2000 were only the "tip of the egg roll," as Senator Robert Brownback (R-Kansas) quipped. Those disturbing and harmful episodes have set the stage for something worse yet to come. Historically, xenophobia and racism heighten during times of economic depression. Yet the anti-Asian 1990s were marked by unprecedented prosperity, a high tech boom driven by the intellectual and entrepreneurial creativity of Asian Americans, especially immigrants from China, India, and Pakistan. Would the economic tailspin of 2001 bring more scapegoating for Asian Americans? How can Asian American communities prepare for the possible onslaught?

Helen Zia

These were some of the issues to discuss on September 11, 2001 for the panel at the Smithsonian. The event, of course, never happened. But racial profiling against "Middle Eastern-appearing people" followed with a vengeance—more than 700 reported hate incidents in only a few weeks, with several deaths. Among them were South Asian Americans, particularly members of the Sikh faith. To the list of those killed by international terrorists, we now have a list of people killed in hate crimes by domestic terrorists.

Each day after September 11 has brought on some new uncertainty—and some new erosion of the principles that have made our country great. Yesterday it was the argument of Peggy Noonan, a *Wall Street Journal* columnist who claimed that we must all "accept the necessity of racial profiling." She said that all Americans have to sacrifice some of our liberties in this post-September 11 world. If it turned out that blond women in blue jeans like her were profiled as terrorists, she said, she wouldn't like it but she would "suck it up" and accept it. I said to myself, yes, so generously offered by someone who doesn't truly expect such a request to be asked of her.

I wondered how she would respond if the blond teenage son she mentioned in her column were subjected to profiling at high schools because law enforcement finally noticed the profile of teenage mass killers at suburban schools like Columbine. I wondered how she would respond if her sons were subjected to the same police scrutiny that young men of color experience each day. I wondered if she would just "suck it up" if every blond family was rounded up and imprisoned indefinitely, living in horse stalls for the next several years, as Japanese Americans were forced to do during World War II. That was just yesterday's news.

The next day, I read that the government is considering using torture to obtain information from some of the estimated 1,000 prisoners who at the time of this writing are being held in indefinite detention for unnamed charges. It may be necessary to drug them or to use force or other torture to get these prisoners to talk. If the American people can't bring ourselves to accept the use of torture by our government, then the suggestion of one official is to ship the prisoners to another allied country, like Israel, where torture is used in interrogations.

More news: the White House and National Security Advisor Condoleeza Rice warned news media executives against publishing or broadcasting "propaganda" from the enemy including possible "coded messages," from Osama bin Laden. The implication was that the news media is playing into the enemy's hands. Within hours, network executives promised more judicious "editing" [read—self-censorship] in the future. None of them want to be seen as unpatriotic by refusing to cooperate with the administration's crusade against terrorism.

This bit about "coded messages" from Osama bin Laden reminded me of the accusations made against Los Alamos scientist Wen Ho Lee. Until September 11, Wen Ho Lee was the poster child for excessive government law enforcement powers and racial profiling. FBI agents had to persuade a federal judge to imprison Dr. Lee because he was so dangerous, so inscrutable, such a threat to national security he should be locked up, pretrial. Their arguments were so chilling that Dr. Lee was held in solitary confinement and maximum security, complete with shackles and chains. The FBI argued that Dr. Lee's mere "hello" might contain a secret message for agents from China—messages that could result in the production of an advanced nuclear warhead. The FBI warned that Ninja warriors from China might arrive in black helicopters at the mountaintop laboratories of Los Alamos to spirit Wen Ho Lee away. Never mind that Ninjas are Japanese warriors, not Chinese, or that it would be very tough for helicopters of any kind to go unnoticed in the secluded and heavily guarded laboratory town perched atop thin, finger mesas.

This was the same FBI whose intelligence failed to detect any clues of the events of September 11, and which now has unbridled policing powers, thanks to the anti-terrorism bill that was gift-wrapped for President George W. Bush. Among other morsels for the FBI and law enforcement, the anti-terrorism act allows noncitizens to be detained indefinitely. It allows the government to detain individuals without charging any crime or even an immigration violation. It also provides no meaningful opportunity for a hearing to determine the reason for an individual's detention. All details of arrests and detention are secret, sealed under court order. All in the name of national security. Of course, "threat to national security" was the same justification used to incarcerate 120,000 Japanese Americans during World War II, and to keep Wen Ho Lee in shackles and chains.

During World War II, the media had a special beat for the patriotic drum. They ran stories about Japanese American farmers who could grow tomatoes that would point to U.S. airbases, guiding Zero pilots to their targets. The esteemed Edward R. Murrow, patron saint of American journalism, announced on his radio broadcasts that any Japanese fighter pilots who made it to Seattle would surely be wearing University of Washington sweaters. And the news media is no different today.

There is great danger in the calls from the White House and Condoleeza Rice to news executives, seeking to restrict information to the public and to increase the self-censorship that already takes place inside the newsroom. Some 78 percent of the American public gets its information about the world beyond their homes from television news or from the Sunday paper. An entire worldview is shaped from newspaper factoid journalism and the eight minutes of evening news—the actual news time that gets crammed between commercials and infotainment. While the dumbing down of news has led to the dumbing down of the public, it also places tremendous power on the factoids and those eight minutes. So the media is losing whatever arguable independence it had before September 11; some twenty national journalism organizations have signed letters criticizing the government's overt efforts to limit what the media makes available to the public.

Sir Edmund Burke of England had it right when he first coined the phrase "the Fourth Estate" in the 1700s. The first three estates were Church of England, the House of Lords, and the House of Commons—all the basic institutions of England. The Fourth Estate was the reporters' gallery, and there was clear recognition of the media's institutional power, even then.

Asian Americans, of all people, should be concerned about and actively watchful over the media's power. The few times in our history when we rose from deliberate "invisibling" and obscurity, it was to be used as a hammer, a wedge, toward someone else's divisive agenda. We've been the 'heathen Chinee," the "hordes of hungry Hindoos," or the countless string of other hateful names that raised the ire of white workers; and the persistent "model minority," to divert the civil rights movement and bring down affirmative action. Asian Americans have been played both as the bystander and the weapon. Indeed, one of the miracles of modern media was the overnight conversion of Asian Americans from the Fifth Column and the Enemy Within, to the Modern American Success Story.

Today, we find news stories of yellow Asian Americans attacking brown Asian Americans—sick players in this patriotic zealotry, weird mutants of equal opportunity hate. This is not the time for any Asian Americans to breathe easy and sigh, "At least it's not us, this time." It is us, every one of us. If Asian Americans of every color and religion aren't speaking out against these travesties, then we are part of the problem, collaborators in our own oppressions.

Not long after September 11, I drove down to San Diego from San Francisco with my partner Lia. We didn't want to fly—not because we were fearful, but to avoid the camouflage uniforms, the automatic weapons, the searches and the reminders of the military state we are rapidly becoming. Near San Diego, I pulled into a gas station. The entire shift was immigrant labor—Latinos, Arabs, East Asians. The young Latino cashier shoved a plastic license plate frame into my face. It was decorated with a painted American flag. "You should buy this, only $3.95." I muttered a, "No thank you," and he tried again, "Don't you love the flag?" This time I said, "I wear the flag in my heart, not on my car." He tried again. "You can show you are American." I thought of my immigrant parents and felt sad for all the immigrants who are now so compelled to have the most prominent American flags on display. I took my change and said, "I am American. You are too. Even without a flag."

I actually do have an American flag, made of heavy canvas. It's folded in a neat triangle. The last time it was unfurled, it decorated the coffin of a laundryman and a World War II veteran, David Bing Hing Chin—the father of Vincent Chin. He died six months

Helen Zia speaks on anti-Asian violence and Vincent Chin at Confucius Plaza, New York City.
© 1992, Corky Lee

Helen Zia

before Vincent was beaten to death by two white autoworkers in 1982. Mrs. Lily Chin gave the flag to me when she moved to China, after spending forty of her sixty years in the U.S., as a naturalized American. She left her home in Michigan because it was too painful to be reminded that her son was killed out of xenophobic hate, struck down like an animal, and then discarded by a justice system that didn't believe an Asian American could be the target of racism. She gave the flag to me because she didn't want it anymore.

For the past fifteen years, I have kept this flag in a safe place. I took it out a few weeks after September 11. Not out of sentimentality, I confess, but because a professor asked me to find a document related to Vincent Chin's case. When I searched through my files, there was the flag. Its colors were as vibrant and strong as ever. The indigo blue. The deep blood red. As I held the canvas triangle of red, white and blue, I gave silent remembrance to Vincent and David Bing Hing Chin. Other names came upon me as well, those of the new victims of domestic terrorism, the new names and stories that keep popping up in my email—Balbir Singh Sodhi, Adel Karas, Surjit Samra, and so many others. I thought of those who died in the World Trade Center, the Pentagon, and the hijacked planes. . .as well as those killed by the Taliban—the countless women stoned and executed over recent years, and how the U.S. and member nations of the International Coalition against Terrorism had ignored the demands of women around the globe to stop the Taliban's femicide. Pictures of the civilian casualties in Afghanistan also came to mind—the families blown apart by errant "surgical strikes," the starving children ambushed by hidden land mines as they rush to grab an air dropped meal. As I hugged the flag, I remembered that this country was founded in defense of liberty, against tyranny. This is also what it means to be American.

As I finish writing this essay, the book on what happened to Wen Ho Lee will soon be published. I hope it will dampen some of the exuberant demands for racial profiling, some even made by those who have been racially profiled themselves. I hope Asian Americans will use our special experiences in this nation's history to speak up, as Americans, to offer some light on these dark topics. We have much experience to share that will strengthen this nation. As the Rev. Dr. Martin Luther King admonished: "Darkness cannot put out darkness. Only light can do that."

Notes from a New York Diary

Jessica Hagedorn

9:20 A.M., September 11, 2001

Fear, the rush of adrenaline, mounting hysteria. I open my door to an eerie sight: hundreds of people are standing in the middle of Washington Street, looking worried and lost. My neighbors, my friends, the maintenance workers who take care of my building, total strangers—all staring at the huge, ugly black clouds engulfing what once was the World Trade Center. There are those poised with their camcorders and cameras, ever ready to document any catastrophic event. I, too, stare at the smoke and flames, mesmerized by the awesome beauty of destruction. The sky is a hard, brilliant blue. It is the end of the world, yet the sun is blazing and it is a crisp, gorgeous morning. We are very much alive. All around me, eyewitness accounts are repeated like some gruesome mantra: *Not one plane, but two. Not two, but four. Not accidentally, but on purpose. I saw the whole thing go down, bodies falling from the sky.*

    I think of the troubled Mindanao region of the Philippines, where I have just been. Where the surreal and the real are one and the same. Where the sunsets are the most glorious on earth and acts of violence are a daily occurrence. Where an equally vicious sense of humor seems the only sane and logical response. Chaos reigns, life is cheap and everything is possible in the Philippines, where I was born. The people adapt, the people survive, the people retain their grace and sense of irony and humor. But thirty years in New York have made me soft—I am cocooned by arrogance and

JESSICA HAGEDORN is author of *Dogeaters* (Penguin, 1991), *Danger and Beauty* (Penguin, 1993), *The Gangster of Love* (Penguin, 1997), and *Burning Heart: A Portrait of the Philippines* (Rizzoli International Publishers, 1999). She is editor of *Charlie Chan is Dead: An Anthology of Contemporary Asian American Fiction* (Penguin, 1993).

privilege, prone to First World delusions. I thought I lived in the toughest city in the world and was therefore safe.

Nine-one-one-zero-one: sinister perfection. The numbers are high; the numbers signify creativity, pride, ambition and power. A numerologist's nightmare, perhaps—or source of infinite satisfaction?

11:15 A.M.

Hordes of dazed office workers stumble up from Battery Park, from Wall Street, from the ruins of the World Trade Center and whatever hell they've seen. White dust coats their faces and shoes, giving them a ghostly appearance. I run in the direction of P.S. 3, the neighborhood elementary school which Esther, my younger daughter, attends. I am determined to pull her out of class; I cannot bear not having her with me. And where is the rest of my family? Are they safe? Do they know that the world has ended? I try my cell phone, though I know better. The Verizon building is located in the World Trade Center area, so phone lines are down.

The sidewalks and streets are teeming, bodies swirl around me, swirls of constant motion. For some strange reason, no one wants to go indoors. Safety in numbers, I guess. It's a somber party in the streets, a macabre fiesta. Car radios are turned up at maximum volume so everyone can hear the latest bulletin. Esther calmly informs me that her fifth-grade class watched from their window as the second plane plowed into the Twin Towers and exploded into flames. Her words stun me into silence. "We need to buy water," I finally say, feeling like an idiot. We head towards the nearest D'Agostino's supermarket, but the entire West Village has beat us to it. It is not yet noon, but there is only one shopping-cart left, which Esther grabs. She's acting more clear-headed than her mother. The supermarket is packed with grim, quiet people. The air hums with anxiety, but everyone's doing their best to act calm and respectful. Lines of shoppers snake around the displays of cheeses and frozen meats. Hipsters, starlets, hustlers, wide-eyed mothers cradling restless infants—we're all in panic mode, but aren't ready to admit it. Carts are loaded with Pampers, bread, pasta, Kotex, toilet paper, six-packs of beer. I resist the sudden urge to laugh hysterically. There's something terribly funny about the situation. Or is the correct phrase "terrible and funny"?

In a state of siege, what does one truly need? The bananas are gone. Bottles of water fly off the shelves. There are no more "C" and "D" batteries, but plenty of double "A's." I ponder the meaning of this, feeling a bit crazy. An adrenaline high, the thrill of fear. At last, it's our turn at the check-out stand. I have managed to purchase four measly bags of groceries for the Apocalypse, while the people in line ahead and behind me have stocked up on at least a year's worth of non-perishable goods. On our way home, my ten-year-old daughter reveals in a soft voice that she is afraid. It is a heartbreaking moment. All around us, a city in shock. We walk home. The persistent wail of sirens is grating and continuous.

Five Weeks Later

I eat without appetite. Rent movies I don't watch. Channel-surf from soundbyte to soundbyte, unable to sleep. Concerned relatives who live far away call to ask when am I moving out of New York. "You're just sitting ducks," goes one of the more insensitive remarks. Fuck you, I want to say, but don't. Should I quote Yogi Berra? *The future ain't what it used to be. . . .* Or: *It ain't over until it's over.* Instead, I stop answering the phone altogether. I thank God, Allah, Buddha, the Virgin Mary, Krishna, my own mother and of course, Saint Sebastian and Jesus Christ for the invention of "caller i.d."

My dreams are fragmented, bleached. In one, the pristine image of three empty suitcases arranged in a neat row seems innocuous and mundane, but fills me with anxiety and dread. *(What to pack in case of the next attack? Passports? Manuscripts? A year's supply of Cipro? Bottles of purified water? I just don't know.)*

In another dream, I walk down a desolate street. The sun is shining; it is a gorgeous, crisp morning. I feel someone behind me and turn my head. A teenage boy rides a bicycle towards me, screaming. But what? I cannot hear him. His face is terrifying—grotesque, distorted, full of hate.

Shall I tell you about the smell? The sweet, nauseating smell of burning rubber, melting plastic and dead bodies? Yesterday was another beautiful day in Manhattan. Warm, sunny, breezy. But the warmer and windier it is, the worse it gets. The smells are everywhere downtown, carried by the wind. Time to summon the shamans. To exorcise the angry spirits, and bless the living and the dead. You can feel it, most days. Bad energy buried in the rubble.

Ground Zero

You ask me to write something about war, peace and race, but I cannot. Words fail me. "The Big Picture"—what it all means, who's really behind it, civil wars, unholy wars, crusades vs. fatwas vs.

jihads vs. ethnic cleansing vs. doves vs. hawks—the complications and mess of history are a blur to me at the moment. But here's one thing maybe I can share with you, one small thing that recently came to mind. One Sunday morning, I finally got up the courage to take a walk as far down Greenwich Street as I could. I wanted to see it for myself. Not on a T.V. screen or in a photograph, but the actual World Trade Center ruins in all their devastating, physical reality.

Ground zero. An apt name, stark and poetic. Here was, *is* a vast, smoldering graveyard of blackened, twisted steel and rubble, right in the middle of my city. The twin towers—once derided and admired as potent symbols of global commerce and architectural arrogance—had, in a matter of minutes, been reduced to a horrific heap of trash. I was immediately reminded of Smokey Mountain, the legendary garbage dump in the Philippines. Another awesome, burning landscape etched in my memory. So cruel yet accommodating, Manila's poorest of the poor figured out a way to live there. But our New York version of the ugly mountain is so much more gargantuan in scale, it literally takes your breath away. Ground Zero. The hauntingly familiar, acrid smells of death and decay waft through an open window in my apartment. Days of anxiety, days of mourning, days without sleep.

Paper cranes at Union Square Park, September 14, 2001, New York City. (NOTE: altered sign in upper left hand corner.)

© 2001, Corky Lee

The Dreamer. ("It was taken by my uncle in Mumbai. I was more interested in the traditional birthday celebrations going on for my younger sister than what my mother had told me earlier about India becoming independent soon.")
Photograph by Rattan Dessai, circa 1946/1947

Existing at the Center, Watching from the Edges

Roshni Rustomji-Kerns

Mandalas

For the last fifteen years I have been writing down notes, sketches of some of the wars I have lived through and yes, often with a survivor's guilt. Notes on the back of receipts, scraps of papers, note cards, letters, books, bookmarks—whatever is at hand. I find it difficult to put these together in any formal, traditional format as I attempt to make sense of the unending wars I have watched and lived through. Wars that have taken the shape of an adult's slap on a child's face, of the red, orange, green, blue and yellow flames engulfing the body of a monk or the body of a woman, of the stooped shoulders and the traumatized eyes of a man or woman whose dignity has been broken through conquest and poverty and of the corpses, the obscene slaughter of human beings and the earth in the name of God, truth, revenge and justice. Seeing, hearing, smelling, tasting and touching war, sometimes from the very center and sometimes from the sidelines that has led me to a pattern of war existence that seems terrifyingly close to walking within a mandala. A journey without any detachment or insight leading to any kind of understanding, wisdom and action against the very nature of war

Roshni Rustomji-Kerns has lived in India, Pakistan, Lebanon, the U.S. and Mexico. She is Professor Emeritus at Sonoma State University and currently a visiting scholar at the Center for Latin American Studies at Stanford University. She is coeditor with Miriam Cooke of *Blood into Ink: South Asian and Middle Eastern Women Write War* (Westview Press, 1994), and editor of *Living in America: Poetry and Prose by South Asian Writers in America* (Westview Press, 1995), and *Encounters: People of Asian Descent in the Americas* (Rowman and Littlefield, 1999).

and towards the essence of peace. Wars remind me of age-old hauntings begging to be exorcized from the body of our planet.

October 31, 2001

El Dia de los Muertos. The Day of the Dead

The two little girls sat beside me, laughing as we made silly sentences out of words. They in English and I in Spanish. When we came to the words, ghosts and *fantasmas*, they became very serious. They asked me, "*Tía*, why does that ghost woman make awful noises and carry away children so we can never see our families again?" One of their teachers had gone in for a multicultural Halloween. She had turned off the lights and told them the story of *la llorona*. The weeping woman who haunts so much of Mexico and the South West of the United States which was of course taken by force from Mexico which was of course taken by force by the European conquistadors which was of course taken by force by— and so on and so forth.

According to the accepted legend, *la llorona* wails as she wanders all over the countryside and through desolate places in towns searching for naughty children she can take away. She cries and looks for children because she has killed her own children because of her pride and insanity. I have heard men talk about how they too have encountered *la llorona* when they were staggering home from an evening of drinking. Those who remembered to make the sign of the cross survived. Those who didn't never reached home again. One of the men who had seen her told me, "*Una guerra. Una mujer contra todos los hombres.*" Why, I asked. Because, he said, one man dishonored a woman and made her so *loca*, so insane that she killed the children she had by him.

The summer after the Zapatista uprising, a Zapoteca selling shawls across from my *Mamacita*'s house in Oaxaca stopped me. She asked me if I had heard the cry of *la llorona* the evening before. I told her that I had heard the woman who sold tamales crying out her wares late into the night throughout Colonia Jalatlaco, the Colonia where the house is located. Her cry, "tamaaaaleees, tamaaa-lees" was so *triste*, full of sorrow and fatigue that it reminded me of the laments of women all over the world as they try to sell what little they have, what little they can make in order to feed their children. The woman selling shawls told me her version of the *la llorona* legend. It is a version I have not yet encountered in any book.

According to the woman, it was the rich and powerful European lover of the beautiful Indian woman, she who was later called *la llorona*, who had killed the two children she had borne him. He had done it to prove his love to his European *novia*. To prove that the two children and "that" woman were of no importance to him. As far as the storyteller was concerned, *la llorona* had never raised her hand against her children. When I asked her about the version where *la llorona* killed her children rather than see them slowly starve to death, the woman shrugged her shoulders and said, "It may have been a blessing. Have you ever seen a child slowly die of hunger?"

I tried to tell my two little companions this version of the story. They were still afraid. It did not matter who killed the children, the children were still dead. And *la llorona* was still searching for children to carry away to the land of the ghosts never to see their families again. One of the girls remembered a priest telling her about the children's crusade, "many hundreds of years ago" and how brave those children were. The other little girl described the children soldiers she had seen on the T.V., "nearly as old as we are." Before we continued to create more sentences, the two girls decided that no one had killed *la llorona*'s children. They had just run away and hidden so that they wouldn't have to go live in a war. "In wars," said the older girl, "people are hungry. They die. By bombs, by being hungry."

1947

I was moving towards my ninth year. One evening, the bells of the Hanuman Temple—at the end of the road, across the *maidan* where the dust rose and blew towards all our houses in summer—stopped. Just like that. They stopped and I haven't heard them since. A silence without a past, present or future.

The next morning, the past and the future became the now. The "there" of the rumors of a savage war became the "here" of refugees. People, strangers, suddenly appeared, flooding the streets of Karachi. My mother said, "To count them as if they are numbers is wrong. Each one is a single person. Think, Roshni, think what must each person be feeling!" I saw tears in my beloved grandmother's eyes as she spoke of orphans, children born of rape, women who would die of rape or be forced to live with the memory of violence and the reality of abandonment. I tried very hard to understand. Looking back after nearly fifty odd years, I don't know what I understood. I did realize that now we were independent. The land had been divided and there was bloodshed. My friend Asha told me about how her favorite aunt had wept as the red *tilak* on her forehead and the red *sindhu* in the parting of her hair was rubbed off when she was widowed. All that auspicious red of marriage and of families joining together turned to blood across the land. One morning, Asha didn't come to school. I asked when she would come back. Was she ill? Had she gone to visit her grandparents in Lahore? The teacher just shook her head. Asha disappeared from my life. I learned about a new flag, and we were given sweets in school for our newly won independence and the birth of a new country.

A week later, about lunchtime, my grandmother and mother spread their much-cherished white damask tablecloth elegant with its finely darned patches across our big dining table. When we had to write the autobiography of an object for an English class, I wrote an autobiography of that dining table. A few years ago, I went to Karachi to empty out the old house because the landlord had sold it to be demolished and made into a parking garage. I refused to watch as the dining table was taken away. My autobiography didn't speak about the day my grandmother and mother spread that tablecloth and asked me to sit at the table on a chair that could be seen from the front door. My grandmother sat at the head of the table and could also be seen from the front door. We were to carry on conversations with imaginary people supposedly sitting with us at the table. I already had a reputation for holding long conversations with myself and with people no one else could see. I don't know who Granny spoke to but I selected to speak to Madame Curie, Florence Nightingale, Rukhmanidevi, Fatima Jinnah, Rabindranath Tagore, Sarojini Naidu and a woman I decided to call Florencia—the greatest flamenco dancer of all times. My mother and father went to the front of the house and spoke to the crowd that had gathered there. "No, she isn't here," they said. "She didn't come to work today. She spoke about leaving for India. We can't help you."

I felt someone's head against my legs, and my grandmother warned me with her eyes not to raise the tablecloth. I reached down and felt the head and face of Dossa, one of my favorite, most-loved older persons. She had come to our house every morning to sweep the floors, and she and my grandmother were the only people in the house I wasn't allowed to question, answer back or tease. A few days earlier, she had arrived at our door with two policemen. Karachi was under curfew from night to dawn. When the policemen tried to stop her from coming to the house early in the morning she wouldn't stop walking. When one of the policemen tried to explain "curfew" to her, she beat him up with her broom and lectured him on the sanctity of work. They accompanied her to the door to protect her from harm. And now she was hiding, her face pressed against my legs, trembling as her pathetic, alcoholic son led a group of men to our door demanding that we give him his mother so that she too could be converted and not have to leave their land. After all, he said, God was God no matter what he was called. This didn't quite appeal to some of his new friends, and they took him off to explain matters to him.

I felt something break inside of me when I saw Dossa crawling out from under the table and through the back corridor as my grandmother walked behind her to shelter her until they both reached the backdoor. I saw my grandmother bend down and help Dossa stand up. My uncle, who was right outside the back door, nearly picked up Dossa as he led her away to what we hoped was safety. She was to have arrived safely in India. I don't know.

A month later, I stood at the same backdoor holding my father's hand. We were facing a man holding the hand of his daughter. The man was begging my father to find him some space for his family. My father was explaining that he couldn't. The girl was younger than I, but I knew we could be friends. She looked as if she liked reading and listening to stories and making up stories. The man wept as he turned away. The girl turned around, and we waved at one another. My father, too, was crying. His beautiful dark face looked as if someone had smeared dead gray ashes on it.

Many years later I heard that my father had turned the top floors of the school where he was the principal as a place of sanctuary for refugees.

My mother told us about the horrors that the refugees who were now citizens of Pakistan had lived through. She was among the many citizens of Karachi—old and new—who set up workplaces where women who had become refugees could work and make new lives for themselves. There was agony, but there was also hope. One of the first Pakistani patriotic songs I heard (I think it was the National Anthem for a brief time) was composed on our piano. People question that, but I remember sitting quietly in a corner listening to the different variations of the melody and the words. But the wars continued, and my mother got tired of trying to explain to me why people kill one another, why people hate, why didn't we stop such things and other questions. One day she said, "Find the answers for yourself." Very Buddhist at heart, my mother.

1958-1961

I used to imagine that Nasima and Arjuman who had traveled with me from Pakistan to Lebanon were somehow two parts of the little girl at our backdoor. It was their gift of friendship and laughter and serious discussions about the what and the why of Pakistan that made Pakistan truly one of my lands, a *desh* (I don't quite understand the concept of nations) for me.

Lebanon was the heartbreakingly beautiful land where I saw a boy, his face masked with blood, leap from a balcony moments after men in uniforms had entered the building. I stood below surrounded by the aroma of strong coffee and the smell of freshly shaved wood, a loud thud interrupting the sounds of Fairouz singing as the boy fell to the sidewalk. That day I learned about the cruelty of men towards boys who could be their sons. It was the first time I heard the indescribable scream of a woman as she watches her child being killed.

Beirut was the city where I passed the wall of lemon trees on my way to the lighthouse and saw two women embracing and weeping. I wanted to console them, but didn't know how and for what. One of them turned to me and said, "Binti, daughter, we cry for our lemon trees we will never see again in our home. Our Palestine." The other woman showed me the key to the house she had left behind. The house, she had just learned, didn't exist anymore. I didn't have any words, so I did what I had seen a woman do to another woman who had lost her husband, her two children and her old father on the way to Karachi from Bombay. She had wiped the grieving woman's face with her bare hands. Six months later, I tripped and hurt my knee. I went to the student health services and the nurse who treated me was the woman with the key.

The campus of the American University of Beirut was where a young woman was pointed out to me on my first day as a Junior. I was told, "She was there. She watched as her father was hanged. She insisted on going. She is carrying on the fight." I don't remember her face, but she had a body that said, "I refuse to break." And, yes, I often saw her laugh and smile.

And then there was the funeral of a classmate that I didn't attend. One of my friends told me that the mother had screamed at the corpse of her son not only for dying but also for having killed other mothers' sons. Later, I heard the same story during the Nicaragua war between the Sandanistas and the Contras and then during the Zapatista uprising for justice.

1962-1963

From the Cedars of Lebanon where the gatekeeper Humbaba fought Gilgamesh and his beloved companion Enkidu to Durham, North Carolina and a campus graced with "ye olde Europeanee" buildings that reminded me of the castles and the churches from my childhood books of fairy tales. A beautiful campus with a glorious library.

I boarded a bus to go to the house where I had been invited for tea. Being a rather nervous bus rider, I sat in one of the first rows of the nearly empty bus. The driver pulled over, came to me and said quite gently, "Don't you know the rules?" I shook my head. He bent down, picked me up, seventy-eight pounds of a sari-wrapped bewildered graduate student and placed me most carefully on a seat at the back of the bus. The books and movies at the USIS in Karachi and the professors from the USA in Beirut had not told me about segregation. I told my hostess about the incident. She said, "Oh dear, I am sorry. Only colored servants take that bus." I showed her my brown hand. She smiled, shook her head and remarked that she was surprised that the bus driver hadn't realized that I was a foreigner. Foreigners were to be treated with the same respect as whites. Otherwise there would be international incidents.

One Sunday afternoon late in the summer of my year in Durham, I stood on a sidewalk on the main street next to an African American family. A grandmother, a grandfather, a father, a mother and two boys. Both boys had their grandmother's smile. The mother admired my sari and asked me if it was handwoven. We carried on a conversation as we watched a phalanx of policemen approach the group of young people trying to enter a restaurant across the street. When the first "thwack" of a baton against human flesh reached us, the grandma moaned and nearly fell over. The mother held her up. The four menfolk stood still, their fists so tight that their arms were shaking. I remembered standing on the terrace in my mother's home in Mumbai (that is how my grandmothers always pronounced the city), watching the police beating up processions of people calling out for freedom, calling out Gandhiji's name. Neither the people being beaten up in that procession in Mumbai nor the people on that street in Durham raised a hand against their attackers. I haven't yet decided if that is really the only right way to defend ourselves.

When I ended up at the Duke Hospital after completing my thesis, the bus driver who had placed me so gently but firmly at the back of the bus came to visit me with a bunch of handpicked flowers. He said that I should get well soon and that he was very sorry to hear about the war between India and China. I told him that my paternal great-great-grandmother was Chinese and ever since I had heard about the war, I had chilling nightmares about dragons and tigers tearing at one another.

1968-1977
Berkeley, California
Memories for stories:

1. Demonstrations against the War in Vietnam. I meet a man at a party who has walked in all the demonstrations in Berkeley. His son tells me with great delight that whenever a woman teacher in Mexico was mean to him and his other American friends, they would call her "an ugly *puta*." According to him they should know that Americans are to be respected.

2. People in Karachi have a difficult time believing my letters about Berkeley. Especially when I write that there are young men and women in ragged clothes (some deliberately torn or patched) begging in the streets around the University.

3. Coming out of the library one evening with no one around me, I see a lone policeman enter the lane. He lobs a canister of tear gas at me.

4. Entering a women's restroom in Dwinelle Hall late one evening and finding a woman with a mop in her hand. She has tears on her face. She turns to me and asks, "How is this going to help to end the war? I won't be paid extra for this extra work. The war won't end. My boys will die in that place while you march and dance in the streets." She points to the row of toilets. They are filled to overflowing with garbage, with rotten fruits, newspapers, old clothes, chicken bones, even pages torn out of books. Angry students have filled up the toilets as a sign of protest against the war mongering authorities. The woman throws down her mop and walks away.

5. Bumper stickers. "Mary Poppins Is A Junkie." I have to have this one deciphered for me. "Question Authority." I am confused. Is this a car driven by a person who is an authority on questions, or is the person telling us to question people in authority? I am told that Berkeley is a War Zone.

6. Sitting in a professor's office with other students as a car comes hurtling down across the green lawn and stops just short of plowing into the office window. We are translating the *Gita*.

7. Walking down University Avenue in a sari. A young woman stops me and says, "Free yourself. Get rid of all those yards of clothing." The woman is wearing a long skirt from India. Is she a friend or foe?

8. Listening to Joan Baez and Bob Dylan at Jock and Emily Brown's house where I live. Jock Brown goes to Vietnam.

9. Hearing the Blues.

10. Reading James Baldwin and learning more about the war I saw in North Carolina.

11. The smoldering anger, fear, frustration in Lebanon turns further inwards. Civil War. One more motherland that has nurtured me in flames. Blood doesn't put out fire. I read: The Worst Wars are Civil Wars. And later: All Wars are Civil Wars. I still wonder at the different uses of the word "civil."

12. I watch televised images of the American war in Vietnam as I learn to translate the *Mahabharata* and the *Iliad*. The women of all the fighting sides stream onto the battle of Kurukshetra mourning their dead, Achilles mourns the death of his beloved companion and drags Hector around in the dirt as his old parents watch, and Vietnam is transformed into a blazing fire of trees and human flesh. There must have been sounds with those images but all I remember is silence as the pictures flashed across the screen while I translate word-by-word the stories of other times, other places where wars raged, the innocent and the guilty were killed and glorious words were spoken. One night, after completing a very long paper I dream that I am running with the women on the field of Kurukshetra, I am screaming, my hair is unbound, I wear no ornaments. Hecuba appears calling for her son. A woman stops me and says, "Who are you on this land? You were not walking with us to Oklahoma."

1975

A student sat in my office at Sonoma State University. He looked like a grown-up version of a Renaissance cherub. There was a sweetness to him that needed protection yet there was nothing childish about him. We discussed the *Gita*. He told me the following story.

After his first tour of duty as a Marine he had volunteered to go to Vietnam again. He couldn't remember what had fired his zeal. Yes, he said, he had seen war, both the inhuman and the human side of it. Towards the end of his second tour of duty, he and his buddies were pulling out bodies from a village set on fire by the Americans. He said, "We burned it by mistake, and we were now trying to save as many of those villagers as we could. We were carrying the burned but alive bodies to the boats. I was carrying someone very light. I looked down and saw that I was carrying an old woman. She looked exactly like my grandmother back in Michigan. Old, wrinkled, wiry and beautiful. She died in my arms. I went out of my mind. I was sent back home."

He made me realize how some people eat war and grow fat and greedy for more. How others eat war and are killed. And how some transform the poisons of war into *amrita*, nectar not only of immortality but also of peace. And then he and his wife gave me a beautiful silk-screened banner with the image of the Lady of Guadalupe. They had decided to earn their living making and selling banners with the symbols of all the world's religions.

The last time I saw the student, he had graduated and was selling his banners on Telegraph Avenue. He no longer reminded me of a cherub. He had the detached, loving look of a bodhisattva.

1987

My mother died. The day after the funeral we found out that the Karachi policemen had towed away the cars parked outside our house during the funeral. The mourners weren't happy, but they will most probably recall the day my mother was taken to the *dukhmo*, the Tower of Silence, as the day the police towed away their cars and hopefully they will smile even as they shake their heads.

As I touched my mother's wedding ring and her glasses—I had never seen her without the ring and seldom without her glasses—I could hear her talking to me. And what struck me was how often she had spoken to me about the utter horror and uselessness of war and the evils of injustice. She never said, "That's how the world is." She always implied that our lives would be rather worthless if we didn't work against evil. I was six years old when the USA dropped the bombs on Hiroshima and Nagasaki.

I looked at my mother. Her calm, rather stern face was absolutely still. Absolutely without a trace of emotions. I remember thinking that this was how my mother would look when she died. My mother was born in Japan.

September 2000

We shouldn't have been office mates. We are far too committed to one another as friends and much more interested in the histories of our families than in some of the academic work we need to complete. After all, we are both Indians, and we are comfortable enough with one another to make jokes about it. About Columbus refusing to ask anyone the way to the real India, about blankets and sheets and such nonsense. We both love literature. She is completing her dissertation and I read some of the chapters. She is a storyteller telling stories about stories and storytellers in her family, her community, her world. I read her narrative about her family, the journey on the Trail of Tears and the final arrival in Oklahoma. She writes about the nuanced and multilinear, many circled techniques of storytelling used by her grandmother. I read about how her grandmother was sent out with food for the wounded warriors hiding in a cave when she was a very little girl. I catch a hint that my friend's grandmother had seen a man die of his wounds when she was a child. Wounds received in the defense of his land and his family. But I don't know how the story really ends. What is connected to what other part? Did her grandmother ever tie up all the threads of the stories about her family, people deprived of their ancestral lands, made invisible in their own land? Can grandmother's stories be tied neatly—for the sake of an academic dissertation—into the stories of the indigenous women of Bolivia fighting for their land and their lives? And my friend, whom I call *Damyanti*, the Victorious One—says, "Roshni, there isn't an end to that story." And I realize that as I live in the Americas, I too am implicated in the story of the rape of this land and of the continual attempts at the destruction of the first peoples of this land. I understand the woman in my dream. I had not been forced to walk with my friend's family to Oklahoma. And I feel the pain I felt when I saw Dossa crawl away from our house in Karachi. I don't know if she arrived somewhere safely. I leave the office, drive home, walk to the edge of the Pacific Ocean, stand on the sand and pray the ancient Zoroastrian prayer of health and safety for everyone who dwells in these lands. A prayer of healing the women in my family taught me. I wonder if it will work.

September 11, 2001

Thursday, a week after. A dear friend I call *hermanocito* sent me an email. It was about a man who had barely escaped being beaten up. He was threatened because he has a beard and wears a turban just like my "adopted" *bhai*, my brother." Just before I received the email, I had been talking with my neighbor whose wondrous eight-year-old daughter had been asking, "But why do those people hate me, Mummy? I am an American." And then I turned on the T.V. and saw what is now Afghanistan for me.

Food was being distributed. Names were being called. The names were of adult males. But most of the adult males were dead or gone, and so the children were coming up to pick up the food allocations. No women. There were a few little girls. A name was called out. Silence. No one came up. And then one of the men smiled sadly and went to the group waiting for food and called a tiny girl. She had wild curly hair and the beautiful eyes of child-hood. It seemed as if she was too young to recognize her father's name and most probably he was dead or fighting toward death. She came forward and picked up the bag they handed to her and began dragging it. Someone showed her how to sling it over her shoulder. And she did. The bag was as big as she was. Maybe big-ger. And then they put a cardboard box in front of her. She stood there looking at it and tried pushing it with her feet. The man who had brought her forward smiled sadly again and gestured that he would bring it to her house later. It was that small gesture of com-passion and the tiny girl-child going back into the crowd with her bag over her shoulder that shattered me. I sat screaming, bleed-ing from the womb that my body hasn't possessed for over thirty years.

Maybe it is good to write about the horrors we bring upon our-selves. Writing, after all, is a political act. I understand that peace and justice is what we have to keep on working towards in our own ways to keep from shriveling up in body, mind and spirit. Compassion. I am haunted by the image of the little girl carrying the bag of food over her shoulder. War—and yet the hope of peace.

War against the Planet

Vijay Prashad

The bombing has begun. Kabul is being bombed. So say the television anchors and the newspapers—all in passive voice, all with an air of inevitability.

I can hear whispers from my neighbors: finally, it is here, and I hope it goes away soon. We don't want to be burdened by it, for it may force us to make moral choices that are far too uncomfortable. Better to pretend that it is has not happened, or else that its inevitability makes it inconsequential.

There is more activity when a storm is on the horizon, when most folk rush to the supermarket to buy provisions and to fill their cars with gas.

Tons of firepower drop from Herat to Jalalabad—cars line up from Kabul to Peshawar through the Khyber Pass, like a row of fireflies, unsure if the border will be open or closed. During the entire eighteenth century, one-and-a-half million people crossed the ocean from England to the Americas. In three weeks, about this number of Afghans have made their way to a neighboring country, eager to get out before the bombardment inevitably begins. That they are in cars tells us something about their class position. Middle-class and elite Afghans left the country in waves, first in the late 1970s to escape the radical egalitarianism of the Communist regime, then in the 1980s to escape the ravages of the mujahidin assault on the cities, again in the 1990s to escape the radical Islamism of the Taliban and the Northern Alliance, and now to escape the rowdy guns of the U.S.-UK armies.

VIJAY PRASHAD is Professor of International Studies at Trinity College, Connecticut and author of *The Karma of Brown Folk* (University of Minnesota Press, 2000) and *Everybody Was Kung Fu Fighting: Afro-Asian Connections and the Myth of Cultural Purity* (Beacon Press, 2001).

Some say that the U.S. has only now lost its "virginity," that it has remained unsullied from the Old World dilemmas in its New World Dreams. The pretence of innocence that coddles the consciousness of many of those who live in the land of the dollar occludes our role in the history that led up to 9/11. Of course those who died in the buildings did not directly participate in the history and those who transformed the planes into bombs had the indecency to kill innocent civilians for the crimes of a culpable imperialist state and its corporate retainers. 9/11, an event against the Geneva Convention, brought the war stateside, a war that has been ongoing for some time now, at least for five decades.

Indeed, five decades ago the United States assumed charge of that band of nations that stretches from Libya to Afghanistan, most of whom are oil rich and therefore immensely important for global capitalism. The civilizational mandate held by France and Britain came to a close when World War II devastated Europe, and it fell to the U.S. to adopt the white man's burden. It did so with glee, indeed on behalf, for the most part, of the Seven Sisters, the largest oil conglomerates in the world (most of them U.S.-based transnational corporations).

Alliances forged with right-wing forces in these regions found fellowship from the U.S., just as the Left fashioned relations with the USSR. The United States participated in the decimation of the Left in north Africa and west Asia, from the destruction of the Egyptian Communist Party, the largest in the region, to the rise of people like Saddam Hussein to take out the vibrant Iraqi Communist Party, and of the Saudi financier Osama bin Laden to take down the Communist Afghan regime.

We hear that 9/11 was the "worst terrorist attack in history," but this ignores the vast history of bombardment, in general, tracked by Sven Lindquist in his new book *The History of Bombing* (New Press, 2001), and it certainly ignores the many terrorist massacres conducted in the name of the United States, for instance, such as at Hallabja in Iraq or else in South America by Operation Condor. These are just a few examples. But what is that history before 8:45 A.M. on 9/11, and will it show us that "retaliation" misses out the fact that the U.S. has been at war for many decades already?

I. The Afghan Concession

In 1930, a U.S. State Department "expert" on Afghanistan offered an assessment which forms the backbone of U.S. social attitudes and state policy towards the region: "Afghanistan is doubtless the most fanatic hostile country in the world today." Given this, the U.S. saw Afghanistan simply as a *tool* in foreign policy terms and as a *mine* in economic terms. When the Taliban (lit. "religious students") entered Kabul on September 27, 1996, the U.S. state welcomed the development with the hope that the new rulers might bring stability to the region despite the fact that they are notoriously illiberal in social terms. The U.S. media offered a muted and clichéd sense of horror at the social decay of the Taliban, but without any sense of the U.S. hand in the manufacture of such theocratic fascists for its own hegemonic ends. In thirty years, Afghanistan has been reduced to a "concession" in which corporations and states vie for control over commodities and markets without concern for the dignity and destiny of the people of the region. Oil, guns, landmines and heroin are the coordinates for policymakers, not the shadowy bodies that hang from the scaffolds like paper-flags of a nation without sovereignty.

Shortly after the Taliban took power in Kabul, the U.S. State Department offered the following assessment: "Taliban leaders have announced that Afghans can return to Kabul without fear, and that Afghanistan is the common home of all Afghans," announced spokesperson Glyn Davies. The U.S. felt that the Taliban's assertion in Kabul would allow "an opportunity for a process of reconciliation to begin." Reconciliation was a distant dream as the troops led by the Tajik warlord, Ahmed Shah Masood, and the troops led by General Abdul Rashid Dostum and the Hazara-dominated Hezb-e-Wahdat party disturbed the vales of Afghanistan with warfare. Citizens of the advanced industrial states mouthed clichés about "timeless ethnic warfare" and "tribal blood-feuds" without any appreciation of the history of Afghanistan that produced these political conflicts (in much the same way as the media speaks of the Tutsi-Hutu turmoil without a sense of colonial Belgium's role in the production of these politico-ethnic conflicts).

In 1964, King Zahir Shah responded to popular pressure from his subjects with a constitution and initiated a process known as "New Democracy." Three main forces grew after this phase: (1) the communists (who split into two factions in 1967, Khalq [the masses] and Parcham [the flag]); (2) the Islamic populists, among whom Burhanuddin Rabbani's Jamiat-i-Islami from 1973 was the main organization (whose youth leader was the engineering student, Gulbuddin Hikmatyar); (3) constitutional reformers (such as Muhammad Daoud, cousin of Zahir Shah, whose coup of July 1973 abolished the monarchy). Daoud's consequent repression against the theocratic elements pushed them into exile from where they began, along with the Pakistani Jamaat-I-Islami and the Saudi Rabitat al-Alam al-Islami, to plot against the secular regime in Afghanistan. In 1975, for instance, the theocratic elements, led by Hikmatyar in Paktia, attempted an uprising with Pakistani assistance, but the "Panjsher Valley incident" was promptly squashed. The first split amongst the theocratic elements occurred in the aftermath of this incident. Instability in Afghanistan led to the communist coup in 1978 and the eventual Soviet military presence in the region from 1979. The valiant attempts to create a democratic state failed as a result of the inability of hegemonic states to allow the nation to come into its own.

From 1979, Afghanistan became home to violence and heroin production. Money from the most unlikely sources poured into the band of mujahidin forces located in Pakistan: the U.S., the Saudis (notably their general intelligence service, al-Istakhbara al-'Ama), the Kuwaitis, the Iraqis, the Libyans and the Iranians paid the theocratic elements over $1 billion per year during the 1980s. The U.S.-Saudi dominance in funding enabled them to choose amongst the various exiled forces—they, along with the Pakistanis, chose seven parties in 1981 that leaned more towards theocratic fascism than toward secular nationalism. One of the main financiers was the Saudi businessman, Osama bin Laden. Five years later, these seven parties joined the Union of Mujahidin of Afghanistan. Its monopoly over access to the U.S.-Saudi link emboldened it to assassinate Professor Sayd Bahauddin Majrooh in Peshawar in 1988 when he reported that 70 percent of the Afghan refugees wanted a return to the monarchism of Zahir Shah (who waited in a Roman suburb playing chess, a pensioner of an unnamed Gulf State who are now eager to call in his debt by sending him back to rule). Further, the Interim Islamic Government of Afghanistan called a *shura* (council) in 1989; the seven parties nominated all the representatives to the body. All liberal and left wing elements came under systematic attack from the *shura* and its armed representatives. The U.S.-Saudi axis anointed the theocratic fascists as the heirs to Afghanistan.

With over $1 billion per year, the mujahidin and its Army of Sacrifice (Lashkar Isar) led by Hikmatyar (who was considered the main "factor of stability" until 1988) built up ferocious arsenals. In 1986, they received shoulder-fired Stinger missiles that they began to fire indiscriminately into civilian areas of Afghanistan. Asia Watch, in 1991, reported that Hikmatyar paid his commanders for each rocket fired into Kabul. Claymore mines and other U.S.-made anti-personnel directional fragmentation mines became a staple of the countryside. Today, about ten million mines still litter the vales of Afghanistan (placed there by the Soviets and by the U.S.-Saudi backed mujahidin). In 1993, the U.S. State Department noted that landmines "may be the most toxic and widespread pollution facing mankind." Nevertheless, the U.S. continues to sell mines at $3/mine (mines cost about $300-$1,000/mine to detect and dismantle). Motorola manufactures many of the plastic components inside the mines, which makes the device undetectable by metal-detectors.

The CIA learned to extend its resources during the Southeast Asian campaigns in the 1970s by sale of heroin from the Golden Triangle. In Afghanistan, the Inter-Service Intelligence (ISI) [Pakistan's CIA], the Pakistani military and civilian authorities (notably Governor Fazle Huq) and the mujahidin became active cultivators, processors and sellers of heroin (a commodity which made its Southern Asian appearance in large numbers only after 1975, and whose devastation can be gleaned in Mohsin Hamid's wonderful novel, *Moth Smoke*). The opium harvest at the Pakistan-Afghan border doubled between 1982 and 1983 (575 tons), but by the end of the decade it would grow to 800 tons. On June 18, 1986, the *New York Times* reported that the mujahidin "have been involved in narcotics activities as a matter of policy to finance their operations." The opium warlords worked under cover of the U.S.-Saudi-Pakistani axis that funded their arms sales and aided the conveyance of the drugs into the European and North American markets where they account for 50 percent of heroin sales.

Heroin is not the only commodity flogged by the mujahidin. They are the frontline troops of an ensemble that wants "commercial freedom" in Afghanistan so that the Afghan people and land can be utilized for "peaceful" exploitation. The California-based oil company Unocal ("the spirit of 76"), then busy killing the Karens and other ethnic groups in alliance with the Burmese *junta* and with the French oil company Total, had its eyes on a pipeline from Central Asia to the Indian Ocean, through Afghanistan. Only with an end to hostilities, at any cost, will the international corporations be able to benefit from the minerals and cheap labor of the Afghans. So far, the corporations have reaped a profit from sales of arms to the Afghans; now they want to use the arms of the Afghans for sweatshops and mines.

For corporations and for corporatized states (such as the U.S.), an unprincipled peace allows them to extract their needs without the bother of political dissent. The Taliban briefly offered the possibility of such a peace. Formed in 1994 under the tutelage of the ISI and General Naseerullah Khan (Pakistan's Interior Minister), the Taliban comprises southern Pashtun tribes who are united by a vision of a society under Wahhabism which extols a form of Islam (*Tariqa Muhammadiya*) based on its interpretation of the Quran without the benefit of the centuries of elaboration of the complexities of the Islamic tradition. In late September 1996, Radio Kabul broadcast a statement from Mullah Agha Gulabi: "God says that those committing adultery should be stoned to death. Anybody who drinks and says that that is not against the Koran, you have to kill him and hang his body for three days until people say this is the body of the drinker who did not obey the Koran and Allah's order." The Taliban announced that women must be veiled and that education would cease to be available for women. Najmussahar Bangash, editor of *Tole Pashtun*, pointed out shortly thereafter that there are 40,000 war widows in Kabul alone and their children will have a hard time with their subsistence. Further, she wrote, "if girls are not allowed to study, this will affect a whole generation." For the U.S.-Saudi-Unocal-Pakistan axis, geopolitics and economics make the Taliban a worthy regime for Afghanistan. Drugs, weapons and social brutalities will continue, but Washington extended a warm hand towards Mullah Mohammed Omar and the Taliban. U.S. foreign policy is driven by the dual modalities of containment (of rebellion inspired by egalitarianism) and concession (of goods which will bring profit to corporate entities). Constrained by these parameters, the U.S. government was able to state, in 1996, "there's on the face of it nothing objectionable at this stage."

Certainly, on October 10, 1996, the State Department revised its analysis of the Taliban on the basis of sustained pressure from Human Rights and women's groups in the advanced industrial states as well as pressure from the conferences held by Iran (at which numerous regional nations, such as India participated). In conflict with its earlier statement, the U.S. declared "we do not see the Taliban as the savior of Afghanistan. We never really welcomed them." The main reason offered for this was the Taliban's "uniquely discriminatory manner" with women. The U.S. State Department would have done well to mention the heroic attempt made by the communist regime to tackle the "woman question." In late 1978, the regime of Nur Mohammad Taraki, President of the Revolutionary Council of Afghanistan, promulgated Decree

No. 7 which aimed at a transformation of the marriage institution by attacking its monetary basis and which promoted equality between men and women. Women took leadership positions in the regime and fought social conservatives and theological fascists on various issues. Anahita Ratebzad was a major Marxist leader who sat on the Revolutionary Council; other notable leaders included Sultana Umayd, Suraya, Ruhafza Kamyar, Firouza, Dilara Mark, Professor R. S. Siddiqui, Fawjiyah Shahsawari, Dr. Aziza, Shirin Afzal and Alamat Tolqun. Ratebzad wrote the famous *Kabul Times* editorial (May 28, 1978) which declared that "Privileges which women, by right, must have are equal education, job security, health services, and free time to rear a healthy generation for building the future of the country. . . . Educating and enlightening women is now the subject of close government attention." The hope of 1978 is now lost and the pessimism must not be laid at the feet of the Taliban alone, but also of those who funded and supported the Taliban-like theocratic fascists, states such as the U.S., Saudi Arabia and Pakistan.

The real reason for the U.S. frustration with the Taliban was its recalcitrance toward global capitalism (as an example, the Unocal scheme fell apart). The Taliban, created by many social forces, but funded by the Saudis (such as bin Laden) and the CIA, was now in the saddle in the center of Asia, and it soon became a haven for disgruntled and alienated young men who wanted to take out their wrath on the U.S. rather than fight against the contradictions of global capital. Bin Laden, the CIA asset, became the fulcrum of many of their inchoate fears and angers.

II. Oil, Guns and Saddam

During the Gulf War of 1991, a decade ago, the U.S.-Europe discovered the Kurds for a few years. The Kurds and the Kuwaitis provided the war aims for the Alliance, since we kept hearing how Saddam Hussein's armies had exploited both. Oil is not the reason, we were repeatedly told; we are only concerned for the ordinary people of the region oppressed by these madmen, such as Saddam Hussein, Hafez al-Assad and the Ayatollahs. We heard little about the recently closed Iran-Iraq war, about the various contradictions in the region, indeed about the role of the U.S.-Europe for several decades in the fabrication of the regimes that ruled here. As the cruise missiles fell on Iraq, we did not then hear that the first major aerial bombardment in modern times took place in December 1923 when the Royal Air Force pummeled the rebellious

Kurds (they felt the wrath of the guns again in March 1924, not being disciplined firmly enough by Headmaster Britain).

In 1932, the British put in place the puppet royal dynasty, the al-Saud family to rule the Arabian Peninsula as Saudi Arabia. This regime was to protect the "interests" of global capitalism, particularly after oil was discovered there in the early 1930s. The British put King Faisal over the newly created Iraq, a Sunni leader over a predominantly Shi'ite land. Workers movements in the region came under attack from these regimes, many of which violently crushed democratic dissent in the name of the dollar. Henry Kissinger was later to create political theory of a policy that had been long in the works: that the U.S. should lock arms with any political leader who will resist the will of socialism, who will ensure that international capitalism's dictates be maintained and who can therefore be a "factor of stability." The rogue gallery of this policy includes a host of CIA assets, such as the Noreiga, Marcos, Pinochet, Suharto, the Shah of Iran, the various Gulf Sheikhs, and latterly such fundamentalist friends as the BJP in India. Even when some of these leaders flirted with the Soviets (Saddam and al-Assad), their usefulness to U.S. policy prevented a break in their links to the CIA, mainly to contain domestic left-wing dissent. The Ayatollah may have been a natural asset, but his regime was stamped by a radical and patriarchially egalitarian Shi'ism that terrified the Oil Kingdoms, whose tenuous rule was now bolstered even further by the armies of the imperial powers and their proxy state at this time, Iraq. When the Iran-Iraq war broke out, people spoke of it as a sectarian war between Shias and Sunnis, but few pointed out that Iraq has a large Shia population and that Iraq fought primarily with the backing of the U.S. and its alliance to "contain" the Iranian revolution and the rule of the Mullahs. Saddam, then, was friend not foe.

During these years, no one mentioned the Kurds. For decades the communist movement grew amongst the Kurds, both in Turkey and in northern Iraq. But by the early 1970s, the CIA entered the battlefield to cut down the left and bolster the right. Between 1972 and 1975 the CIA paid $16 million to the eccentric and untrustworthy Mullah Mustafa Barzani as a "moral guarantee" of U.S. support for this activities. In 1959, Barzani had expelled the communists from his mainly Iraqi party, and he had sent Iranian Kurds to their death in the camps of the Shah. Barzani was an asset that the U.S. cultivated, and is now a close ally of Saddam Hussein, another U.S. asset. In 1975, Marxist-Leninists within the Kurdish resistance formed the Patriotic Union of Kurdistan (PUK), which pushed many Kurds to the Left, including those in the Iraqi Kurdish Front formed in 1988. Saddam Hussein was given the green light by Washington to take out the PUK, and he conducted chemical bombing on them in 1983 (at Arbil) and most spectacularly in 1988 (at Halabja, where five thousand died, and many thousands continue to suffer). The outrage of Halabja created a momentary stir in the Left media, but nothing was done then because Saddam was a U.S. ally and asset—it returned to do ideological work during the Gulf War. As many died at Hallabja as on 9/11, but their death does not factor in when NPR announces that 9/11 was the "worst terrorist attack in history." When terror is conducted in our name, then it is not terror but "retaliation."

III. Revenge or Justice?

President Bush promises to get those who did the bombings in New York and Washington, but he also promises that those who harbor them will feel the wrath of the U.S. This is the most dangerous statement so far. Not only does it violate all manner of international laws, it ignores the fact that the U.S. has harbored these criminals for years, mainly at the expense of the global Left. Saddam and bin Laden are products of the U.S., even as they, like Frankenstein's beast, turn against their master now. The lesson is not to continue the madness, to go after the symptom with $40 billion of firepower. The lesson, for all democratic-minded people, is to undermine the basis of our global insecurity. Our grief is not a cry for war.

First, those people who conspired to do the horrendous deed on 9/11 must be found, arrested and brought to trial. The path of justice should not be short-circuited by the emotions of the moment. The bombardment of Afghanistan will not make the work of justice any easier.

Second, our fight in the U.S. continues, as we continue to point out that U.S. foreign policy engenders these acts of barbarism by its own desire to set up strong-arm "factors of stability" in those zones of raw materials and markets that must be subservient to U.S. corporate interests. Vast areas of anger, zones of resentment will continue to emerge—this is not the way forward. Another indiscriminate bombardment will bring forth more body bags for the innocent. Berkeley's Congresswoman Barbara Lee voted against the war with just this logic: "I am convinced that military action will not prevent further acts of international terrorism against the United States. However difficult this vote may be, some of us must urge the use of restraint." She takes her place in the great American tradition of Jeannette Rankin, twice U.S. Congress-woman and the only person to vote against U.S. entry into both world wars.

History shows us that the U.S. was not innocent on 9/11, even as thousands of innocent people died. We should not confuse these two things: the terrorists made no distinction between those who conduct political and economic terror over their lives, between a regime that they dislike, corporate interests that they revile and innocent people who live in the same spaces. The terror of the frustrated works alongside the terror of the behemoth to under-mine the powerful and democratic urges of the people. Both of those terrors must be condemned.

Oakwood students from Birmingham, Alabama representing National Association for Prevention of Starvation (NAPS) march through Chinatown after driving in two vans for two days to reach New York City, September 15, 2001.
© 2001, Corky Lee

Breadseller.
Bazaar, Kashgar.
© 2001, Eric Chang

Organizer Raza Mir addresses crowd at the conclusion of silent rally at Jackson Heights, September 22, 2001. Sign on chest reads: "Islam is not the enemy. War is not the answer. Let's work to end the cycle. Pass it on..."

©2001, Corky Lee

Nothing to Write Home About

Amitava Kumar

It was 10 A.M. and I was still asleep. I was woken up with the news by an editor from India who had just seen the second plane slam into the World Trade Center. Actually, when the phone rang it was my wife, Mona, who picked it up. It would be more accurate to say that I woke up to the sound of her sobbing. Mona's younger brother arrives at the WTC at 8:42 each morning. He was late that day because he had worked in his Wall Street firm till 4 A.M. the previous night. On September 11, he couldn't even make it to his office: the announcement came on the subway that there had been an emergency. He came out of the station and was soon covered with ash. He walked to the ferry, away from the smoking towers. But we did not know this. We were not able to reach him or his office; we sent an email instead. He carries one of those cool little contraptions that allows him to receive and send email messages from anywhere. We waited anxiously to hear from him. The first email message I received was from the editor who had earlier called with the news. She wanted to know if everything was alright, and then she added that she had felt "vulture-ish" asking for a quick essay from me, but that was part of the reason why she had called. Over the next two hours, there were other notes from editors. I had not even brushed my teeth. We had heard nothing from Mona's brother. We were waiting. Mona's parents had moved from Pakistan to Canada over the past couple of years. Her father, a sixty-four-year-old retiree, woke up his eldest son with tears in his eyes. He had seen the news on television. He was now waiting for the phone to ring. You could imagine this happening in homes

AMITAVA KUMAR teaches at Penn State University and is the author of *Passport Photos* (University of California Press, 2000). His writings have recently appeared in *Harper's*, *Transition*, the *New Statesman*, and the *Nation*. He is a literary columnist at Tehelka.com.

all over America and abroad. Then, the email came from Mona's brother. It said "I'm ok." We were relieved. I felt that I had now been freed to write. I wrote several dispatches over the next few days for three separate news outlets in India. It would not be wrong to say that I experienced September 11 and its aftermath as an event to be reported to readers. I do not know whether this is good or bad. I can say that there is a coherence that I found in this act: reporting for an audience that was far away on another continent, I was allowed to distance myself from grief. I found courage to offer criticism when, if I were writing for an American newspaper, I would have felt myself constrained. When I read some other writers whose voices were filled with mourning, I felt guilty and somehow shabby. It was as if I had arrived drunk at a funeral. But, nevertheless, the feeling of coherence remained for me, simply because I had in each of these pieces asked myself what I ought to feel and do as a writer. And it is this that I was trying to communicate to readers in India. What I offer below are excerpts from some of those reports. The last dispatch I have included here, written still with the hope that words would stop bombs and missiles from being launched, makes the most explicit attempt to ask what we as writers are required to do now. Even when our words have failed to stop bombs. The first reports of the U.S. and British attacks mention that fifty tomahawk cruise missiles were launched on Afghani people yesterday. These attacks were followed by the dropping of 37,500 food packages and leaflets. What leaflets? We are told that these are leaflets telling people that the war is not against them but against bin Laden. So, I guess, the people have to weigh the evidence of what is falling on their heads, bombs and leaflets, and decide what they want. If this parody of caring must be carried out—death followed by cards—why not at least drop translations of our writings protesting what the U.S. government has done in the past and is doing now? I do not want anyone in Afghanistan and elsewhere to believe that many voices were not raised against the bombing of their homes.

—October 8, 2001

Dispatch 1/Excerpt/ September 11

On Another Plane

The first time I had visited the World Trade Center was when I took my younger sister, Divya, and her little child there. We wanted to see New York City from the top floor. The elevators raced to the top in seconds: their speed was such that little metal signs outside the doors warned pregnant women not to step in them.

My niece, Mishu, will turn seven on Sunday. She lives with her parents in a suburb of Washington, D.C. Today, after the explosion at the Pentagon, my sister began to worry about Mishu. My mother also called her from Patna: she wanted to know if we were all safe. After my mother's call, Divya went to Mishu's school. Other parents were already there, picking up their kids.

Mishu was happy to get off early from school. She saw her father waiting by the car and this pleased her too. She wanted to know how come her father wasn't in his office in downtown Washington, D.C. Mishu's friend, Faria, was also being picked up by Divya. Faria is a little older than Mishu. She looked at my sister and asked, "Is everything okay?"

Younger children have a prescience about them. Mishu's questions to her mother became more anxious. What can you tell a child about the attack on the Pentagon building if her chief excitement at the moment is her coming seventh birthday?

Divya said that she began telling Mishu a story about "bad guys." It worked for a while. In the evening, like most of us, Mishu had already achieved an education on CNN. She asked my sister, "What is a terrorist?"

There, I thought, was the crux of the matter. I asked my sister what was the answer she had given Mishu. My sister said, "She has seen films. So, I told her that these men were like the ones she had seen in *Mission Kashmir*." [*Mission Kashmir* is a recent Bullywood film that has, among its cast of characters, a ruthless Afghan *muja-hadeen* leading Kashmiri Muslims in a bloodthirsty fight against the Indian state. The film, like many others of this genre in recent Indian history, is painted in the colors of the Indian flag.]

And then, wanting to tell Mishu more about India, as perhaps many other Indian parents here do, Divya began telling her child also what she sees as India's history. She told Mishu about Khalistan and the desire on the part of some Sikhs for a separate homeland. The bombings and killings that had gone on in that struggle. At the end of that story, my sister said, Mishu asked her, and I quote her exact words, "Was their wish fulfilled?"

Divya said to Mishu, "No." And, she told me, Mishu said to her, "Thank God."

Oddly enough, I too had been thinking of the Sikhs today.

I was thinking of the barbarity that was meted out to the thousands of Sikhs living in Delhi and elsewhere in the riots that followed the assassination of Indira Gandhi in October 1984.

In the next few days in the U.S., as the death toll is announced, there shall be an orgy of fresh violence, perhaps not in any widespread manner on American soil, but certainly elsewhere. Once it is confirmed that there has been an Arab hand behind today's tragedy, a greater military might will be unleashed in foreign lands. In this country, in community halls, in bars, in homes, in comedy clubs, in classrooms, in films and on television, there shall be fresh charges of hate against Arab and other minorities.

Propaganda will build its own prison camps of disinformation and bigotry. And the armed forces will erect their twin towers there. Will Indians in the U.S., given the dominance of the Hindu right at home, remain untouched by all of this?

I remember the way in which in a DTC bus or in the streets, for several days after the riots in Delhi, those very Sikhs who had been your neighbors till yesterday suddenly looked so incongruous in our midst, so very alien.

In the U.S., Arabs and others who "look like them," which would also mean Indians, will take on that subdued, hard-to-place passiveness, that had overcome the Sikhs in the winter months of 1984.

Who will teach the Americans this history? Who will teach Mishu this history?

On the radio today I heard a young lawyer talking to a reporter. The lawyer's voice shook with what I imagine was hurt and pride when she said, "I cannot believe this is happening in our America."

Such innocence. Such ignorance.

An Indian living in the U.S. will never say this. We have no such illusions of invulnerability. We bear the scar of more painful histories. We look at what has been unfolding on our television sets today, and we are able to put ourselves on another plane.

This is the plane on which we are familiar and unsurprised, even if shocked, by the erupting conflagrations of our times. We are veterans of conflict. We have seen it all. We will even advise people on how to deal with terrorists. And here, like experts in war who think they know all, we run the risk of making a fatal error.

We will take the arrogance that we learned at home and make it a part of our life in America. We will teach our children to make the whole world our Kashmir. We will become guns trained at the heads of the innocent.

Not Just Falling Buildings

"For journalists, we face the largest assignment of our careers," the writer said at the end of her article. "Americans will need not just the news but perspective, not just the images but understanding. They will need from us our very best."

These were fine, stirring words. But, I found that I wasn't doing too well in the perspective department. What did those words mean anyway?

The article I was reading was on the Poynter Institute website. I had come to it because a few hours after the planes had crashed into the twin towers of the World Trade Center, Sree Sreenivasan of the South Asian Journalists Association sent out a memo on his listserv. The memo said that this website offered suggestions to reporters covering the story of the attack.

I confess I considered for a while stringing together a sentence about the Statue of Liberty near the World Trade Center and my sudden awareness, at moments like these as I walked on the streets, that I was a foreigner. But, I gave up that attempt and began worrying wholeheartedly about the loved ones I hadn't heard from.

On the streets near my house, I saw people embracing each other or crying. I knew that it wasn't that they lacked perspective. They had a perspective—perhaps that is why they were able to cry. And there I was—aware that Americans needed from me "my very best"—hunting for perspective.

An old friend from college, Sankarshan Thakur, now an editor at the *Indian Express,* sent an email. His whole note, starting with the words "THIS IS AN S.O.S.," was written in block letters. When I saw those words, my first thought was "Oh no, he has a relative in New York City whom he cannot find. . . ."

But, I quickly realized that all that was needed from me was a report. More perspective. Sankarshan had even specified the length. 1,800 words. Dryly, at the end of his note, he had added "By the way, hope you are safe."

My friend's note really made me think. What was I going to write?

I went back to the Poynter Institute website. This time I read an article that made it clear that more than catastrophic events, what needed to be stressed was courage and creativity. Catastrophes cannot be equated with humanity. "They may define news and history," the writer said, "but not a civilization."

Even though I didn't entirely get it, I read those words for the same reason one drank Horlicks in one's childhood. For strength.

The writer's wisdom was laid out in clean, muscular prose: "The things that truly define us take time: the emancipation of slaves, the achievement of rights, the creation of new technologies, the curing of disease, the building of communities. Not just Hiroshima, but the Marshall Plan. Not just the AIDS epidemic, but Jonas Salk."

I think I finally understood what the first writer had meant by perspective. I still had a problem. The second writer wasn't telling me what the other half of the equation was. I tried to formulate this for myself. I only got the first half of the sentence: "Not just falling buildings, but. . ."

I tried to remember what had happened in the last few hours. My wife's brother, who works on Wall Street, had sent an email saying he was safe. We were very relieved. He is going to get married to his high-school sweetheart this December in Karachi. Then, I had found out that my friend Rakesh had sprinted away safely from the falling debris. I broke down and cried on getting his news. Other friends were reaching out with gestures of love and concern.

I went back to the writer's examples. And suddenly, a thought came to me. For every person in a given country, for example, Afghanistan, for every person who turns to terror, there are millions who go on with their lives, in the worst of conditions, without raising a finger to harm anyone else.

The above fact should be self-evident but it needs to be said here, in this country, recovering from what has been a terrible, devastating attack.

So, yes, as the writer advised me in his column on the website, I want to be upbeat. I, too, want to stress virtue, and I can only do it by emphasizing the humanity of entire nations who are now being charged with this crime.

As the talking heads on American television have begun bristling with threats of armed retaliation, it is necessary to say this over and over again. The Arab people are not just terrorists, but teachers. Not just terrorists, but patient mothers. Not just terrorists, but children wanting toys.

Or, to hell with cliches! They are not just terrorists, but a man worried about his second ulcer. Not just terrorists, but a woman wanting books. Not just terrorists, but a family terrified of terrorists who come in tanks.

I returned once again to the Poynter website and found an article written by an American journalist who had been working, on the morning of the attack, with a group of visiting Saudi journalists. One of the Saudis had told the writer, "This is not an attack against America. This is a crime against humanity."

By making that statement, the Saudi journalist had expressed his own humanity; and by reporting it, the American journalist had expressed his.

But, I beg to differ from both. Let me first say that the devastation that was visited on the people in New York City on Tuesday did, indeed, affect human beings very deeply all over the world. Ordinary individuals in different nations mourn this tragedy. I do too. But, my grief for this loss does not in any way contradict my understanding that this was indeed an attack on America. In fact, we need to be emphatic on one point. If Osama Bin Laden was indeed responsible for Tuesday's attacks, then America was attacked by its own creation.

Today, Secretary Colin Powell mentioned Bin Laden as a possible suspect. This is the first time a U.S. administrator has publicly named him. Yesterday, Tony Blair has already declared his resolve to "dismantle the machinery of terror." The governments that both these men represent were active in arming and building the arsenal of the Afghani mujahideen ever since the 1970s. The attack on Tuesday, if indeed it was the handiwork of Osama Bin Laden, is a matter of U.S. militarism and murderous intrigue coming home to roost.

I remember very clearly the 1996 photograph of the Afghan President Najibullah and his brother Shahpur Ahmadzai in Kabul. The two men dangled several feet above the ground, hung to death, while a Taliban militant faced the photographer. The former President was clad in sneakers and jeans. His face was half-turned away from the camera. Looking at the photograph, one could not see that the Taliban had cut Najibullah's genitals and stuffed them in his mouth.

I was reminded of this photograph when I read Suemas Milne in the *Guardian* today. Milne recalled that particular moment of Taliban ascendancy: "But by then Bin Laden had turned against his American sponsors, while U.S.-sponsored Pakistani intelligence had spawned the grotesque Taliban now protecting him. To punish its wayward Afghan offspring, the U.S. subsequently forced through a sanctions regime which has helped push 4 million to the brink of starvation, according to the latest UN figures, while Afghan refugees fan out across the world."

What happened in New York City is not just about falling buildings. It is also about nations that have been devastated by the machinations of the U.S.

The truth is that the spread of Islamic fundamentalism in countries like Afghanistan, Pakistan, and Palestine is to a very large extent also a result of U.S. policies in those regions.

How much of "understanding" and "perspective" will we need in order to be able to convey this to the U.S. administration now once again preparing for war?

Dispatch 4/September 20

Signs Taken for Wonders

Yesterday, on the Interstate Highway 70, barely an hour outside Washington, D.C., I was passing through the typical, sunlit landscape of early fall. The leaves on the trees in the surrounding hills were touched with the colors of autumn. Yellow, gold, red, russet, and, here and there, quiet explosions of orange.

I stopped at a McDonald's for coffee. The U.S. flag as well as the red flag of the fast-food chain hung on half-mast, mourning the deaths from the attacks on September 11. My wife, Mona, went to the women's room. On the walls of the toilet, she found fresh, neatly printed slogans in a school-girlish hand: "God Bless America, Home Sweet Home," "No Freeloaders," and "America Love It or Leave It."

In a few minutes, we were back on the highway, the car passing hilly meadows where horses gently plucked on grass. But, this serenity, so becalming, was deceptive. Like the language of the graffiti, tinged with innocence, it hid a deep disturbance. This disturbance can be given a name: it is a nationalism that is laced with grief and anger. Its assertion of pride is underlined with menace. It serves as a warning to those who would dissent.

The British writer Martin Amis has commented that the United Airlines Flight 175 was "an Intercontinental Ballistic Missile" aimed at American innocence—an innocence which was revealed to be "a luxurious and anachronistic delusion."

But, Amis is being optimistic. I say this because innocence, mixed with hubris, persists all across this grieving nation. Let's go back to the graffiti. What could be more innocent than the understanding that the only way of being a valuable part of a nation was through unquestioning love?

Does even being in love mean that anymore? Did it ever?

We need to be skeptical of innocence, especially at the level of language. We cannot take signs for wonders. Indeed, such skepticism is practiced even by the intelligence authorities when they comb through the messages of those that they have been watching. I read in the *New Yorker* recently that officials "look for telephone calls using code words to warn that something is going to happen—sometimes innocuous phrases, such as 'There is a wedding tomorrow' or 'You should come home.'"

I advocate skepticism or doubt as an alternative to fundamentalism. Doubt and concern can be a weapon against the absolutism not only of the terrorists but those who would wield terror in return. We need to read, against the grain, the loose use of words like "freedom" and "justice." Freedom to bomb from on high or freedom to live lives free from attacks? Justice in terms of fierce retribution or justice as the right to live without duress?

One can hear that note of doubt, a skepticism voiced against the righteousness of our rulers, in a public letter to President Bush written by the parents of one who has been missing in the rubble of the World Trade Center. Phyllis and Orlando Rodriguez wrote in their letter: "Your response to this attack does not make us feel better about our son's death. It makes us feel worse. It makes us feel that our government is using our son's memory as a justification to cause suffering for other sons and parents in other lands."

The twin towers were like alphabets linked to words like America and power and security. The towers were destroyed by men who fiendishly read that meaning in a clear way. For them to be doubtful would have meant an openness to possibilities about the contrary meaning of the buildings. Then, they would have had to concede that in those towers were ordinary men and women with their irreplaceable lives.

The hijackers held close to themselves their own form of murderous innocence. Now, the rest of the world, particularly President Bush, must not blithely parrot that same language when they seek to "bomb Afghanistan back into the Stone Age."

Medina. Old walled city, Kashgar.

Today
September 11, 2001

Russell C. Leong

Today, it's another city
They say.
Another New York. Another L.A.
Another America changed forever.
Newscasters, generals, and presidents say.

Today, it's another city
They say.
Bring third world terrorists to justice.
Look for someone slightly darker
    (than even me)
Maybe a guy not so slant-eyed, taller,
Who speaks Arabic,
Not Chinese or English.

Today, it's another city
They say.
He, or she, or they, may be praying or plotting
In a mosque. In a temple. In a church.
In a truck, car, or plane.

Today, it's another city
They say.
Nah. Mexicans don't qualify as the enemy.

RUSSELL C. LEONG is the editor of *Amerasia Journal*.

They just cross borders, everyday, they say.
Not even Chinese, or Russians are enemies
That's another place, another time.

Today, it's another city
They say.
But what if the enemy lurks within?

> *Within the alley of the aorta.*
> *Within the barrio of the brain.*
> *Within the gutter below the skin.*
> *Within the bullet of the eye.*
> *Within the twist of the blade*
> *Within your back?*

Dead or alive, I'm a different person
Than who I was yesterday.

Look me in the eye, I say.
For it's another city, today.

Sunday bazaar, Kashgar.
© 2001, Eric C. Chang

Sumi Koide, New York City JACL Chapter President and Inderjert Singh, candidate for New York City Council, at teach-in and youth speakout forum held at New York University, September 22, 2001.

© 2001, Corky Lee

II. Civil Liberties & Internment

Soldier posting Civilian Exclusion Order No. 1 together with instructions for
evacuation procedures. March 23, 1942, Bainbridge Island, Washington.
Seattle Post-Intelligencer/Executive Order 9066, Maisie and Richard Conrat
(Los Angeles: UCLA Asian American Studies Center, 1992)

Thinking through Internment

Thinking through Internment:
12/7 and 9/11

Jerry Kang

Jerry Kang giving address at "Struggle for Social Justice: A Symposium on Recognition, Reparations, and Redress," Spring 2001, UCLA.

© 2001, Mary U. Kao

What 12/7 Has to Teach about 9/11: Race Matters

The terrorist attacks on 9-11 have frequently been analogized to Pearl Harbor. In many ways, the analogy is apt. Just as that attack launched us into World War II, the attacks on the World Trade Center and the Pentagon have launched us into a new kind of war, against terrorism. But waging this sort of borderless war poses great risks, not only to the soldiers commanded to fight but also to core American values. In this way, Pearl Harbor raises other disturbing memories, those of the internment.

Like the recent explosions on the East Coast, the bombing of Pearl Harbor on 12-7 shattered our feeling of national security. How could this have happened? Ordinary individuals, prominent journalists, and government officials soon started pointing the finger at the Japanese in America. Viewing these "Orientals" as incurably foreign, speaking foreign languages, perpetuating foreign cultures, practicing foreign religions (Shinto, Buddhism), American society could not distinguish between the Empire of Japan and Americans of Japanese descent. As General DeWitt, in charge of the Western Defense Command, put it, "A Jap's a Jap." In his ominously titled "Final Recommendation," he explained: "[R]acial affinities are not severed by migration. The Japanese race is an enemy race and while many second and third generation Japanese born on United States soil, possessed of United States citizenship have become 'Americanized' the racial strains are undiluted."[1] As government reports rushed to the conclusion that

JERRY KANG is Professor of Law, University of California, Los Angeles School of Law.

Jerry Kang

Japanese Americans aided and abetted the attack, the wheels of the internment machinery began turning.

On February 19, 1942, President Franklin Roosevelt issued Executive Order 9066, which authorized military commanders in the Western U.S. to issue whatever orders were necessary for national security. Although prompted by DeWitt's plan for mass exclusion of Japanese Americans, the Executive Order conveniently made no mention of race or ethnicity. In March, Congress criminalized disobedience of military regulations issued pursuant to the executive order. By December, an efficient, empowered military with the newly created War Relocation Authority had concentrated nearly all Japanese on the West Coast into ten desolate camps, surrounded by barbed wire and armed sentries. All this without the declaration of martial law. All this without individualized determinations of guilt or disloyalty.

The internment was challenged in courts of law, but the Supreme Court affirmed the constitutionality of the curfew and exclusion orders in the 1943 and 1944 cases of *Hirabayashi*,[2] *Yasui*,[3] and *Korematsu*.[4] While protesting loudly that racial prejudice should trigger the highest scrutiny, the Court nevertheless deferred to the government's vague claims of military necessity. Was the internment in fact justified as a matter of military necessity? A Congressionally appointed blue ribbon commission concluded in 1982 that the "broad historical causes which shaped these decisions were race prejudice, war hysteria, and a failure of political leadership,"[5] not any genuine military necessity. In other words, it was a tragic wartime mistake. For that, all branches of the U.S. government have apologized.

What lessons then should we learn from this mistake? One lesson could be that this was just an accident, in a time of war, and that the Supreme Court erred because it was not given complete, accurate information. It turns out that the Executive Branch (Department of War and Department of Justice) suppressed key evidence from the Office of Naval Intelligence, Federal Bureau of Investigation, and Federal Communications Commission. This exculpatory evidence, in the form of smoking gun documents (burned reports, edited footnotes, and the like), was uncovered in the early 1980s[6] and helped eventually reverse the criminal convictions of the World War II litigants.[7] Applied to the present crisis, this lesson would counsel against law enforcement zeal that prevents a fair, balanced consideration of all the facts by our political leaders, the judiciary, and the American people.

But learning only this lesson would be to commit another error. We did not intern *en masse* German and Italian Americans, even though we were at war with those nations too. We did not intern *en masse* the huge numbers of Japanese in Hawaii (where Pearl Harbor is), for doing so would have meant shutting down that economy.[8] We did not abstain from drafting Japanese Americans from the very internment camps that kept jailed their traumatized parents. The Supreme Court knew and understood this. Even without the suppressed evidence, Justice Murphy knew enough to dissent in *Korematsu* and lament that the majority had fallen into "the ugly abyss of racism."

The more important lesson, then, is not that wartime creates mistakes; instead, it is that wartime coupled with racism and intolerance create particular types of mistakes. Specifically, we overestimate the threat posed by racial "others" (in WWII, Japanese Americans; today, Arab Americans, Muslims, Middle Easterners, immigrants, and anyone who looks like "them"). Simultaneously, we underestimate how our response to those threats burden those "others" (in WWII, shattering lives through the internment; today, intimidation and violence by individuals, and racial profiling by the state). Historian Roger Daniels put it more bluntly:

> the general tendency of educated Americans. . .to write the evacuation off as a "wartime mistake" is to obscure its true significance. Rather than a mistake. . .the legal atrocity which was committed against Japanese Americans was the logical outgrowth of over three centuries of American experience, an experience which taught Americans to regard the United States as a White man's country. . . .[9]

Thinking through Profiling

Most people believe that nothing like the internment could ever happen again. Surely, as yet, it seems politically implausible to intern tens of thousands of American citizens of Arab descent in desert camps, for years, without individual determinations of guilt. But what about less severe curtailments of civil liberties, both *de jure* and *de facto*? (Recall that the first step of the internment process was a curfew.) Specifically, consider the hard case of racial profiling. After 9-11 and our retaliation, should we authorize racial profiling of Arab Americans and those who look like them? More specifically, should we use race or ethnicity as a substantial factor to subject someone to a search or special surveillance? During World War II, Japanese Americans were subject to racial profiling that went way beyond search and surveillance, but the idea remains the same.

Utilitarian justifications are now given for what was once unsavory practice: The benefits (stopping another terrorist attack) are said to outweigh the costs (minor inconveniences for those profiled). If we suppose for the sake of argument that cost-benefit analysis is the right approach, how should Americans of good conscience who have learned the internment's lessons think through the issue?

First, we should demand good data. For instance, what data might justify special searches of anyone who looks "Arab" at an airport? There are up to seven million Arab Americans in the United States, up to eight million Muslims, and if we add all those South Asians (1.6 million), Latinos, and African Americans who might "appear" Arab, and discount overlaps, we have a ball park figure of at least 10 million folks. How many of these are bona fide terrorists? Let's say a 100. That is a percentage of 0.001 percent. As rough comparison (admittedly, comparing apples to oranges), consider that in 1999 alone, roughly 350,000 men were arrested for violent crimes. There are about 135 million men alive in America. That is a percentage of 0.26 percent. Should we stop and search all men because they may act violently?

Obviously, these numbers are rough and speculative. Maybe there are 1,000, not 100, bona fide terrorists in our midst. Also, as we have painfully witnessed, one violent terrorist can do far more damage than one violent street criminal. Still, we should demand the best data available from our government. Even if the government can only provide guesses, forcing the government publicly to provide ball park figures is itself a check on reckless profiling.

Second, we should strive to parse the data correctly. Humans are notoriously bad with probabilities. For instance, the fact that 100 percent of the terrorists are Arab-looking men does not mean that 100 percent of Arab-looking men are terrorists. We also fixate on relative probabilities instead of absolute ones. So, even if the Arab-looking man seated to your left is 100 times more likely to be a terrorist than the Aryan-looking man seated to your right (relative), 100 times a number essentially zero is still near zero (absolute). This is an important reminder for our own conduct as private citizens; it is an even more important reminder for public policymakers.

Third, we should not overestimate the benefit. Is racial profiling really that effective? There will surely be "false negatives," those

February 27, 1942,
Oakland, California.

Dorothea Lange,
WRA/*Executive Order 9066*,
Maisie and Richard Conrat
(Los Angeles: UCLA Asian
American Studies Center, 1992)

who turn out to be terrorists who do not fit the profile. Recall that many of the terrorists in the 9-11 attacks hardly behaved as fundamentalist Muslims: They drank alcohol and got lap dances. And shrewd terrorists will respond to Arab-based profiling by sending different types of bodies, which look Asian (consider Malaysia or the Philippines) or pass for White (consider Turkey). We may also waste valuable resources on "false positives," those who fit the profile but who are not terrorists. That is the lesson of scientist Wen Ho Lee, who was unfairly scapegoated as the "spy" who leaked nuclear secrets to China. That is also the lesson of the internment.

Moreover, if profiling is being justified in cold, logical cost-benefit terms, we should dispassionately consider how many statistical

Jerry Kang

59

lives we will actually save. Could we save far more lives by man-dating head-curtain airbags, reducing the national speed limit (thereby decreasing dependence on Middle Eastern oil), discouraging smoking, and encouraging exercise? To be sure, the possibility of death in a car accident feels different than death in a terrorist act. The fear of the former does not paralyze the nation; the fear of the latter does. But that difference does not automatically justify what might end up being a misallocation of life-saving resources.

Fourth, do not underestimate the harm. Just as it is easy to spend other people's money, it is easy to burden other people's liberties—especially racial and ethnic minorities. Just ask a young Black man profiled as a rapist; a Black woman profiled as a drug mule; a Latino profiled as an illegal immigrant; a survivor of the Japanese American internment profiled as a traitor. The leap of empathy is difficult, so we must all try hard to imagine living the life of a "false positive," stopped at airports, bus stops, stadiums, skyscrapers, and malls. Think about the time, the inconvenience, the insult to your dignity. Think about trying to calm your children bewildered by armed men pulling you aside. Now think about this happening every day of your life.

Fifth, understand context and consequence. If the profile is accurate, why is that so? Can we simply take the sociological facts "as they are" and ignore what context made them come to be, ignore how government action based on that profile might perpetuate an unjust past? Moreover, what are the long-term consequences of profiling? Will relegating Arab Americans into second-class status be strategically beneficial in our attempt to bolster human intelligence? Will it fuel propaganda that America represses Islam?

Consider another lesson from the internment. In *Hirabayashi*, the Court noted that because American society had discriminated against the Japanese legally, politically, and economically, they had been kept from integrating into mainstream society:

> There is support for the view that social, economic and political conditions which have prevailed since the close of the last century, when the Japanese began to come to this country in substantial numbers, have intensified their solidarity and have in large measure prevented their assimilation as an integral part of the white population.[10]

In a footnote, the Court continued by detailing federal law that denied Japanese naturalization and prevented their immigration; state law that prevented property ownership and inter-marriage with Whites; and economic discrimination that limited professional and employment opportunities.[11]

Exactly right. But then, the Court went on the explain—in an entirely rational but still disturbing way—that therefore the Japanese posed a greater national security risk.[12] This presents a horrible Catch-22. In essence, the Court said: Because America has treated you badly, you have reason to be disloyal; therefore, America now has reason to treat you still more badly, by restricting your civil rights. The analogy post 9-11 is clear. If state actors racially profile and private actors racially harass, we might be forcing another group of Americans into the same impossible situation. Tomorrow's burdens will be justified by the resentment caused by today's burdens—a vicious cycle.

Sixth and finally, we must consider morality. Only after taking these five steps can any profiling policy be justified "on the numbers." But aren't moral principles embedded in our Constitution supposed to trump utilitarian calculations? Isn't this precisely what the Supreme Court claimed to be doing when it struck down useful affirmative action programs for violating the rights of innocent Whites? Is it now unfair or unpatriotic to hold the conservative Justice Antonin Scalia to his word: "In the eyes of government, we are just one race here. It is American."[13]

Still, we should not be surprised if courts determine that national security in the face of terrorism is—in the lingo of constitutional law—a "compelling interest" and that crude forms of racial profiling, notwithstanding its over- and under-inclusiveness, are "narrowly tailored" to furthering that interest. It would be foolish to think that the courts will necessarily save us from the excesses of the more political branches. That is another lesson of the internment. This is all the more reason to demand that our political leaders publicly make the cost-benefit and moral case in favor of racial profiling before they adopt any such practice.

We are living through times of terror. And liberty does not flourish in fear. Those tutored in realpolitik may pooh-pooh this essay with shibboleths heard during all wars: We have a "fighting Constitution," which is not a "suicide pact." Indeed, in *Hirabayashi*, the Court exclaimed that "[t]he war power of the national government is 'the power to wage war' successfully."[14] A call to remember the lessons of the internment—that racism warps what we honestly believe to be rational calculations, especially in times of crisis—is not a call for weakness or suicide. True heeding these lessons will not make us any more secure against terrorism. But we should remember, even in times of terror, that the Constitution in itself does not make our nation strong. It merely makes us worthy of our strength.

Notes

1. Report of the Commission on Wartime Relocation and Internment of Civilians, *Personal Justice Denied* 66 (CLPEF 1997) (quoting DeWitt's Final Report, 34) (hereinafter *Personal Justice Denied*).

2. *Hirabayashi* v. *United States*, 320 U.S. 81 (1943).

3. *Yasui* v. *United States*, 320 U.S. 115 (1943).

4. *Korematsu* v. *United States*, 323 U.S. 214 (1944).

5. *See Personal Justice Denied*, note 1, 18.

6. See generally Eric Yamamoto, Margaret Chon, Carol Izumi, Jerry Kang, and Frank Wu, *Race, Rights and Reparation: Law and the Japanese American Internment* (Aspen Law & Business, 2001) (reproducing the original suppressed documents), 286-318.

7. See, e.g., *Korematsu* v. *United States*, 584 F. Supp. 1406 (N.D. Cal. 1984).

8. We did, however, declare martial law in Hawai'i.

9. Roger Daniels, *Concentration Camps, North America: Japanese in The United States And Canada During World War II* (Krieger, 1981), xvi .

10. Hirabayashi, 320 U.S., 96.

11. *Ibid.*, note 4.

12. Specifically, the Court wrote: "The restrictions, both practical and legal, affecting the privileges and opportunities afforded to persons of Japanese extraction residing in the United States, have been sources of irritation and may well have tended to increase their isolation, and in many instances their attachments to Japan and its institutions.

"Viewing these data in all their aspects, Congress and the Executive could reasonably have concluded that these conditions have encouraged the continued attachment of members of this group to Japan and Japanese institutions. These are only some of the many considerations which those charged with the responsibility for the national defense could take into account in determining the nature and extent of the danger of espionage and sabotage, in the event of invasion or air raid attack." *Hirabayashi*, 320 U.S. at 98-99.

13. *Adarand Constructors, Inc.* v. *Pena*, 515 U.S. 200, 239 (1995) (Scalia, J., concurring in part and concurring in the judgment).

14. *Hirabayashi*, 320 U.S., 93 (quoting Charles Evan Hughes, *War Powers Under the Constitution*, 42 A.B.A. Rep. 232, 238).

The Loaded Weapon

Eric K. Yamamoto and Susan Kiyomi Serrano

[T]he Court for all time has validated the principle of racial
discrimination in criminal procedure and of transplanting American citizens. The principle lies about like a loaded weapon ready
for the hand of any authority that can bring forward a plausible
claim of an urgent need.

Justice Jackson, dissenting
Korematsu v. *U.S.*, 323 U.S. 214 (1944)

Ahmed's Secret Incarceration

What do you make of Nasser Ahmed's secret incarceration? An
imagined Kafkaesque trial of the absurd? Could it be real, here in
the United States?

Nasser Ahmed spends over three years in prison as a national
security threat. "Secret evidence" in a "secret" government proceeding marks him a bona fide threat to the nation's security. An
Egyptian father of four U.S. citizen children, Ahmed is never
charged with a crime. Even so, the Immigration and Naturalization Service imprisons and then seeks to deport him based on
evidence hidden from Ahmed and his attorney. For an entire year,
the government refuses to even furnish Ahmed's lawyer with a
summary of the evidence. Finally, the government provides a one-
line summary, asserting only that it has evidence "concerning
respondent's association with a known terrorist organization."
The government refuses to identify the organization.[1] Unable to
defend himself against nonexistent charges on the basis of undis-

ERIC K. YAMAMOTO is Professor of Law, William S. Richardson School of
Law, University of Hawai'i at Manoa.

SUSAN KIYOMI SERRANO is Project Director, Equal Justice Society, William
S. Richardson School of Law, University of Hawai'i at Manoa.

closed evidence in a secret proceeding, Ahmed languishes in solitary confinement.

After years of incarceration the actual "secret" evidence is revealed, and it shows that Ahmed has not engaged in any kind of terrorist activity. Nor has he supported any terrorist organizations. The government imprisoned and sought to deport Ahmed on national security grounds because of his "associations." And what were the government's allegations of those associations? Ahmed once was appointed by a U.S. court to serve as a paralegal and translator for the defense team of Sheik Abdel Rahman, who was being tried in a U.S. court for seditious conspiracy. Three years of secret incarceration for doing what the court asked and indeed authorized him to do.

Ahmed's civil liberties nightmare sounds like tortured Kafkaesque imaginings. It is, however, reality. United States reality. One such story among many. And it happened during time of comparative peace, well before the public outcry for revenge abroad and heightened national security protections at home following the September 11 attacks on the World Trade Center and Pentagon. A board of immigration appeals court eventually reviewing Ahmed's case said that Ahmed's blind imprisonment for groundless national security reasons was an injustice. But that was before. Before the "War on Terrorism."

Today, in response to the horrific killing of thousands of Americans and people from countries around the world, the President, Congress and federal agencies, like the Immigration and Naturalization Service, are creating a new regime of national security measures. Some of these measures are needed and only reasonably burdensome—like added checks at airports and increased security at nuclear power plants and government buildings. But others, like secret detentions, are immensely troubling. When the government abuses its national security powers, particularly by targeting members of vulnerable groups, and is challenged, how are the U.S. courts likely to rule?

This is the key question for all concerned about both the nation's security and civil liberties, for all concerned about justice here as well as abroad. Will the judiciary, as popularly believed, stand strong under the Constitution as the bulwark against ill-conceived, harshly discriminatory government action during times of national stress? Will it assure due process and equal protection for those denigrated in the public mind, the very democratic values that make the nation's security worth protecting? Or, taking an implicit cue from the U.S. Supreme Court, might frontline and appeals courts react with more fear than balance and replay in postmodern form the injustice of the Japanese American World War II internment? Recall the potentially prescient dissent of Supreme Court Justice Jackson in the 1944 *Korematsu* case, which upheld the legality of the internment: "The Court has for all time validated the principle of racial discrimination in criminal procedure and of transplanting citizens. The principle stands as a loaded weapon ready for the hand of any authority that can bring forward a plausible claim of urgent need."

The "Law" after September 11

Two months after the deadly plane-bombings in New York and Washington D.C., the U.S. continues to detain over a thousand "suspected" terrorists. Officials have not revealed the names or citizenship of hundreds of those arrested or their places of detention. None has been charged with terrorist crimes. Civil rights groups called for the release of information about these individuals, arguing that the secrecy surrounding these detentions "prevents any democratic oversight of the government's response to the attacks." In the face of charges that the government has been indefinitely jailing innocent people without charges, proper food or access to attorneys, U.S. Attorney General Ashcroft issued a Nixonian non-denial denial: the government has engaged in no "wholesale abuse" of those detained.[2]

In the wake of September 11, the government responded with a spate of laws designed both to address broad threats to the nation's physical security and to salve the nation's damaged psyche. It did so by expanding executive and military powers to pursue what it described as a "war against terrorists"—increased wiretapping and surveillance, communications intercepts, secret property searches, racial investigative profiling, prolonged detentions and accelerated deportations. The government did this in part by curtailing rights of speech, press and association, as well rights to freedom from racial discrimination and incarceration without charges or trial. In signing the far-reaching anti-terrorism "Patriot" bill into law, President Bush vowed that the government would "enforce [it] with all the urgency of a nation at war."[3]

Many among the American public responded with deep concern both for those killed and for the proper balance of national security and civil liberties. Others reacted by looking for scapegoats. Those remotely resembling persons of Arab ancestry were targeted. In Arizona, a man angry about the bombings shot and killed a Sikh storeowner. Men in a car shouting epithets ran over and killed a Native American woman. Airline pilots, reacting to passenger sentiments, banned Arab, Pakistani and Asian Indians from flights for no other reason than their apparent ancestry. High school students in Dearborn, Michigan taunted a Muslim girl wearing a traditional headscarf, kicked her and slammed her into a locker. In Los Angeles, two men mistook a Latino man for an Arab, followed him home and kicked in his front door. In San Francisco, fake blood was smeared across the entrance to an Islamic community center. Businesses, homes and mosques were firebombed and vandalized. Housing evictions, job firings, verbal harassment as well as assaults were reported in alarming numbers.

President Bush cautioned that the U.S. was targeting "terrorists," not Muslims or all persons of Arab ancestry. At the same time the government's actions potentially raised the ugly specter of guilt-by-association ("if you're not with us, you're against us"). This principle, for some, was a coded reference to ancestry, casting suspicion on all persons of Arab descent. Indeed the FBI and INS reportedly commenced racial profiling investigations and detentions; the Justice Department appeared to resurrect support for the formerly discredited secret trials based on secret evidence for the deportation of "dangerous" immigrants—like Nasser Ahmed. Attorney General Ashcroft announced a "wartime reorganization" of the Justice Department to aggressively investigate and prosecute terrorists. The government also launched a "terrorist tracking task force" to root out suspected terrorists who overstay their visas. Attorney General Ashcroft vowed to prosecute those suspected of associations with designated terrorist groups: "If you overstay your visas even by one day, we will arrest you. . . . If you violate a local law, we will hope that you will, and work to make sure that you are put in jail and be kept in custody as long as possible."[4]

Should we worry about the swashbuckling rhetoric of the head of the U.S. Justice Department? Should we be concerned about the new expansive executive edicts, agency actions and Congressional enactments? Don't we have a Constitution that gives the government strong national security powers while protecting the civil liberties of all in America? More specifically, aren't the U.S. courts the bulwark against violations of the Bill of Rights? The answers are that yes, we have explicit constitutional guarantees of due process and equal protection, but that no, the actual performance of our judiciary during times of national stress suggests that the courts will be influenced by popular politics and will subtly renounce their role as constitutional backstop; they will instead defer almost completely to the executive and legislative branches.

We submit that this is how U.S. courts tend to perform during times of national distress—taking a hands-off approach in reviewing government national security actions, even where fundamental liberties are sharply restricted. As a consequence, the courts most often legitimize, rather than check, the actions of the executive and legislative branches reacting to the "ephemeral emotions of their political constituencies."[5] In times like these, we therefore must ask, as a democracy, how do we hold the executive and legislative branches accountable for military or national security actions inimical to the civil liberties of those in America, and who will insure that accountability? Insights from the law of the Japanese American internment help illuminate the complex dimensions to these questions.

Insights from Japanese American Internment: The Hands-off Role of the Courts

The politically popular and legally-sanctioned internment of 120,000 Japanese Americans during World War II illustrates the dangers of political and racial scapegoating during national crisis. On February 19, 1942, President Franklin Roosevelt issued Executive Order 9066, authorizing military commanders to protect West Coast military facilities. Based on fear and racial stereotypes, the government then interned 120,000 Japanese Americans without charges, indictment or hearing. The internees were forced to abandon their homes, farms and businesses with only what they could carry. They lost their property, jobs and sense of security. They endured the desert heat, cold and dust storms in ten desolate camps surrounded by barbed wire and armed guards.[6]

Three American citizens of Japanese ancestry challenged the internment as a violation of the constitutional guarantee of equal protection of laws. In *Hirabayashi*, *Yasui*, and *Korematsu*, the government countered by asserting that the danger of espionage and sabotage by persons of Japanese ancestry on the West Coast justified its extraordinary actions. The government argued that "all Japanese, including American citizens, were, by culture and race, predisposed to loyalty to Japan and to disloyalty to the United States; that Japanese on the West Coast had committed and were likely to commit acts of espionage and sabotage against the United States; and that mass action was needed because there was insuf-

Eric K. Yamamoto and
Susan Kiyomi Serrano

ficient time to determine disloyalty individually."[7] No evidence supported these assertions.

In deciding the cases, the Supreme Court announced that it would subject the government's discriminatory actions to the highest level of scrutiny. "[D]istinctions between citizens solely because of their ancestry are by their very nature odious to a free people." "[A]ll legal restrictions which curtail the civil rights of a single racial group are immediately suspect."

Despite its pronouncements, however, the Court deferred completely to the military's unsubstantiated assertions of "necessity." It simply adopted the military's sweeping conclusions about disloyal Japanese Americans. The Court thus upheld the constitutionality of the internment (specifically, the curfew and exclusion) and thereby sanctioned the government's extraordinary civil liberties abuses. Thousands of innocent Japanese Americans remained imprisoned on account of their race, later to carry into private life the legally sanctioned stigma of disloyalty.

War Plus Racism Plus Law

Forty years passed before unearthed documents revealed that there had been no military necessity to justify the internment, that government decisionmakers knew this at the time and later lied about it to the Supreme Court. In fact, the War and Justice Departments altered, destroyed and suppressed key exonerating evidence from the Office of Naval Intelligence, Federal Bureau of Investigation, and Federal Communications Commission. In extraordinary *coram nobis* proceedings in the 1980s, the lower federal courts reversed course and acknowledged egregious government misconduct in justifying the internment and the resulting "manifest injustice" for all interned Japanese Americans. In 1988, as the U.S. intensified its pro-democracy and human rights fight against communism, Congress passed the Civil Liberties Act. The law provided $20,000 reparations for each surviving internee, mandated a presidential apology and established a civil liberties public education fund.

Despite the *coram nobis* victories and the Civil Liberties Act, the original *Korematsu* case remains on the law books. The Supreme Court "has not overruled or formally discredited the *Korematsu* decision or its principle of judicial deference to government claims of military necessity. Nor has the Court announced in principle that the demanding standards of review now normally applicable to government restrictions of constitutionally protected liberties are unaltered by the government's claim of military necessity or national security." In fact, in a whole range of modern-day cases, courts have deferred to government assertions of national security at the expense of civil liberties.[8] Indeed, U.S. Chief Justice Rehnquist, ignoring the stark revelations of the *Korematsu* and *Hirabayashi coram nobis* cases, recently defended the internment as legally justified, at least as to first generation Japanese Americans. The Chief Justice also opined that the judiciary should defer to the executive branch and military during times of war, even in the face of harsh treatment of civilians in the U.S. on the basis of ancestry, even in the absence of martial law.[9]

In the minds of many Americans the internment is an aberration, a bad mistake during war. Wartime exigencies gave rise to hasty actions. The Supreme Court erred for this reason, not because of individual prejudices and the forces of popular sentiment. In sharp contrast, and in light of the revelations of the *coram nobis* cases, Professor Jerry Kang maintains that the important lesson of the internment is not just that wartime generates unfortunate but inevitable mistakes—akin to the errant bombing of a Red Cross field hospital. Instead, he posits, "wartime coupled with racism and intolerance create particular types of social mistakes"[10]—like the politically popular incarceration of a group by reason of that group's presumed disloyalty.

We add another dimension to Professor Kang's calculus: national security crises coupled with racism or nativism and *backed by the force of law* generate deep and lasting social injustice. Court rulings, in particular, legitimize even extreme, albeit popular, governmental actions—in the 1940s, the internment; yesterday, Ahmed's three-year secret incarceration; today, potentially, groundless detentions, secret trials and deportations and government racial profiling and harassment. Once legitimated by the courts, government excesses and human suffering take on the mantle of normalcy. Once broadly sanctioned by law, hostile or vengeful members of the public sense a license to harm. It is the law's stamp of approval on wartime exigencies plus racism that transforms mistakes of the moment into enduring social injustice.

What Now?:
National Security, Civil Liberties and Democracy

No one doubts the broad powers of government to protect people and institutions. The problem, history tells us, lies in harsh government excess in the exercise of that power.

Eric K. Yamamoto and
Susan Kiyomi Serrano

The most far-reaching recent government national security law is the hastily-enacted, 342-page "USA Patriot Act" (Uniting and Strengthening America by Providing Appropriate Tools Required to Intercept and Obstruct Terrorism Act). Signed into law only six weeks after the attacks, the law authorizes expansive new powers for law enforcement agencies to wiretap phones, track Internet traffic, conduct secret searches, examine private financial and educational records and prosecute anyone who supports a "terrorist." The law also allows the government to detain immigrants for seven days without charges and permits the possible indefinite detention of non-citizens without meaningful judicial review.[11]

Because the law creates a new, broadly defined crime of "domestic terrorism," groups engaged in acts of political protest could be deemed terrorist organizations and their members criminally prosecuted as "terrorists." The American Civil Liberties Union warned that "Americans who oppose U.S. policies and who are believed to have ties to foreign powers could find their homes broken into and their telephones tapped." Those found providing assistance to designated terrorists could also be charged, even if the assistance is only providing food or shelter. Small monetary contributions of humanitarian aid from the U.S., when administered regionally by a group deemed to engage in terrorist activity, as in areas of Sri Lanka, make the donor a terrorist accomplice subject to prosecution. Analysts warn that the Patriot Act will allow the government to intimidate people of color and immigrants on the basis of innuendo and conjecture. [12]

Even before the Act's passage, government agents targeted Arab Americans and Muslims in the U.S. Several colleges and universities were approached for information about foreign students, students of particular ethnicities and students with strong political leanings. FBI agents entered mosques, interrupted prayer services and harassed worshippers and awakened Arab Americans late at night to interrogate them at length, even though they lacked any connection to terrorists.[13]

Many Americans were also subjected to private attacks and discrimination because they remotely resembled Arabs or Muslims. Commercial airline pilots expelled from their planes Arab Americans, South Asians and others who "looked like terrorists"— the airline "has no choice but to reaccommodate a passenger or passengers if their actions or presence make a majority of passengers uncomfortable and threaten to disrupt normal operations in flight."

Hundreds were physically assaulted, harassed, fired or demoted because of their ethnicity, religion or appearance. Many others were intimidated by law enforcement, profiled at the airports and discriminated against in the schools. Still others received hate mail, death threats and bomb threats. Five people were killed. The Justice Department commenced 170 investigations into hate crimes, including killings, shootings and arson.[14]

What will happen when those profiled, detained, harassed or discriminated against turn to the courts for legal protection? How will the U.S. courts respond to the need to protect fundamental democratic values of our political process—that people are to be treated fairly and equally? No definitive answers emerge. As the internment cases and more recent court rulings suggest, however, the judiciary most often yields to political pressure and declines to hold the government accountable for restrictions of civil liberties during times of national stress. Indeed, court observers warn that the same courts that frowned upon racial profiling in the past will authorize it "more definitively than before" to protect national security.[15]

Korematsu Revisited: The Call for Community Political Education and Mobilization

During World War II Fred Korematsu challenged the constitutionality of the internment and lost. The Supreme Court blindly accepted the government's false assertion of "military necessity." In the 1984 *coram nobis* case, federal judge Marilyn Hall Patel declared the original *Korematsu* case a "manifest injustice." In her ruling, Judge Patel echoed Justice Jackson's "loaded weapon" warning forty years earlier: The *Korematsu* case debacle "stands as a constant caution that in times of war or declared military necessity our institutions must be vigilant in protecting constitutional guarantees. It stands as a caution that in times of distress the shield of military necessity and national security must not be used to protect governmental actions from close scrutiny and accountability. It stands as a caution that in times of international hostility and antagonisms, our institutions, legislative, executive and judicial, must be prepared to exercise their authority to protect all citizens from the petty fears and prejudices that are so easily aroused."[16]

Judge Patel thus exhorted "institutions" during national crisis to be vigilant in order to "protect all citizens from the petty fears and prejudices." Yet, institutions, particularly government, lean hard toward the powerful, not the powerless. On their own

71

they are disinclined to struggle to "protect all." Those institutions, including the courts, however, are responsive in varying ways to political will. They will exercise the vigilance called for by Judge Patel, but only when pushed to do so by the coordinated efforts of frontline community and political organizations, scholars, journalists and politicians. The institutions will respond, but only to up-front education, in-your-face organizing and strategic political mobilization.

The real bulwark against governmental excess and lax judicial scrutiny, then, is political education and mobilization, both at the front end when laws are passed and enforced and at the back end when they are challenged in courts. During World War II internment, at the front end, no one spoke against it. Not the ACLU, not the NAACP. Not even the Japanese American Citizens League. All were silent, feeling vulnerable and fearing the repercussions of appearing to be unpatriotic. And the internment proceeded apace, and the high court legitimated it. Forty years later, at the back end challenge to the injustice, the *Korematsu coram nobis* legal team took a different tack. It engaged a multifaceted legal-political strategy— litigation, community organizing, public education, media storytelling and scholarly writing. Civil rights and community groups and concerned individuals joined the struggle in the courts, Congress and President's office, as well as in the schools, churches, union halls and community centers. The legal process provided a focal point for these efforts, but political education and mobilization shaped the larger public understandings crucial to the success of the internment justice movement.

In today's climate of fear and anger, our first task in protecting both people and key democratic values is to be pro-active at the front end—to prevent post-modern forms of internment. We need to organize and speak out to assure that the expansive new national security regime does not overwhelm the civil liberties of vulnerable groups and move the country toward a police state. We need to mobilize and raise challenges to prevent Ahmed-like secret incarcerations, particularly en masse. Through political analysis, education and activism, our job is to compel powerful institutions, particularly the courts, to be vigilant, to "protect all." Our second task is to be assertive at the back end—to call out injustice when it occurs, to spell out the damage it does to real people in our midst and to our constitutional democracy, and to demand accountability to principles of equality and due process.

Our collective task, then, is to turn Justice Jackson's warning into to an affirmative challenge. The time is now to unload that weapon.

Notes

1. This description is based on the accounts of Professor Natsu Saito, Professor David Cole, and various news articles. See Natsu Saito, "Symbolism Under Siege: Japanese American Redress and the 'Racing' of Arab Americans as 'Terrorists'," *Asian Law Journal* 8:1 (2001), 17, 19-20 (noting that the INS has attempted to deport at least two dozen people on the basis of secret evidence, almost all of them Muslim, most of them Arab Americans); David Cole, "Secret Trials," *Human Rights* 28:8 (2001), 8-9 (noting that the U.S. government detained Ahmed based on his alleged association with a terrorist organization, but would not reveal the name of the group, "much less when and how Ahmed had been associated and what, if anything, he allegedly did for the group"); David Cole, "Secrecy, Guilt by Association, and the Terrorist Profile," *Journal of Law and Religion* 15 (2000-2001), 267, 273-275 (emphasizing that "[m]uch of the evidence declassified in Ahmed's case should never have been classified in the first place" because "Ahmed's association with Abdel-Rahman was no secret; Ahmed served as the sheik's court-appointed paralegal and translator during Abdel-Rahman's criminal trial."); Douglas Montero, "U.S. Secret Evidence Law Terrorizes Innocent Arabs," *New York Post*, January 9, 2000, 22; Jim Lobe, "Opponents of Secret Evidence Make Headway," *Inter Press Service*, June 8, 2000. Saito also reports that the FBI and Immigration and Naturalization Service tried to force Ahmed to inform on Abdel-Rhaman and threatened to deport him and his family if he did not. Even though an immigration judge ruled that Ahmed would be imprisoned and likely tortured if he was returned to Egypt—and was therefore eligible for political asylum—Ahmed was not released until the Board of Immigration Appeals forced the government to reveal its "secret evidence.") See Saito, 19-20. While Ahmed, along with many others, worshipped at the mosque where Abdel-Rahman led prayer, there was no evidence that Ahmed engaged in any terrorist activity. See Susan M. Akram, "Scheherezade Meets Kafka: Two Dozen Sordid Tales of Ideological Exclusion," *Georgetown Immigration Law Journal* 14:51 (1999), 76; Cole, "Secret Trials," 8; "House Holds Hearings on Use of Secret Evidence, Visa Waiver Pilot Program," *Interpreter Releases*, March 13, 2000, 301-302.

2. See Neil A. Lewis, "Detentions After Attacks Pass 1,000, U.S. Says," *New York Times*, October 30, 2001, B1; Joan Mazzolini, "Arab Immigrant's Detention Raises Host of Concerns," *The Plain Dealer*, October 21, 2001, A1; Tamar Lewin, "For Many of Those Held in a Legal Tangle, Little is Revealed," *New York Times*, November 1, 2001 (reporting that detainees have been held for weeks, even after the FBI has cleared them of involvement in the attacks and of even the most minor charges).

3. Eric K. Yamamoto, Chris Iijima and Angela E. Oh, *Law Through Asian American Eyes* (forthcoming).

4. See Elisabeth Bumiller, "Bush Announces a Crackdown on Visa Violations," *New York Times*, October 30, 2001; John Ibbitson, "Antiterrorism Bill Becomes U.S. Law," *The Globe and Mail*, October 27, 2001, A14.

5. Eric K. Yamamoto, "Korematsu Revisited—Correcting the Injustice of Extraordinary Government Excess and Lax Judicial Review: Time for a Better Accommodation of National Security Concerns and Civil Liberties," *Santa Clara Law Review* 26:1 (1986), 7-8.

6. See Yamamoto, Chon, Izumi, Kang and Wu, *Race, Rights and Reparation: Law and the Japanese American Internment* 100-101 (2001).

7. Yamamoto, *Korematsu Revisited*, note 5, 8-9; *Hirabayashi* v. *U.S.*, 320 U.S. 81 (1943); *Yasui* v. *U.S.*, 320 U.S. 115 (1943); *Korematsu* v. *U.S.*, 323 U.S. 214 (1944).

8. See *Rostker* v. *Goldberg*, 453 U.S. 57 (1981); *Haig* v. *Agee*, 453 U.S. 280 (1981); *Regan* v. *Wald*, 104 S.Ct. 3026 (1984); and *U.S.* v. *Albertini*, 105 S.Ct. 2897 (1985).

9. Alfred C. Yen, Introduction, "Praising With Faint Damnation—The Troubling Rehabilitation of Korematsu," *Boston College Law Review* 40 (1998), 2-7; *Boston College Third World Law Journal* 19 (1998), 2-7 (discussing William H. Rehnquist, "When the Laws Were Silent," American Heritage (October 1998), 77-89).

10. Jerry Kang, "What 12-7 Has to Teach about 9-11," September 17, 2001 (unpublished manuscript on file with authors).

11. James Kuhnhenn, "Senate Approves Counter-Terrorism Bill," *Knight-Ridder Tribune Business News*, October 26, 2001; Ann McFeatters, "Bush Signs Anti-Terror Bill, Says Tough Law Will Preserve Constitutional Rights," *Pittsburgh Post-Gazette*, October 27, 2001, A6; Ronald Weich, "Upsetting Checks and Balances: Congressional Hostility Towards the Courts in Times of Crisis," ACLU Report, October 2001, 5; Joan Mazzolini, "Arab Immigrant's Detention Raises Host of Concerns," *The Plain Dealer*, October 21, 2001, A1.

12. Victoria Harris, "U.S., Not Terrorists, Infringing on Americans' Civil Rights," *U-Wire*, October 23, 2001; Margaret Graham Tebo, Immigration Policy: Two Minds With Single Aim, *ABA Journal eReport*, September 21, 2001, at http://www.abanet.org/journal/ereport/immig.html.

13. See Jackie Koszckuk and Sumana Chatterjee, "Muslims, Arabs Assert FBI Abuse," *Pittsburgh Post-Gazette*, September 24, 2001, A8.

14. American Arab Anti-Discrimination Committee, Press Release, September 21, 2001, at www.adc.org/press/2001/21september2001.htm; "Backlash Violence Reports Decrease, Watch Groups Say/Civil Rights Complaints Are on Upswing," *Houston Chronicle*, October 25, 2001, 18.

15. William Glaberson, "Racial Profiling May Get Wider Approval by Courts," *New York Times*, September 21, 2001; "National Briefing Homeland Security: There's A New Law Of The Land," *American Political Network* 10:9, October 26, 2001; Deborah Kong, "Muslims in U.S. Consider Lawsuits," *AP Online*, September 29, 2001.

16. *Korematsu* v. *U.S.*, 584 F. Supp. 1406, 1420 (N.D. Cal. 1984).

Pearl Harbor Revisited

Frank Chin

Frank Chin, 2000.
© 2000, Mary U. Kao

The laughter stopped on September 11, 2001. A day America likened to Pearl Harbor. Till that day we were still laughing at the foolishness of the Organization of Chinese Americans, a self styled civil rights and education organization, linking up with the Japanese American Citizen's League, the group known to have used and abandoned the title "civil rights organization" at their convenience. The OCA might not know what their civil rights organization is or does; in fact there's real doubt that the Organization of Chinese Americans knows what a Chinese American is. In their scrambling around to match their name and title with meaning, I would think the OCA would know that the JACL is the one organization that would sink their credibility as a civil rights group. Everybody knows that. But obviously the OCA didn't.

They invited Norman Mineta, the Japanese American Secretary of Transportation, and former Congressman, to speak and the JACL to give them instruction. Norman Mineta told them that in WWII, his people, the Japanese Americans, had been unfairly interned in concentration camps, and had their civil rights stripped from them. Mineta did not say that the leader of the JACL had asked for the camps, and had advocated the drafting of the Nisei from the camps while their families were held hostage. The JACL at the time was led by Mike Masaoka, Mineta's brother-in-law and political mentor.

Mike Masaoka had convinced Congress that the JACL was the only national organization with the membership and the leadership to represent Japanese American civil rights. He used the

FRANK CHIN is author of *Chickencoop Chinaman* and *Year of the Dragon* (University of Washington Press, 1981), *Donald Duk* (Coffeehouse Press, 1991), *Gunga Din Highway* (Coffeehouse Press, 1995) and *Bulletproof Buddhists* (University of Hawai'i Press, 1998).

words: "civil rights" in describing the JACL. And civil rights described the cases of Gordon Hirabayashi, arrested in Seattle, and Minoru Yasui in Portland, for violating a curfew that applied to Japanese only. Mike Masaoka and the JACL refused to support Hirabayashi and Yasui's case, saying, "The JACL is unalterably opposed to cases to determine the constitutionaliity of the military orders at this time." An act blatantly against civil rights, and there's more, much more.

Masaoka offered a hundred thousand of his people—men, women and children—in concentration camps, as hostages to ensure the loyalty of the men of his proposed "suicide battalion." The army refused the suicide battalion idea, in name only. They did accept an all Nisei combat unit. Masaoka convinced the army that the Japanese Americans were so anxious to "prove their loyalty" that they would volunteer in overwhelming numbers, and leave their families hostage in the camps. Masaoka was embarrassed when Japanese America proved him wrong. It seemed the Japanese Americans were interested in the return of their civil rights before they volunteered. But not the JACL.

In 1944 the government reinstated the draft for Nisei whether they were in camp or not. Now was the time for the JACL to prove they were a civil rights organization. They proved they were not. "Perhaps we Japanese Americans have not yet earned our right to unqualified citizenship." Thus spoke Masaoka, on April 22, 1944. Instead of defending the citizenship of the American-born-and-raised Japanese Americans, he offers a formula for the subjects of the white race to be accepted.

"Therefore, in order to be in a position to legitimately demand that our full citizenship rights and privileges be restored and maintained for all time to come, JACL has worked unceasingly for the reinstitution of the Selective Service ever since the War Department changed its policy and announced that Japanese Americans were not wanted for military service. That arbitrary classification of 4-C granted us was embarrassing and humiliating."

What was embarrassing and humiliating was the JACL's slavish acceptance of concentration camps and white approval—instead of the law—as a condition of their American citizenship. Perhaps embarrassing is the wrong word for what the JACL did. The JACL whipped up America's war of revenge against Japanese-America. They abandoned civil rights and the Japanese culture of their people for one man's vision of a "better American for a greater America," enforced with lies and an intimidating identification with Masaoka's vision of a monstrous white man.

The Organization of Chinese Americans has come across the interesting fact that all of the mainland Japanese Americans to achieve elective office, at any level of government, from dog-catcher to either house of congress have been members of the JACL. The JACL is rightfully known as a patriotic organization that encouraged Nisei men to accept being drafted from camp. The JACL was wrong in its assertion that their recruiting for the 442nd Regimental Combat Team was responsible for the closing of concentration camps. The 442nd might have helped mightily to win WWII, but everything they—and the whole American army—did was irrelevant to any of the issues of camp.

The JACL was performing for the whites, the JACL sent Japanese Americans to camp for the whites, turned against civil rights for the whites, and wanted to prove Japanese American loyalty to the whites. During the forties of WWII, when the Japanese were the despised people of the day, it took no courage for the JACL to satisfy the whites. Such craven behavior was precisely what the whites wanted and expected.

It took real courage for a Japanese American in camp to say he would not answer the call to go to war, like a normal American, until he was a normal American. In Hawai'i, the site of Pearl Harbor, Japanese were not interned, and produced 10,000 volunteers and answered the draft with less resistance than the mainland, where only 805 volunteered from the camps. The numbers suggest that if the mainlanders were not in camps, they would have responded to the call for volunteers and the draft more positively. But the Japanese Americans on the mainland weren't treated like normal Americans; they were interned. In a mimeographed bulletin dated March 4, 1944, the draft resistance tells everyone where they stood:

> Without any hearings, without due process of law as guaranteed by the Constitution and Bill of Rights, without any charges filed against us, without any evidence of wrong doing on our part, one hundred and ten thousand innocent people were kicked out of their homes, literally uprooted from where they have lived for the greater part of their life, and herded like dangerous criminals into concentration camps with barbed wire fence and military police guarding it, AND THEN, WITHOUT RECTIFICATION OF THE INJUSTICES COMMITTED AGAINST US AND WITHOUT RESTORATION OF OUR RIGHTS AS GUARANTEED BY THE CONSTITUTION, WE ARE ORDERED TO JOIN

THE ARMY THRU DISCRIMINATORY PROCEDURES INTO A SEGREGATED COMBAT UNIT! Is that the American Way? No.

And it took real courage for Frank Emi to write and insist on the words he knew would get them arrested:

> We feel that the present program of drafting us from this concentration camp is unjust, unconstitutional, and against all principles of civilized usage, and therefore, WE MEMBERS OF THE FAIR PLAY COMMITTEE HEREBY REFUSE TO GO TO THE PHYSICAL EXAMINATION OR TO THE INDUCTION IF OR WHEN WE ARE CALLED IN ORDER TO CONTEST THE ISSUE.

All the draft resisters wanted was the camps closed—then they would accept the draft. The JACL as a civil rights organization should have supported this clear cut civil rights stand, but instead, they accused the draft resisters of sedition, cowardice and treason, and stood against their civil rights. Whether or not the JACL has ever been a civil rights organization has been a matter of internal debate since Pearl Harbor. Outside of Japanese America and the JACL, there is no debate. It is not a civil rights organization.

Mineta and the JACL's insistence that the WWII monument include Masaoka's words exalting the government moved National Park Service Director Robert Stanton to reject petitions signed by more than a thousand Japanese Americans. Stanton, likewise, refused to read a protest pamphlet prepared by two members of Stanton's board, Francis Sogi, who'd seen service in WWII, in the Military Intelligence Service, and Kelly Kuwayama, a member of the 442nd. "JAPANESE AMERICANS DISUNITED: How a memorial to unify the Japanese American community became a symbol of disunity" at the very least, is an indication of how deep the controversy of the JACL runs through Japanese America.

The Organization of Chinese Americans says it is a civil rights and an education organization. Because of the events of September 11, 2001, its Washington office finds itself in the right place at the right time to speak for us. But don't count on OCA to stand for Chinese America. When asked what Chinese America is, they say, they're really more than Chinese American, that they have Korean American members and Japanese Americans in the organization. When asked to define Korean American and Japanese American, they offer double talk and distraction but no answer.

As an education organization, they seem to be equally inept. Chinese stories one would expect every Chinese to know are foreign to the ears of OCA. Their members manning the phones of their Washington office can tell any number of European children's stories—*The Ugly Duckling, Cinderella, Sleeping Beauty*, a few Jewish stories, *The Golem*, but not one Chinese children's story. Why is it that only in America do we find this contempt for the Chinese children's story? So what Chinese or Chinese American knowledge do they teach?

Their magazine *IMAGE* is full of self-congratulatory stories on working with Norman Mineta and the JACL. The OCA membership is saying things like, "We're the Chinese JACL."

Seen in action, the OCA is right to liken themselves to the JACL. They don't know and don't like Chinese Americans. Where do we go when we need an organization that knows Chinese America—knows the stories, knows the history, knows the facts and knows the difference between a real Chinese-American spy and an FBI face-saving fake, or between a real Chinese American threat and a fake. When the government moves to put us into concentration camps for our own protection—will the OCA, defender of our civil rights—go to the Supreme Court, or will they sacrifice our rights as a proof of our loyalty?

Manzanar concentration camp, July 3, 1942.

Photograph by Dorothea Lange, WRA. *Executive Order 9066*, Maisie and Richard Conrat (Los Angeles: UCLA Asian American Studies Center, 1992)

Frank Chin

Sikh candlelight vigil at Central
Park, September 15, 2001.
© 2001, Corky Lee

How Does It Feel to Be a Problem?

Moustafa Bayoumi

New York City, September 25, 2001

Thankfully, I was spared any personal loss. Like so many others in the city which I love, I have spent much of the past two weeks reeling from the devastation. Mostly this has meant getting back in touch with friends, frantically calling them on the phone, rushing around the city to meet with them to give them a consoling hug, but knowing that really it was me looking for the hug. I dash off simple one-line emails, "let me know you're okay, okay?"

Old friends from around the world responded immediately. An email from Canada asks simply if I am all right. Another arrives from friends in Germany telling me how they remember, during their last visit to see me, the view from the top of the towers. A cousin in Egypt states in awkward English, "I hope this attack will not affect you. We hear that some of the Americans attack Arabs and Muslims. I will feel happy if you be in contact with me."

I am all right, of course, but I am devastated. In the first days, I scoured the lists of the dead and missing hoping not to find any recognizable names, but I come across the name of a three-year-old child, and my heart collapses. I hear my neighbor, who works downtown, arrive home, and I knock on her door. She tells me how she was chased by a cloud of debris into a building, locked in there for over an hour, and then, like thousands of others, walked home. I can picture her with the masses in the streets, trudging bewildered like refugees, covered in concrete and human dust. Later, I ride the subway and see a full-page picture of the towers on fire

MOUSTAFA BAYOUMI is Assistant Professor of English at Brooklyn College, City University of New York.

with tiny figures in the frame silently diving to their deaths, and I start to cry.

In the following days, I cried a lot. Then, with friends, I attended a somber peace march in Brooklyn, sponsored by the Arab community. Thousands, overwhelmingly non-Arab and non-Muslim, show up, and I feel buoyed by the support. A reporter from Chile notices my Arab appearance and asks if she can interview me. I talk to her but am inwardly frightened by her locating me so easily among the thousands. Many people are wearing stickers reading: "We Support Our Arab neighbors," which leaves me both happy and, strangely, crushed. Has it really come to this? Now it has become not just a question of whether we—New Yorkers—are so vulnerable as a city but whether we—in the Arab and Muslim communities—are so vulnerable by our appearances. Is our existence so precarious here? I want to show solidarity with the people wearing the stickers, so how can I possibly explain to them how those stickers scare me?

Before September 11, I used to be fond of saying that the relations between the Muslim world and the West have never been at a lower point since the crusades. They have now sunk lower. The English language lexicon is, once again, degraded by war. George W. Bush's ignorant use of the word "crusade" is but a manifestation. Why don't we ask the Apache what they think of the Apache helicopter? Is there any phrase more disingenuous in the English language than "collateral damage"?

Terror, according to the United States law (Title 18, 2331), is defined as a "violent act or acts dangerous to human life that. . .appears to be intended (i) to intimidate or coerce a civilian population; (ii) to influence the policy of a government by intimidation or coercion." Since 1990, the United States has been the major force behind the longest and most destructive sanctions regime in the history of our modern world. The sanctions on Iraq, according to UNICEF, cause about 5,000 deaths a month of children under the age of five. It is not just a matter of caloric intake for these children but, as documented by Sarah Graham-Brown in her important book *Sanctioning Saddam: The Politics of Intervention in Iraq*, the fact that the food and health infrastructure of the country has been decimated by the sanctions. Meanwhile, the military and political elite have remained unscathed. They may be weaker to their neighbors but, by the pauperization of the population, they are actually more entrenched than ever.

The Clinton administration adopted a cruel status-quo arrangement when it came to Iraq. Claiming on the one hand that the sanctions were directly linked to Iraq's compliance with the United Nation's inspections for weapons of mass destruction, and on the other that the sanctions would only be lifted with the demise of Saddam Hussein's regime, they settled into a structure of "containment." (The Clinton administration, it must be said, inherited this position from Bush Sr. Keeping Iraq weak limited the Shi'a influence in the population and in the region, and didn't risk recognizing Kurdish independence, which would threaten the important ally of Turkey.)

In a putative attempt to discover weapons of mass destruction, the United States has been involved in laying out a most inhumane weapon of mass destruction, for surely there is no other name for the cruelty of the sanctions. Well, maybe, according to the U.S.'s definition, there is another name: terrorism. The sanctions regime is dangerous to human life, and is an attempt to intimidate the policy of a government by coercion, and innocent people suffer by the hundreds of thousands.

For the first four weeks after the attacks, I felt a bubble of hope in the dank air of New York. The blunt smell of smoke and death that hung in the atmosphere slowed the city down like I had never experienced it before. New York was solemn, lugubrious, and, for once, without a quick comeback. For a moment, it felt that the trauma of suffering—not the exercise of reason, not the belief in any God, not the universal consumption of a fizzy drink, but the simple and tragic reality that it hurts when we feel pain—was understood as the thread that connects all of humanity. From this point, I had hope that a lesson was being learned, that inflicting more misery cannot alleviate the ache of collective pain.

When the bombing began, the bubble burst. Where there was apprehension, now there was relief in the air. It felt like the city was taking a collective sigh, saying to itself that finally, with the bombing, we can get back to our own lives again. With a perverted logic, dropping munitions meant all's right with the world again.

Television, the great mediator, allows the public to feel violence or to abstract it. New Yorkers qualify as human interest; Afghans, if they are lucky, get the long shot. In late October, CNN issued a directive to its reporters, for it seems that even a little bit of detached compassion is too much in the media world. "It seems perverse to focus too much on the casualties or hardship in Afghanistan," their leadership explains. "We must talk about how the Taliban is using civilian shields and how the Taliban has harbored the terrorists responsible for killing close to 5,000 innocent people." God forbid, we viewers see the pain ordinary Afghans are forced to endure. CNN must instead issue policy like a nervous state, rather than investigate how cluster bombs, freely dropped in the tens of thousands from the skies, metamorphose into land mines since about 7 percent of these soda-can-sized bombs don't explode on contact. In Canada, in the U.K., across the Arab world, this is becoming an issue. But in the United States, a cluster bomb sounds like a new kind of candy bar.

This is not to say that people in the United States are foolish, but they are by and large woefully underinformed. A study taken during the course of the Gulf War revealed that the more TV one watched, the less one actually knew about the region. In the crash course on Islam that the American public is now receiving, I actually heard a group of well-suited pundits on MSNBC (or its equivalent, I can no longer separate the lame from the loony) ask questions to a Muslim about the basics of the faith, questions like "Now, is there a difference between Moslem and Muslim?" No lie. The USA-Patriot Act, the end of the world as we know it (or at least of judicial review), actually includes the expression "Muslim descent," as if Islam is a chromosome to be marked by the human genome project. About Islam, most people in the United States still know nothing, unlike professional sports, where many are encyclopedias.

The media have basically stopped reporting the number of Afghan dead. But what would happen if CNN were able to report a number greater than 5,000 innocents killed? What would the score then be? After all, hasn't this tragedy turned, perversely, into some kind of television sports event, at least in the United States? We would do well to remember that the conquest for Afghanistan, a quagmire for every empire (Mongol, British, Soviet), was not too long ago called "the great game."

For years, the organized Arab American community has been lobbying to be recognized with minority status. The check boxes on application forms have always stared defiantly out at me. Go ahead, try to find yourself, they seem to be taunting me. I search and find that, in the eyes of the government, I am a white man.

It is a strange thing, to be brown in reality and white in bureaucracy. Now, however, it is stranger than ever. Since 1909, when the government began questioning whether Syrian immigrants were of "white" stock (desirable) or Asian stock (excludable), Arab immigrants in this country have had to contend with fitting their mixed hues into the primary colors of the state. As subjects of the Ottoman empire, and thus somehow comingled with Turkish stock (who themselves claim descent from the Caucauses, birthplace of the original white people in nineteenth century thinking, even though the location is Asia Minor), Arabs, Armenians, and other Western Asians caused a good deal of consternation among the legislators of race in this country. Syrians and Palestinians were in 1899 classified as white, but by 1910 they were reclassified as "Asiatics." A South Carolina judge in 1914 wrote that even though Syrians may be white people, they were not "that particular free white person to whom the Act of Congress had donated the privilege of citizenship" (that being reserved exclusively for people of European descent). What is it DuBois wrote: "How does it feel to be a problem?"

In the twenty-first century, we are back to being white on paper and brown in reality. After the attacks of September 11, the flood to classify Arabs in this country was drowning our community like a break in a dam. This impact? Hundreds of hate crimes, many directed at South Asians and Iranians, whom the perpetrators misidentified as Arab (or, more confusingly, as "Muslim": again as if that were a racial category). In the days following the attack (September 14/15), a Gallup Poll revealed that 49 percent of Americans supported "requiring Arabs, including those who are U.S. citizens, to carry a special ID." Fifty-eight percent also supported "requiring Arabs, including those who are U.S. citizens, to undergo special, more intensive security checks before boarding airplanes in the U.S." Debate rages across the nation as to the legitimacy of using "racial profiling" in these times (overwhelmingly pro). The irony, delicious if it were not so tragic, is that they are racially profiling a people whom they don't even recognize as a race.

The U.S. government is flirting with the idea of institutionalizing torture. (Police departments around the country must be overjoyed to know that their methods might be getting an institutional stamp of approval.) Recently, the Justice Department revealed that it is letting investigators monitor conversations between terrorist suspects and their attorneys, throwing the idea of privileged communication to the winds of time past. Isn't the notion of due process the reason why many of us left autocratic regimes behind in the first place to come to the United States? Aren't we destroying the village in order to save it?

⊕ ⊕ ⊕

An old story told about Ford motor cars says that in their early years, Ford offered prospective automobile buyers the option to have their cars in any color, just as long as it was black. More and more, Operation "Enduring Freedom" resembles Mr. Ford's edict. It is the appearance of choice without any real choice. You think you are getting what you want, but it is all an illusion.

It is axiomatic to say that war polarizes positions, but that doesn't make it any less worth considering. War forces stark demarcations between good and evil, makes Manichean distinctions in black and white. We can see how the rhetoric being used by both Osama bin Laden and George W. Bush reflect each other. It has become "if you are not with us, you are against us," according to Mr. Bush, and "either you are a believer or an infidel," for bin Laden. The religious rhetoric of bin Laden scares many in the United States, yet never have I heard so many "God bless Americas" in such a short time. The U.S. rightly decries the tragic loss of innocent lives from the September 11 attacks, but excuses itself of the innocent deaths in Afghanistan as a necessary corollary of war. "I say bomb the hell out of them." This is Senator Zell Miller, Democrat of Georgia, as quoted in the *New York Times*. "If there is collateral damage so be it. They found our civilians to be expendable."

This is, of course, not to say anything about the attacks of September 11. These horrific, terrible, and inexcusable acts have no foundation in any ethics of any kind. Such crimes against humanity are to be rejected out of hand, denounced and done away with in any world which operates on principles of ethics, the sanctity of human life, belief in the ideas of human dignity and opportunity. How do we get there?

From the fall to the fallout, I have been living these days in some kind of limbo. The horrific attacks of September 11 have damaged everyone's sense of security, a principle enshrined in the Universal Declaration of Human Rights, and I wonder if for the first that I can remember in the United States, we can start to reflect on that notion more carefully. All the innocents who have perished in this horrendous crime deserve to be mourned, whether they be the rescue workers, the financiers, the tourists, or the service employees in the buildings. An imam in the city has told me how a local union requested his services for a September 11 memorial of their loss since a quarter of their membership was Muslim. Foreign nationals from over eighty countries lost their lives, and the spectacular nature of the attacks meant that the world could witness the United States' own sense of security crumble with the towers. The tragedy of September 11 is truly of heartbreaking proportions. The question remains whether the United States will understand its feelings of stolen security as an unique circumstance, woven into the familiar narrative of American exceptionalism, or whether the people of this country will begin to see how security of person must be guaranteed for all. Aren't we all in this together?

So perhaps there is a way in which this is a Manichean struggle of sorts, not between different peoples or different faiths but between different ideas of the global versus the universal. On the one hand, there is a way in which globalization means the long stretch of the American imperial hand, along with IMF structural adjustment programs and World Bank initiatives, which have led to less democracy and fewer freedoms in the poorer parts of the world. Globalization here has also meant the United States versus the world—think of the Kyoto treaty, or opting out of the World Court or sneaking around the ABM treaty or the moratorium on landmine use. Otherwise, globalization can mean eking out a universal applicable for all, trying to make an international court of justice a workable reality, believing in the United Nations as an idea and as a mission. There is either a way in which the other becomes so "other-ed" that we can't even see whom we are destroying, or there is a way in which the destruction of any innocent life is the destruction of ourselves. In that regard, I think the choice does fall along two different poles. Choose one, and the future may be bright, multicolored even; choose the other, and the future is black.

Overheard on a city bus, days after the attacks: "They will take them, like they did the Japanese, into camps. I think that's what they're going to do." In *Koremastu* v. *United States*, the infamous Supreme Court decision on Japanese internment, Justice Black wrote:

> It is said that we are dealing here with the case of imprisonment of a citizen in a concentration camp solely because of his ancestry, without evidence or inquiry concerning his loyalty and good disposition towards the United States. Our task would be simple, our duty clear, were this a case involving the imprisonment of a loyal citizen in a concentration camp because of racial prejudice. Regardless of the true nature of the assembly and relocation centers—and we deem it unjustifiable to call them concentration camps with all the ugly connotations that term implies—we are dealing specifically with nothing but an exclusion order.

In this exercise in rationalizing racism, Justice Black's backward logic is underscored by *his* taking offense at the term "concentration camp."

Of course, the Japanese American experience is not far from everyone's mind these days. Two months after the attack on Pearl Harbor, President Roosevelt signed Executive Order 9066, which led to the internment of over 110,000 Americans of Japanese decent. Without any need for evidence, anyone of Japanese ancestry, whether American-born or not, could be rounded up and placed in detention, all of course in the name of democracy and national security. What is less well-known is that in the 1980s, a multi-agency task force of the government, headed by the INS, had plans to round up citizens of seven Arab countries and Iran and place them in a camp in Oakdale, Louisiana in the event of a war or action in the Middle East.

Will we see the return of the camps? I doubt it. How do you round up some seven or eight million people, geographically and economically dispersed throughout the society in ways people of Japanese descent were not in the 1940s? I suspect that this time we are not in for such measures, but we are already in the middle of something else. Over 1,000 people, most non-citizens, most Arab and Muslim, have been taken into custody under shadowy circumstances reminiscent of the disappeared of Argentina. Targeted for their looks, their opinions, or their associations, not one has yet to be indicted on any charge directly related to the attacks of September 11. Now, being Muslim means you are worthy of incarceration. INS administrative courts are the places where much of this happens, since non-citizens are the weakest segment of the population from a judicial point of view. Islam in this scenario becomes both racial and ideological.

In 1920, Attorney General A. Mitchell Palmer launched a nationwide assault on suspected communists and rounded up thousands without any judicial review (this event, an egregious abuse of authority, launched the ACLU). It too was directed mainly at immigrants to this country, and was covert and indiscriminate. This is what Palmer had to say about it: "How the Department of Justice discovered upwards of 60,000 of these organized agitators of the Trotsky doctrine in the United States, is the confidential information upon which the government is now sweeping the nation clean of such alien filth." John Ashcroft may be more circumspect in his language, but what we are facing now is a combination of both Yellow Peril and the Red Scare. Call it the Green Scare if you will, and recognize it is as a perilous path.

Final words are reserved for Khalil Gibran, from *The Garden of the Prophet* (1934):

> Pity the nation that acclaims the bully as hero, and that deems the glittering conqueror bountiful.

In the Spring of 1994, I was driving back to Albuquerque from El Paso when I noticed this mushroom cloud. Minutes later, a convoy of military vehicles rushed past me at a frantic pace. I knew that there would be no report of this event in any newspaper anywhere.

© 1994, Stephen Lee

90

What Does Danger Look Like?

Stephen Lee

I don't know what compelled me last winter to drive to Santa Fe and walk through the remnants of a World War II internment camp. Was it a suspicion of something more or a dare that it shouldn't be done? Either way, it was awkward. New Mexico is my childhood home, where I learned the world, and one does not tend to question the place of first belonging. And whatever the reason for going, I know this much: my impulses had everything to do with the same age-old questions that befuddled our nation following the 9/11 tragedy—who are we, and what does danger look like?

That I went to Santa Fe was no strange fact. I grew up in Albuquerque and we often go—the five of us, my brother, sister, father, mother, and myself—whenever I visit them, though as a child we made a habit of going monthly and always with a cooler full of soda and *kim bap*. Only fifty miles of highway separate Albuquerque and Santa Fe, but it seems like more because of the sky. New Mexico is defined by its sky, an ocean inverted, and it is awesome—its size dwarfs everything. It exists in mostly shades of blue, though dusk and dawn betray its pink, purple, and red hues.

Santa Fe housed only one of many internment camps the U.S. government had set up during World War II. This particular site was reserved for what the government considered to be the most dangerous elements of the Japanese American community. First-generation Japanese men from all over the western United States were torn from their families and forced to endure the Santa Fe altitude and winters, an austere seven-thousand-foot view pockmarked by barbed wire and hypocrisy. This 28-acre area was not

STEPHEN LEE is Publications Assistant for *Amerasia Journal*. He received his M.A. in Asian American Studies, University of California, Los Angeles.

meant for families; only the men came, a group of lonely farmers—the dangerous and the dastardly.

The day I went to Santa Fe was the kind of day my father loves. He deeply loves New Mexico. I suspect it has something to do with the weather. He grew up in Korea, that trenchant peninsula. Humidity capsized his youth. Humidity is oppressive to him, my father insists, the weight of it. To him, arid air is freedom, even when gone awry. Dustdevils, a New Mexican staple for example, though magical and frightening, are bearable because at least they're wind—air in motion—not still air pregnant of water ready to spill open.

As I was driving up I-25, I had only a vague idea of where I was going. I tried contacting the obvious sources for help—the local chapter of the JACL, the Santa Fe Office of Tourism, historical societies—but I was met by answering machines and did not receive a single return phone call. I next tried the Internet and had better luck. I punched in words like "Internment Camps" and "Santa Fe," and though many hits came up, they hardly mentioned the Santa Fe camp. Even when they did, they did not disclose the specific location. Who would think to include major cross streets and address to a War Department relic?

A pair of articles from publications probably not well-known outside of their home regions morseled out the most useful information. The headline of an article in the *Corpus Christi Caller* on October 25, 1999 read "Internment Memorial Rankles Bataan Vets" and in the *Amarillo Globe-News* on October 28 of the same year, the headline read "Santa Fe OKs Plaque Marking Internment Camp." The articles covered both the proposal of an internment camp marker and the mixed community responses to the Santa Fe City Council's eventual decision to O.K. the historical plaque. The decision squeaked through as Mayor Larry Delgado provided the tie-breaking vote to pass and authorize the bronze plaque. Consequently, a plaque would be "placed at a city park" located "on a hilltop overlooking the 28-acre site—now a residential neighborhood—where the camp was located"; this was the extent of the information I was able to find. Looking at a Santa Fe city map, I guessed Frank Ortiz Park in the northwest part of town was the best candidate.

Why was the community response mixed? Unfortunately, many people of color in the West must inherit the weight of the rest of the world; they, we, are at the mercy of U.S. foreign policy decisions as they play out thousands of miles away. Political conflicts, war wounds, struggles for sovereignty, all of this collective pain can gather itself within the geography of a face, usually nonwhite, like mine or a Sikh airline passenger's. Deborah Baker, the AP journalist covering the plaque proposal, interviewed Bataan death march survivors, and one eighty-eight-year-old veteran, Manuel Armijo, in response to the city's decision to establish a marker, was quoted as saying, "It's just like asking us to turn the other cheek. . .why can't they wait till I'm dead? It just opens up old wounds. And it hurts." Armijo's horrific experiences in the Bataan death march still haunt him over fifty years later and half way around the world. The memories weigh on him like a dull autumn light; the part of me that would usually grow angry at his insensitivity and conflation (what do Japanese imperial soldiers have to do with imprisoned American farmers of Japanese descent?) instead relents and gives way to chagrin. But the lesson nevertheless does not lose itself in grieving for him. The implications of his words are still problematic. What strikes me is that most Americans don't know war and its anguish intimately the way Armijo does, and yet they nevertheless share the same bitterness, xenophobia, and fear—a soft, gushy spot raw to the touch—that can overwhelm during times of national crisis and overrun the ability to think logically and sort through the muck. This is inexcusable.

That day I stopped in the Plaza for lunch. Eagerly, I sat with my steaming hot plate of beef and red chile enchiladas, relished the aroma that settled in my nostrils and stomach. I gazed out the window at the passers-by, took in that place that is the southwest of America's imagination. Those of us from Albuquerque don't think much of Santa Fe—it seems too much like Thailand. The locals in their attempts to please the tourist industry create a certain image of themselves, giving others only what they want. The décor: adobe walls adorned with roasted chile ristros, mute Indian merchants perched atop blankets woven with an even deeper silence, the Loretto Chapel and its magical staircase. The ambience is as much a commodity as the jewelry peddled on the sidewalks. The tourists here aren't gleeful as they are in the Grand Canyon or New York City. There is a look of melancholy in their blue and gray eyes as they stroll (tourists that stroll indeed!) as if they were reliving some distant memory or perhaps more accurately, living out some fantasy. Bang Bang Westerns and hippie renegade artists and celebrity refugees like Gene Hackman and Val Kilmer find their homes here. That day my eyes wandered with avarice. With anonymity behind a reflecting window, I stared into the face of one Indian boy, no more than fourteen years of age, selling turquoise bracelets, and he looked neither eager to sell nor eager to be there. This boy's hair reminded me of the blackness in the Tiger's Eye marbles I used to play with as a child. I remembered my youth and how I used to hate my hair because it always looked dirty, the way its blackness seemed to always catch and show off sand. I shuddered as I recognized that same resignation of my youth in that brown boy's eyes.

After lunch, I left the Plaza and begin to head west in search of the camp. The radio was off and silence had molded itself into a passenger, not to be treated irreverently. As I drove away from the city's center, I encountered fewer stoplights and more stop signs. The roads began to narrow. I remained steadfast on a nondescript street that felt like an artery with anonymous cul-de-sacs whipping off it like capillaries.

After a bout of right turns taking me up and around hotels and bed and breakfast lodges, I wound up and through rows of adobe residences and without noticing, stumbled into a neighborhood with no fences and no clear marks between properties. Go up, I told myself. The camp was atop a hill.

The homes in this neighborhood were property of the affluent. Since I was on the northern end of town, I wondered if any of them commuted to Los Alamos for work, which lay only thirty minutes up I-25. Los Alamos wears the local distinction of being one of the few places in the state where neither an indigenous nor Hispanic influence exists or at least not apparently. It is a science and therefore military outlet, so the population is disproportionately high for whites and Asians and low for Hispanics. The hand-and-glove relationship between Asians and national laboratories in New Mexico is remarkable. In Los Alamos with its now famous National Laboratories, the 2000 Census shows that of the city's 18,000 members, 3.8 percent is Asian whereas Asians comprise only 1.1 percent of New Mexico's population as a whole. As a child, Los Alamos became a place where I could expect to find faces that resembled mine and in that recognition, safety. It was there I could find men with the same immigrant slouch of my father. I never talked with them, but I would see their faces, their black hair and white coats. It wouldn't be until years later when Wen Ho Lee was manacled there that I would learn the irony of me, an Asian American, finding refuge in, of all places, a town built upon a national energy laboratory.

Finally, as I climbed the nose of what seemed like an endless hill, I came into a flat clearing. It was Frank Ortiz Park. It was just as the article described it—a city park, immemorable and homely. It was covered in snow and in its sandy bare spots, I saw it had all the fixings—jungle gyms, swing sets, slides, and from the long stretches of flat white, I assumed a lush lawn. The whiteness defined the place and reflected the sun's glare. Trees spotted the landscape. Piñons held their green, while the Aspens looked like elderly fingers grown cold to the touch and without a glove to protect them.

The men, the prisoners: did they ever get used to it all? No women, no families to look after, only themselves to contemplate, a flag to stare at staring back at them. Did that place ever approximate home? I quickly parked and disregarding the seven inches of snow, marched squarely into the field of white, the bottoms of my khakis darkening from the wetness. How long before these men got used to the chilling cold? Maybe never.

I walked in no particular direction. I was searching for the plaque and saw nothing. Making my way through the flat white-

During the Christmas of 2001, I drove up to Frank Ortiz Park in Santa Fe. I wanted to see if a plaque commemorating the internment camp had been erected yet. Disappointingly, I found nothing. The wind chill and high altitude made the cold quite unbearable.

Stephen Lee

ness, I passed the lonely swing sets cupping the melting memories of snow and slowly trudged up the trail that lead up to the ridge. Somehow I managed to do so without falling once. As I mounted the ridge, for the first time I was able to see back the way I had come and stared in disbelief at the vast patchwork of greens and browns and blues and whites.

But where was that plaque?

For an hour I searched. My footprints crisscrossed themselves in the whiteness, each step pressing deeper into the virginity of the snow, robbing it of its strength. By the time I was done, the snow had been trampled, and I was beside myself in irritation. I had wasted an entire day and found nothing.

Then the redundancy of the place hit me.

This story had been told before, I told myself, but it was only whispered between elders over drink late at night. I realized that even before men with Japanese faces hated this place for imprisoning them, Indian men stood from afar and stared at this same desolate land longing for home. What was once imprisoned was stolen. What was once stolen was a native link. Now all of it had been forgotten and buried beneath a neighborhood with an expensive view.

I turned my neck to glance at my car and for the first time noticed how stiff my neck had become. I began to roll my head to work the knots out, and as I rolled my head from side to side, I found a rhythm that took on the cadence of a black gospel song, like the kind Aretha used to sing. Resigned, I couldn't help but think that this place had no memory of itself because the air was too dry to catch the tears of heartbroken men.

Every story has its origins somewhere. On September 11th, when those God-defying planes struck our beloved towers, most Americans were shocked at what they saw. Meanwhile, the rest of the planet, though sympathetic to our grief, seemed to just shrug a teethy shrug: everyone else seemed to already understand that what happened was a part of something bigger, a continuation of a larger story.

That day, I sunk into television and news addiction, turning to it for solace. I needed the words of others to stitch together what my eyes witnessed but disbelieved. The disbelief seemed to encompass everyone: it was the first time I had ever seen news anchormen unsure of themselves. As the day wore on, the looping image of the plane crashing into the second World Trade Center

This photograph was taken by my father when I was very young during one of our many family car trips. I'm not sure which New Mexican creek this is, but it seems to best capture the essence of La Llorona.

tower tamed my disbelief and made things real, but a foreboding fear remained. But unlike most Americans, my fear wasn't so much of additional attacks; my fear was for the safety of Arab, Middle Eastern, and South Asian Americans. I knew that anyone who "looked like a terrorist" was a potential target for anger-turned-mob violence. My fear was of the inevitable compromises our government would take with our civil liberties. I wondered how many of us could become a suspect in the hunt for the "evil doers." My fear was for the future. Just as I kept a wary eye open for signs of new internment camps, I prodded those around me to remember the past so we wouldn't keep telling the same stories over and over again.

As a youth in New Mexico, I grew up with mainly ghost stories. The one I like best is *La Llorona*—the weeping woman. This is a story told to me by my Mexican friends. The story goes that a New Mexican woman, in a fit of anger against her abusive husband, took her vengeance through their children. She threw them into the

Rio Grande river to hurt that misery-giving man the only way she could. She heaved and upon hearing the splash of her two beloved children, was reawakened into reality and understood her mistake, the horror of her actions. She began desperately running to retrieve them, but to no avail. Her heart broke open like an egg, and she lost herself to insanity. The story goes that she wanders at night by the river having taken the wind as her voice and still searching for her children. Parents warn their own children that they must be good, otherwise *La Llorona* will come for them. They would say, "Shh! Listen! You can hear her footsteps!"

It is a strange thing admitting that as a grown man of twenty-five living in California, whenever I catch the sound of wind at night, I look over my shoulder to make sure *La Llorona* isn't there to snatch me away. I'm always looking for her footsteps.

What I worry most about in these coming months and years, in a post-9/11 world, are those footsteps—will we remember the stories behind them? We forget that bipedal Lucy was mortal. When she died, she left her loved ones anguished despite her immortal footprints. And how will we make sense of these stories? When history's footsteps—*La Llorona's* footsteps—creep into our early morning sleep, we have to choose to either ignore them or turn about face to confront them. This is our choice and even if we make this choice once, or even twice, we will be asked to make it again.

When Mothers Talk

Janice Mirikitani

What do we talk about?

Kitty litter. Miracle brands
that protect us from odor.

Our children, the amazing adolescent years,
my daughter's rebellion to find her voice.
Your son tells you of his "mother filter"
that sifts out mother messages.

September 11, 2001.
We replay the vision of towers crumbling,
bodies falling from windows,
heros and sheros entering hell over and over,
saving lives, giving up their own.

The dust.

The shaking of our economy.

We laugh about my Nisei mother,
hiding her coffee can of money under the mattress.
World War II, depression times
before we were sent to American prison camps.

JANICE MIRIKITANI is poet laureate of San Francisco. She is author of *We the Dangerous* (Berkeley: Celestial Arts, 1997), *Love Works* (San Francisco: City Lights Publishing, 2001), and is executive director and president of Glide Church/Foundation, where she has directed programs for the poor for over thirty-five years.

We cry together about the phone calls
from flight #77.
The inconsolable loss of a child, of a beloved.
6,330 missing.
Growing numbers of the dead.

We feel distracted. Kitty litter.
Our cats' sensitivity to moods
running in circles lately.

We are uncomfortable.
Vulnerable. Attacked.
We want security.
Protect our children and our cats.
Feel safe in our homes,
Drink the water without fear,
travel without checking out
who's boarding the plane.

How do we teach our children not to hate?

How do we climb out
from this rubble of despair?

We share recipes of rice casseroles.

Our country calls to arms
without a clear target,
refugees once more uprooted in Afghanistan,
women oppressed, children without hope,
casualties of war.

In California, a Sikh child is almost torched.
A Sikh woman chased by a car, beaten.

Rice recipes. Jap profiling.
Those camps containing the innocent.
Children behind barbed wire.

We shake our heads about the rising cost
of electricity, heat, shoes and meat, civil liberties.
The consequence of our government raiding natural
resources,
collusion with despots, multinational sweatshops,
a billion people starving in this world.
Proliferation of violence.
Possibility of military draft.
Futility of war
and racial profiling in America.

Kitty litter.
No time for despair.

Mothers must cook.
Teach about sanctity of life.

Love them all
children who are growing up
so fast
we can hardly catch
our breath.

9/29/01

Janice Mirikitani

Benazir Bhutto, former president of Pakistan, lights candle and prays
in traditional Muslim stance, Union Square Park, October 6, 2001.
© 2001, Corky Lee

Why Children Did Not Knock at My Door on Halloween This Year

Ifti Nasim

There was no knock at the door
my cats were waiting in the foyer,
listening to the steps passing by.
Children were knocking at the door
of the apartment in front of mine.

"Trick or treat. Trick or treat."
My money jar full of quarters
looked so empty.
What happened? Who played
these dirty tricks on me?

Thirty-one years as a law-abiding citizen
I am still a foreigner. Foreigner
with a crude face and features of
a terrorist. My color—two shades
darker than an average white man
is not accepted anymore.
My café ole color, once I was so proud of,
is a guilt trip for me now.
My ethnicity has become a crime.

Ifti Nasim is co-founder of Sangat/Chicago, a Southasian lesbian/bisexual/transgender organization. He is also president of the Southasian Performing Arts Council of America. He lectures on sexual diversity among South Asians in diaspora at universities in the U.S. and abroad. A widely published poet, writer and activist, his latest book is *Myrmecophile, Selected Poems* (Philadelphia: xlibris, 2000).

Inside mosque. Kashgar.
© 2001, Eric Chang

Mean streets of Chicago have become meaner.
"Go back to your country. Go back to your country."
They yell at me.
And I am a citizen of the USA
with no country.
Airports, train stations, shopping malls, schools,
hospitals wherever I go,
I am watched and scrutinized.

I yearn for the freedom I came here for.
Right now I am worse than a black slave.
I am tired. I am tired.
I feel like Rosa Parks
and there is no bus for me
because I am not only two shades darker
than an average white man
but I am also a Muslim.

Chicago
10-31-2001

Chinatown, New York City, September 2001.
© 2001, Corky Lee

Sikh candlelight vigil at Central Park, New York City, September 15, 2001. Approximately 2,500 people attended, including those coming in from New Jersey.

© 2001, Corky Lee

Colonialism, Globalization and Culture:
Reflections on September 11th

Arif Dirlik

September 11 has cast a shadow on how we think, what we say, and what we do. The shadow weighs with particular heaviness on the people of the United States; but few around the world have been untouched by it. We stand at a crossroads. There is little question in my mind that the criminal network responsible for that foul deed needs to be brought to justice. But care must be exercised so that the demand for justice does not turn into injustice of its own. The grief caused by the wanton murder of innocent civilians easily turns into anger. A longing for revenge, if unchecked, is likely to bring destruction and further grief to untold numbers of innocent people. The other alternative is to mourn, and find in the mourning an occasion for reflection on those circumstances, that we may work our way out of the spiral of violence that already has brutalized many, and now threatens to consume us all.

It may seem difficult at a moment of national crisis to look past the collapse of the World Trade Center, and the thousands buried in the rubble, and to include in the mourning the millions who have been victimized by the concatenation of brutal events that are as much a part of the historical record of modernity as any record of its achievements. And yet this may be exactly what that tragedy calls for. There is no demeaning or trivialization here of the event itself. On the contrary. It may be comforting in an immediate sense to view what happened in New York City and Washington, D.C., as an aberration—the doing of a handful of misguided fanatics— that may be corrected with their punishment so that history may be

Arif Dirlik is Knight Professor of Social Science at the University of Oregon, and Professor of History and Cultural Anthropology at Duke University.

returned to its intended path. The price to be paid for such evanescent comfort is a disregard for the history that produced the fanatics themselves, and a failure to recognize the historical significance of the event itself. Such recognition, and what lessons we may derive from it, are the best tribute we may pay to all the innocents who were buried under the rubble of destruction on September 11.

A contribution by John Gerassi to the discussion of the intellectual and emotional distress occasioned by September 11, "I Cry," captured the significance of the event by placing it within the context of a series of similarly tragic events that long have been endured by people in different places at different times over the last half century, in the making of which the United States has played a central part.[1] The historical context is not intended to excuse the event, or to explain it away, but to mark it as the most recent of the tragedies of global modernity as it has been shaped by the United States power over the last half century. In an ironic way, September 11 underlines the common history that the United States shares with the rest of the world not just as the architect of this modernity but also as its victim. Americans are used to their wars being fought elsewhere, often in places that most of them would be hard put to locate on a map. September 11 brought the war home (though in a much more difficult sense than facile comparisons with Pearl Harbor suggest). The sense of anxiety and insecurity created by the event in the United States is the daily lot of millions around the world. As we ponder our unaccustomed plight, we may be more sympathetic to theirs; at least one hopes so. The sympathy may be an essential first step toward resolution of at least some of the problems that have led to one tragedy after another around the world.

This said, it is difficult for me to go along with a habitual radical response to the event that takes recourse to the past not to understand the event historically, but to cover up the novel problems it presents to lay the responsibility on "history." Many a radical contribution to the discussion of September 11 begins with heartfelt expression of dismay at the criminal acts of terror in New York City and Washington, D.C., and proceeds from there to catalogue the injustices the United States has visited upon the world, as if the latter were sufficient to explain what happened, and the explanation obviated the need to do anything about it. History is important so that we may look past the immediate event, and the punishment it calls for, to the resolution of the deep-seated problems to which terror may be one response, though by no means the only one. If people around the world express some ambivalence toward an event they find shocking otherwise, the resentment toward the United States that lies at the basis of the ambivalence has to be taken seriously. But none of this explains the criminal act by a self-appointed network of terrorists whose activities have taken on a logic of their own, which no pretense to speak in the name of the oppressed can conceal. The despicable bin Laden, his mentally deranged minions, and the fascist Taliban may evoke sympathy among millions, but just as we must be careful to distinguish the sympathizers from the perpetrators of the deed to remain within the bounds of justice, we must also take care not to confuse sympathy for the terrorists with complicity in the deed and, therefore, a common propensity to terror. As Bruce Cumings writes:

> In the past month many on the Left, in my view, have made the fundamental error of framing the terrorist attacks against the sorrier aspects of the American record abroad, when in fact nothing that has happened since the United States was founded could sensibly justify such wild, wanton and inhuman recklessness. It is as if I were to get upset about the war in Vietnam thirty years ago or American carpet bombing of North Korea fifty years ago. . .and decide to commandeer a Mack truck, load it with explosives and run it headlong into the Sears Tower.[2]

Radical responses to September 11 have suffered from an intellectually and politically debilitating historicism that assumes that the event needs to be comprehended within the context of a history structured by capitalism and colonialism—which ignores that capitalism and colonialism also have histories, and that they may not have the same meaning, or the same consequences, at all times or places. It is necessary, in other words, to distinguish the immediate context from the historical legacies that produced it; most relevant being the necessity of recognizing how the subjects of history perceive, interpret and act upon past legacies under different circumstances. The alternative is entrapment in the same categories that, in the eyes of its perpetrators, legitimized the activities that produced the heinous undertaking of September 11. Especially important here is the question of why retrograde regimes that participate in a global capitalist economy may nevertheless engage in terror against it out of a professed concern for cultural integrity. The contradiction is one that is particular to contemporary globalization. It involves issues of political economy, as well as issues of culture.

Progressive critics have focused for the most part on problems of globalization in its political/economic aspects. The focus here is on the inequalities perpetuated or generated by economic globalization, as it seeks to bring the whole world into a market economy. Economic globalization also implies the attenuation of democracy, as people around the world lose control over (or are deprived of the possibility of controlling) their daily lives, and are denied participation in the making of decisions that shape their lives. This in turn is continuous with the millennial victory of capitalism, and of the colonialist turn it has taken for the last few centuries. Its ideological expression is a Eurocentric or, presently, a United States-centered developmental ideology. Globalization, viewed in this perspective, is the latest stage of EuroAmerican imperialism—which also renders suspect any claims to the liberating promise of globalization. What happened on September 11, it follows, was a product of, and a response to, this situation.

There is at one level little cause for disputation in this diagnosis. What gives pause is its coincidence with the diagnoses offered by rightwingers in Europe and the United States, who have suggested already that there may be links between the terrorist attacks on the United States and the anti-globalization protests in Genoa, Seattle, or other places; not because there is any serious credibility to be attached to such suggestions, but because progressives now have to explain their differences from reactionary responses to globalization, as well as their relationship to what used to be called the Third World. If progressives in Europe, the United States, and elsewhere in the world all hold Wall Street (the symbol of capitalism) and the Pentagon (the symbol of United States power, and its ability to undermine the sovereignty of others) to be responsible for the ills of globalization, how do they distinguish themselves from the brainwashed half-wits who thought that attacking those same targets, and killing as many innocent people as possible in the process, would take them to some Quranic paradise?

One aspect of the discourse on globalization that has been overlooked consistently is the cultural contradictions it has generated, which could be viewed also as the cultural contradictions of capitalism in its contemporary phase. Progressive well-wishers of globalization see in it both the promise of a "global village," and an age of infinite recognition of and respect for cultural difference, which would make little sense to anyone who has ever lived in a village, but has become a liberal faith nevertheless in the United States and Europe. There is little reflection in this discourse on how and where cultural difference is to be located. The result is to identify culture with nations, civilizations, or just "cultures," which lifts culture out of its context in social relations, ignores its historicity, and contributes to its reification.

September 11, at least on the surface, has vindicated those such as Samuel Huntington who have been suspicious of globalization as a unifying idea, seeing in it instead the bleak prospect of a "clash of civilizations."[3] While this discourse is equally off the mark in its identification of culture with "civilization," it at least recognizes the importance of power in shaping culture. It is a geopolitical idea, the goal of which is not to nurture tolerance and mutual understanding, but to deal with the realities of power in shaping culture. Interestingly, because he views culture as a geopolitical problem, Huntington is more willing than his liberal counterparts to recognize the impossibility of locating culture. Seemingly reversing his own earlier position in his *Clash of Civilizations*, he says in a recent interview that "Osama bin Laden wants it to be a clash of civilizations between Islam and the West. The first priority for our government is to try to prevent it from becoming one." More interestingly, he denies that he ever viewed Islam (or other civilizations) as a "unified bloc," and paraphrases Henry Kissinger to query, "if you want to call the Islamic world, what number do you call?"[4]

There has been much talk in the last six weeks of Islam, which has revolved around the intricacies of Islam and how they may help us understand what happened. It is probably a tribute to the intellectual changes of the last three decades that President Bush in his September 20 address to the nation drew a distinction between Islam and its perversions. Since then, the talk of good Islam/bad Islam has become part of the discourse on September 11, what Mahmood Mamdani describes appropriately as "culture talk." As Mamdani argues persuasively, "culture talk" takes religion out of its social and political context, and seeks to find a direct causal relationship between religious belief and political act; in effect depoliticizing the whole issue, which has been a characteristic of cultural discussion in the United States and Europe at least over the last decade. Similarly, the good Islam/bad Islam distinction, suspiciously resonant with our Moslems/their Moslems, is vacuous in ignoring that Islam, like all religions and other systems of belief, is open to interpretation and appropriation for a variety of causes, and the language of good/bad simply has the effect of taking politics out of Islam.[5] The more important question is whether Islam (or Christianity, or any other religion) should control political power. It is a question of secular versus religious politics. That this basic question is ignored in the discussion may be an indication of how we have not just learned to resign ourselves to reactionary revivals around the world (including our world), but even to celebrate them in national and global multiculturalisms.

The ambivalence toward September 11 to which I referred above is not just a matter of Islam versus Christianity, but is a product of the legacy of colonialism. The discussion of colonialism, however, has been marginalized by the preoccupation with Islam. It is not only Moslems who feel ambivalent, but all those who have suffered from colonialism, which has not found its way into the discussion. On the other hand, non-Moslems may have little reason to find comfort in the despicable bin Laden's division of the world into the world of Islam and the world of the infidels, any more than they have in accepting the pronouncements of a Jerry Falwell or a Pat Robertson. "Culture talk" also depoliticizes the world of Islam by focusing on good/bad Islam, while ignoring that many who live in so-called Islamic societies, and have Moslem stamped in their birth certificates (such as myself) not only are not sympathetic to the claims of Islam, but absolutely oppose religious efforts, "good" or "bad," to capture the public sphere.

For all the talk in United States and (to a lesser extent) European scholarship over the last decade about cultural crossings, porous boundaries, etc., what has been happening in the world at large is not the erasure but the proliferation of boundaries. National boundaries seem to be disappearing not because they are weakening, but because within and across national borders new boundaries have been added to earlier ones, defined not by politics but the reification of cultures. Whatever the discontents of nationalism, and they are many, the nation-state also nourished off and sustained a notion of the public. The idea of the public is now being torn apart in the First World by the claims of autonomous ethnic cultures, while it is invaded in Third World societies by the invasion of religious despotism which, in its totalitarian claims, makes a mockery of any notion of the public. "Globalization" has produced the questioning of cultural boundaries, but it also has generated the reification of cultural difference. Even the discussion of capitalism, perhaps the most universalistic of contemporary discourses, has found itself challenged by questions of cultural difference.

The question is not whether or not "culture matters," as the title of a recent volume puts it,[6] but where we draw the boundaries of culture. The answer to this question, ironically, has been of the most conservative kind; at least in the theoretical literature (in contrast to marketing and advertising literatures, which comprehend culture in a much more concrete, anthropological sense): the identification of culture with fictive civilizational claims. Those who have the power to represent those claims also take it upon themselves to define what their cultural content may be.

This tendency is obviously inconsistent with the evidence of cultural complexity. The so-called civilizations are not characterized by cultural homogeneity; even their boundaries are blurred. They are internally fractured both culturally and ideologically; so that the "clash of civilizations" is not merely across civilizational boundaries, wherever they may be located, but internal to their constitution. Civilizations, if they ever existed except through political and military enforcement, have infiltrated one another as modernity has emerged as a global condition. Islamic ideas of justice are not external to "the West" any more than human rights discourse is a foreign idea in Islamic societies, as there are constituencies that represent these discourses that are located across so-called civilizational boundaries. Civilizational claims, in other words, are off-ground abstractions imposed upon the diverse populations that are contained within those boundaries.

The revival of civilizational claims with globalization suggests that it is no longer possible to view relations of power in the world in terms of earlier paradigms of colonialism or neo-colonialism. While a critique of the devastation wrought by globalization is as necessary as ever, we need to recognize that increasingly, others than the United States and Europe are complicit in its functioning, and benefit from it—including those who were encompassed earlier within the "Third World." The Third World, which served in an earlier time not just as a descriptive term (of a global condition) but also as the source of alternative political visions of humanity, is no more. In some ways, what happened on September 11 may also symbolize the death of the Third World, of any remaining hopes that the so-called Third World might serve as the source of hopes for a different kind of world. The progressive common visions of an earlier period of national liberation movements have been overtaken by conservative retreats into civilizations that, as cultural abstractions, now serve as excuses for denying rights to their constituencies. While we need to criticize the policies and activities of powers such as the United States for generating, or being oblivious to, the disastrous consequences of globalization, such criticism needs to be accompanied more than ever before by critique of the leadership in these other societies that are no less disastrous. The Taliban started its terror at home, and against women. Pointing to the part United States anti-communism played in the emergence of Taliban is historically instructive, but it does not do away with the responsibility of Taliban leaders for their criminal activities. I may add here that this necessity of a double-critique—both of the powers that dominate and shape the world, and of reactionary culturalist responses to it that legitimize oppressive politics—is better grasped by those in the "Third World" engaged in social and ideological struggles than by intellectuals in Europe and the United States who, rebelling against a legacy of Eurocentrism, are often too anxious to pledge allegiance to the cultural claims of fictive civilizations.

In his contribution to the discussion of September 11, Henry Giroux observes the emergence of a public unity around the event, and hopes that this unity can go beyond temporary assertions of national chauvinism to regenerate a notion of the public that has been undermined by the attack on public institutions under a neo-liberal regime.[7] Giroux has been an eloquent analyst of the destruction of the public sphere in the United States by the marketization of society. I think we need also to consider how an excessive concern with ethnicity and cultural "integrity" may also contribute to the undermining of the social at both the national and the global level, by rendering politics into identity politics. Culturalism, which is both attendant on the neo-liberal economic regime and a product of its voracious social appetites, also needs to be challenged at both the national and the global levels. Ethnic cultural assertion is a weapon of those who are marginalized in the dominant society, but it needs to look beyond itself in the reconstruction of the public. Liberal multiculturalism is an indispensable companion of economic neo-liberalism, which seeks to contain genuine difference, which is situational and historical, with pieties about preserving cultural integrity. Whether promoted by national governments or the United Nations, "culture talk" is inevitably captured by those who make some claim to cultural purity and, therefore, the prerogative of speaking for entire societies, which sacrifices the political prerogatives of billions of people to elites with their own political agenda, extinguishing any hopes not only for economic but also political democracy. It may be instructive to remember here that the perpetrators of September 11 direct their venom not just at the United States, but at native elites as well who have "sold out" to the United States. Likewise, apologists for "globalization" identify anti-globalization protestors with the Taliban and bin Laden. Those who are concerned with justice and global peace would do well to heed such identifications, and define where they stand vis-à-vis either camp.

Everyday welfare, justice and democracy seem to me to be a good point of departure, and places offer a way of challenging this situation of cultural reification across all civilizational "boundaries." As Arturo Escobar has put it cogently, "culture sits in places."[8] Culture, understood not in the abstract or in terms of the ideologies of power, is inextricable from the practices through which people define and conduct their everyday lives, in the process generating ever new cultural practices as their circumstances change. It is, in other words, as alive as the lives that it defines and expresses. As Vijay Prashad has put it, "tradition and culture are not givens; rather, they need to be constantly remade in ways that enable us to live creatively, to struggle in the creation of a good society of the future."[9] The production of new cultural forms in the concrete interactions of everyday life may be the best defense we have against the reifications of culture that imprison people in ethnic spaces, divide them from one another in everyday life, and undermine any significant sense of the social—and the public.

There are trans-place cultures, needless to say, that are generated by the interactions of places, and of places with other social and political entities (including other "civilizations"), but culture, to be meaningful as an aspect of life, needs to be located in everyday life in its historicity, and in all its variability across places. It is this culture that proves intolerable to the forces of homogenizing power. We are complicit in such intolerance to the extent that our language legitimizes abstract cultural claims that presuppose boundaries of nations, regions or civilizations.

Places have been maligned in the literature of modernization; especially, sadly, in modernizationist radical literature that has viewed them as locations of parochialism and backwardness—which may say more about the prejudicial commitments of modern liberalism and radicalism to cosmopolitanism and the nation-state than about the politics of place, or, as I would prefer it, place-based politics. Politics that can be transformative and yet respectful of place-based difference has not found its way into either liberal or radical agenda until recently, as it defies the most fundamental assumptions of either liberal or Marxist "political science," which for all their differences share in common a fetishistic scientism that privileges generality over difference—and take for granted the civilizing mission of the state. The result has been to abandon the politics of everyday life to the most conservative forces.

What is at issue here is a transformative conception of place that is insistent nevertheless on the necessity of respecting the integrity of places. Places are marked by their particular historical legacies and practices of oppression and exploitation, which need to be addressed in any progressive conceptualization of place. This in turn calls for the injection into places of ideas and hopes that have their origins outside of places (which is also the reason for the preference for "place" over "community"). On the other hand, for such transformation to be effective and genuinely democratic, it must seek not to homogenize places by the ideologies and practices of larger structures of political economy, but to recognize the logic of heterogeneity, which includes listening to the voices of those who inhabit places. Theory, with all its ideological presuppositions, at some point needs to give way to concrete empirical circumstances; and where that point lies needs to be determined by those who live in places, and not the purveyors of abstractions who claim omniscience by virtue of being outside of places. Roland Robertson has captured this dialectic with the term "glocality."[10] What we might add is the question of agency in the resolution of the contradictions thrown up by glocality. A place-based perspective is most important in recognizing agency to those who live in places.

The misogynist deeds of the Taliban are a reminder of the importance of women in any conception of place. This is not simply out of prejudice for feminist agenda that exclude men, but out of a recognition of the increasingly heavy burden that women around the world have had to carry both as protectors of home and the bearers of labor as labor has been "feminized." Women are privileged because they represent the "bottom line" in oppression, but also because they have increasingly taken the initiative to challenge such oppression (I must note that this statement may need qualification in light of the abuse and brutalization of children, who also suffer from voicelessness). The abuse of women's bodies at home or work is a universal problem, although its malignity differs from place to place. Any recognition of the importance of women in preserving and sustaining "home" needs also to recognize the plight of children. If home is a place for nurturing children, women also have had to carry a burden in nurturing and preserving the humanity of their children, who are under the constant threat of brutalization by hunger, war, and pestilence, including the pestilence of ideological indoctrination. Women have taken the lead in environmental protection, on which the preservation of bodies and home may depend, and providing it with accessible metaphors. Finally, the insistence on public recognition of private existence has changed our understanding of what the "public" means. There is a certain danger here to be sure; because the intrusion of the private into the public also invites the intrusion of the public into private life, which is not necessarily benign in its consequences. But the transformative effects of the changing relationship is unquestionable, and needs serious reflection. It is necessary to recognize the importance of women in all these areas. It also may tell us why women's agency is evidently threatening to reactionary apologists for patriarchal power—from the Taliban in Afghanistan, who first unleashed their terror on women, to the Jerry Falwells and Pat Robertsons of the United States, who see the terrorist attack on the United States as God's punishment for feminists and gays, whom one commentator describes, appropriately, as "the American Taliban."

September 11 is a reminder once again of the need to bring to the surface deep-seated structures of oppression that are lost all too easily in ideological concerns with cultures and civilizations. This means, also, that we turn our attention from abstract promises of progress and development, or cultural preservation, to progress that preserves life at the most fundamental level of everyday life. Those buried under the rubble of the World Trade Center, and even those at work at the Pentagon, were where they were because they were simply following their everyday routines of work and labor. Their momentary extinction is a reminder of the fragility of human life, not just in the United States but in Afghanistan, where life is difficult enough without Taliban despotism, and the terror from the sky that Taliban terrorism has bred. Compassion for both is what made Gerassi cry, and kept him crying. Let us hope that once the tears are dry, we can see our way more clearly out of the tragedies of our making.

Notes

1. I am grateful to Fatma Alloo, friend and colleague, for sharing with me this piece by Gerassi which was published in Tanzanian papers.

2. Bruce Cumings, "Some Thoughts Subsequent to September 11th," http://www.ssrc.org/sept11/essays/cumings.htm, 2

3. Samuel P. Huntington, "The Clash of Civilizations?" *Foreign Affairs* (Summer 1992): 22-49, and, Samuel P. Huntington, *The Clash of Civilizations and the Remaking of World Order* (New York: Simon and Schuster, 1996).

4. "A Head-On Collision of Alien Cultures," interview with Michael Steinberger, *The New York Times*, October 20, 2001

5. Mahmood Mamdani, "Good Muslim, Bad Muslim—An African Perspective," http://www.ssrc.org/sept11/essays/mamdani.htm.

6. Lawrence E. Harrison and Samuel P. Huntington, eds., *Culture Matters: How Values Shape Human Progress* (New York: Basic Books, 2000).

7. Henry A. Giroux, "Reclaiming the Social in a Time of Crisis: Democracy After September 11th." I thank the author for sharing this paper with me.

8. Arturo Escobar, "Culture Sits in Places: Anthropological Reflections on Globalism and Subaltern Strategies of Globalization," *Political Geography* 20 (2001): 139-174.

9. Vijay Prashad, *The Karma of Brown Folk* (Minneapolis: University of Minnesota Press, 2000), 156.

10. Robertson in turn traces the term as a verb, glocalize, to Japanese (*dochakuka*): "Glocalize is a term which was developed with particular reference to marketing issues. . ." Roland Robertson, "`The Search for Fundamentals' in Global Perspective," in Roland Robertson, *Globalization: Social Theory and Global Culture* (Thousand Oaks: Sage Publications, 1994), 164-181, 173.

Silent peace rally by South Asians in Jackson Heights, Queens.
© 2001, Corky Lee

Coming Full Circle
North American Labor History Conference
Wayne State University, October 19, 2001

Grace Lee Boggs

I want to thank Elizabeth Faue for choosing "Coming Full Circle" as the title for my talk this evening. I don't know what inspired her to choose it—I saw it for the first time in the conference brochure—but it captures the feeling I often have these days, that I/ we are in the midst of a great turning. To begin with, I was born during World War I, which historians like Eric Hobsbawm view as the real beginning of the twentieth century because it put an end to the illusion of nineteenth-century Europeans that they had reached the apogee of civilization.[1] Now, providentially, I have lived long enough to witness the death blow dealt by September 11 to the illusion that unceasing technological innovations and economic growth can guarantee happiness and security to the citizens of our planet's only superpower.

In the last few years I have also become increasingly conscious that I began my movement activism in the early 1940s when, in the wake of the Great Depression and the sitdown of millions of factory and office workers all over the country, the writings of public intellectuals and academicians began to reflect the influence of Marx's ideas of class and class struggle.

Now, sixty years later, in the wake of unceasing revolutions in technology, the mobility of corporations, the social movements of the last forty years and the demise of Soviet Communism, the fundamental tenets of Marxist-Leninism are in disarray.

Immanuel Wallerstein has summed up the precarious state of these tenets in this passage from *After Liberalism*:[2]

GRACE LEE BOGGS has been a Movement activist and theoretician for nearly sixty years. Her autobiography, *Living for Change*, was published by the University of Minnesota Press in 1998.

1. The two step strategy—first take state power, then transform society—has moved from the status of self-evident truth (for most persons) to the status of doubtful proposition.

2. The organizational assumption that political activity in each state would be most efficacious if channeled through a single cohesive party is no longer widely acceptable.

3. The concept that the only conflict within capitalism that is fundamental is the conflict between capital and labor—and that other conflicts based on gender, race, ethnicity, sexuality, etc. are all secondary, derived or atavistic—no longer has wide credence.

4. The idea that democracy is a bourgeois concept that blocks revolutionary activity has been giving way to an idea that democracy may be a profoundly anti-capitalistic and revolutionary idea.

5. The idea that an increase in productivity is the essential prerequisite of socialist construction has been replaced by a concern with the consequences of productivism in terms of ecology, the quality of life, and the consequent commodification of everything.

6. The faith in science as the foundation stone of the construction of utopia has given way to a scepticism about classical science and popular scientism, in favor of a willingness to think in terms of a more complex relationship between determinism and free will, order and chaos. Progress is no longer self-evident.

In other words, we can no longer depend on the profound philosophical and strategic concepts that gave birth to the concept of the Left and guided twentieth-century revolutionaries all over the world. So twenty-first-century revolutionaries need new ideas and strategies for our anti-systemic struggles, and academics also need new paradigms for their work.

Long before reading this remarkably succinct summation by Wallerstein, I had come to similar conclusions as a result of my movement experiences, especially after being deeply involved in the Black Power movement in Detroit during the 1960s. Since then, together with Jimmy Boggs until his death in 1993, I have been engaged in the arduous and exciting process of exploring and creating these new ideas and strategies.

What I would like to do this evening is review the process by which I came to these conclusions. My aim is to do this in a way that will be useful to you as movement historians, even if many, perhaps most, of you find my projections difficult to accept.

Having been born female and Chinese American, I knew from early on that changes were needed in our society, but not until I left the university in 1940 with a Ph.D. in philosophy did it occur to me that I might be involved in making those changes. At that point, confronted with the need to make a living, I realized how unlikely it was that I would ever do so as a university professor. In those days, even department stores would come right out and say, "We don't hire Orientals." Luckily for me, my awakening coincided with the beginning of World War II and the emergence of the March on Washington Movement demanding jobs for blacks in the defense industry. I became involved with the MOW movement and was so inspired by it that I decided that what I wanted to do with the rest of my life was become a movement activist in the black community. Towards that goal I joined the Workers Party which, through the South Side Tenants Organization, had brought me into contact with the black community.

Inside the Workers Party, after nearly twenty years in classrooms, I was primarily interested in getting my feet wet in practical activities. But I was also an intellectual who, having studied Hegel, was acutely aware of the power of ideas to be both liberating and limiting. From Hegel I had gained an appreciation of how human beings have evolved over many thousands of years as they struggled for Freedom (or what we today call "self-determination"), constantly striving to overcome the contradictions or negatives which inevitably arise in the course of struggle, constantly challenged to break free from ideas which were at one time liberating but had become fetters on our minds because reality had changed, and to create new ones that make more concrete and more universal our concept of what it means to be free. In my last year of graduate work, I had also been drawn to the American pragmatists George Herbert Mead and John Dewey who helped me to unthink the sharp separation between the True and the Good which was entrenched in nineteenth century thought and to recognize that individuals can only develop to their highest potential through their involvement in community.

That is why, inside the Workers Party I was immediately attracted to the Johnson-Forest Tendency led by C.L.R. James, the West Indian historian (his best-known work is *The Black Jacobins*), and Raya Dunayevskaya, a Russian-born self-educated intellectual who had once been Trotsky's secretary. C.L.R. and Raya appealed to me in the first place because, unlike most radicals in that period, they emphasized the significance of the independent Negro struggle for the making of an American revolution. They were also avid students of Hegel. So their Marxism and Leninism were very different from that of most Marxist-Leninists. Instead of being economist and determinist, their Marxism was infused with the humanism of Marx's early Economic Philosophical Manuscripts. Instead of focusing on Lenin's strategies for the seizure of power, they emphasized his profoundly democratic vision that "Every Cook Can Govern."[3]

I spent ten years in New York working closely with C.L.R. and Dunayevskaya, while also learning the nuts and bolts of radical organizing by doing the Jimmy Higgins work of a party member. But I was delighted when the Johnson-Forest Tendency came to the conclusion in 1951 that both the Workers and the Socialist Workers parties were too stuck in the ideas that they had derived mainly from the Russian Revolution to recognize the new social forces for an American revolution—Blacks, rank-and-file women workers, and youth—that had emerged out of the socializing experiences of World War II. So we decided to set out on our own to launch an independent newspaper called *Correspondence*, that would be written and edited by representatives of these new social forces and published in Detroit.

That is why I moved to Detroit in 1953 and soon thereafter married Jimmy Boggs. Living and working with Jimmy in the black community of Detroit, I began to see the relationship between ideas and historical reality in a completely different light. C.L.R. and Raya were both powerful intellectuals and I had learned a lot from working with them. But their ideas about workers had come more from books and from struggles with other radicals whose ideas about workers also came from books, than out of real life. Jimmy, on the other hand, was what Gramsci called "an organic intellectual" whose ideas came mainly out of his life experiences. Born in Marion Junction, Alabama, a tiny country town with two stores on its main street, he had moved to Detroit after graduating from high school. Working on the line at the Chrysler Jefferson plant, he became a rank and file militant, absorbing from the left wing forces in the UAW (whom Reuther had not yet red-baited out of the union) the fundamental concepts of class, race and socialism that helped him to see himself as a continuation of thousands of years of human struggle to be free or self-determining. After World War II, he experienced the decimation of the work force by automation. As a result, he was very conscious of the tremendous changes taking place in his reality and of himself as a worker who had lived through three different epochs of human struggle to extend our material powers: agriculture, industry and automation. Because he had this dialectical sense of constantly changing reality and of himself as a historical person, he also had the audacity, the *chutzbah*, to recognize—as he did in *The American Revolution: Pages from a Negro Worker's Notebook*[4]—that Marx's ideas, created in a period of material scarcity, could no longer guide us in our period of material abundance, and that it was now up to him to do for our period what Marx had done for his.

When I began living in Detroit in the 1950s, Jimmy was still mainly engaged with his fellow workers in struggles in the plant against automation and speed-up (which workers in the plant called man-o-mation). But by the 1960s he had concluded that because unions were unable or unwilling to struggle with management over the fundamental questions raised by Hi-Tech, the workplace was no longer the main site of struggle, and revolutionaries should focus instead on the profoundly new questions about how to live and make a living that were being asked by the "Outsiders" in the community, who were mainly black young people. As he put it in *The American Revolution*: "Thus at this point when the labor movement is on the decline—because it can't solve the issues raised by Hi-Tech—the Negro movement is on the upsurge."[5]

During the 1950s I mainly listened and learned from being with Jimmy in the many meetings he held with workers from his plant and people in the community. However, by the 1960s I felt I had been living in the black community long enough to play an active role in the black power movement which was emerging organically in a Detroit that was becoming majority black. So while Jimmy wrote articles and made speeches challenging black power militants to face the questions of Hi-Tech, I was doing a lot of organizing.[6] Thus I was one of the main organizers of the Grassroots Leadership Conference at which Malcolm made his famous speech. And I was the coordinator of the 1964 Michigan Freedom Now Party, the first all-black party to get on the ballot in a major election.

Then, in July 1967, the Detroit rebellion exploded, forcing us to rethink the Marxist-Leninist ideas about revolution which the Left accepts as self-evident.

In 1967 Jimmy and I had each been in the radical movement for twenty years or more, but we had never felt compelled to address head-on the question of what is a revolution and how do you make it. Now, with rebellions breaking out all over and young blacks joining the Black Panther Party by the tens of thousands, we had to ask ourselves whether there is a fundamental distinction between a rebellion and a revolution. Out of that questioning, we concluded that although rebellion is a stage in the development of revolution, it falls far short of revolution. As we wrote in *Revolution and Evolution in the 20th Century*,[7] rebellions are important because they represent the standing up of the oppressed, break the threads that have been holding the system together, shake up old values so that relations between individuals and groups within the society are unlikely ever to be the same again. But rebels see themselves and call on others to see them mainly as victims. They do not see themselves as responsible for reorganizing the society, which is what the revolutionary social forces must do in a revolutionary period. They are not prepared to create the new values, the new truths, relationships and infrastructures that are the foundation for a new society. So that while a rebellion usually begins with the belief on the part of the oppressed that they can change things from the way they are to the way they should be, they usually end by saying "*They* ought to do this and *they* ought to do that." In other words, because rebellions do not go beyond protesting injustices, they increase the dependency rather than the self-determination of the oppressed.

We also recognized that those who purport to be revolutionaries but deny or evade this lesson of history and continue to celebrate or encourage rebellions do so mainly because they view themselves as the leaders of angry, oppressed but essentially faceless masses. If or when they gain power, they may make some reforms but they are powerless to make fundamental changes because they have not empowered the oppressed prior to taking power.

That is why, beginning with 1968, Jimmy and I felt that our main responsibility as revolutionaries was to go beyond "Protest Politics," beyond just increasing the anger and outrage of the oppressed, concentrating instead on projecting and initiating struggles that involve them in assuming the responsibility for creating the new values, truths, infrastructures and institutions that are necessary to a new society. Now that the rebellions of the late 1960s have broken the threads that have been holding the system together, we said, now that urban rebellions have become part of the American political landscape, now that the constant revolutionizing of production has created everlasting uncertainty and compelled people in all layers of society to face with sober senses our conditions of life and our relations with our kind, now that capitalism has defiled all our human relationships by turning them into money relationships, revolutionaries urgently need to project new ideas and new forms of struggles that involve the potentially revolutionary social forces in exploring in theory and practice new concepts of Work, Education, Community, Citizenship, Patriotism, Health, Justice, and Democracy, transforming and empowering themselves as they struggle to transform their reality.

In the 1970s we did this exploration mainly in pamphlets and statements, for example, "Education to Govern," "Crime Among Our People," "Beyond Usual Politics," "The Energy Crisis and You," "Towards a New Concept of Citizenship," "But What About the Workers?"[8]

By the 1980s, however, Detroit had been turned into a wasteland by Hi-Tech and de-industrialization, and it had become obvious that Detroit's first black mayor, Coleman Young (who had been elected because the rebellions had demonstrated that only Black Political Power could keep blacks from rebelling) didn't have a clue as to how to rebuild Detroit. All he could come up with were megaprojects like the GM Poletown plant, which required bull dozing 1,500 houses, 600 small businesses and six churches to build a plant that GM promised would employ 6,000 workers (it has never employed more than 4,000), at the same time that it was closing down the Fisher Body and Cadillac plants which together employed 30,000. That was in 1980.

A few years later an increasingly desperate Coleman Young decided that the secret to Detroit's revitalization was a "Casino industry" which he said would employ 50,000 workers. To struggle against (and eventually defeat) this proposal, we joined a broad coalition of community groups, blue collar, white collar and cultural workers, political leaders, clergy and professionals who together embodied the rich ethnic and social diversity of Detroit. In the course of the struggle, Coleman called us "naysayers" and challenged us to come up with an alternative. Jimmy welcomed the challenge. In a speech entitled "Rebuilding Detroit" he insisted that to rebuild Detroit we need to think of "a new mode of production based upon serving human needs and the needs of the community and not upon any quick get-rich schemes." "We have to get rid of the myth that there is something sacred about large scale production for the national and international market and begin thinking instead of creating small enterprises which produce food, goods and services for the local market and combine craftsmanship or the preservation and enhancement of human skills with the new technologies which make flexible and customized production possible."[9]

Based upon this vision we began in the 1990s to create programs like Detroit Summer, an intergenerational, multicultural youth program to rebuild, redefine and respirit Detroit from the ground up (which has just completed its tenth season) and to join networks like the Detroit Agricultural Network which connects thousands of Detroiters who have created hundreds of community, youth, church and school gardens on the vacant lots that have turned Detroit into a prairie. We also began a Mural Message Movement (AC3T) bringing artists and schoolchildren together to create community by designing huge murals that hang on school walls. Inspired by the new energy in the community represented by these projects, students and faculty in the University of Detroit Mercy School of Architecture have since created ADAMAH, a vision of a community based on urban agriculture, both as starting point and as metaphor, for a 2.5 square mile area on the east side of Detroit not far from the Boggs Center.[10]

Meanwhile I have been writing a weekly column on the Fresh Ideas page of the *Michigan Citizen* describing and analyzing the potential for a new movement that is emerging in Detroit and the country. For example, "Detroit: Place and Space to Build Anew," "Another World is Possible," "Freedom Schooling," "Restorative Justice," "Participatory Democracy," "Beyond Protest Politics," "The World of 2050 Will Be What We Make It."

As a result of these activities involving the hands, heads and imaginations of diverse citizens, Detroit, like the Zapatistas in Chiapas and the Tree Huggers in India, is becoming an example of what has been called "Grassroots Post-Modernism,"[11] the movement emerging in the Two-Thirds world that has never been industrialized to challenge Western ideas of development and the three sacred cows of modernity: 1) that there is only one universally valid way of understanding social reality; 2) the exclusive and general validity of Western-defined notions of human rights; and 3) the notion of the self-sufficient individual, as contrasted with people in community, which is how all human beings lived until the onset of capitalism in Europe 500 years ago.[12]

In the last few years people have been coming from all over the country to go on the Boggs Center tours that give them a view not only of the devastation that global capitalism has produced but also of the new life emerging on vacant lots and, through the ADAMAH video, a vision of how Detroit could actually be rebuilt, redefined and respirited from the ground up. Europeans are especially fascinated because they fear a Detroit in their own future. A delegation from the British Parliament was scheduled to come here on September 28 but cancelled because of September 11.

Last weekend the Boggs Center organized a tour for a very diverse group of movement activists en route to a Retreat at the Fetzer Institute in Kalamazoo. The Retreat was one of the series of "State of the Possible" Retreats that are being convened by the Positive Futures Network, publishers of *YES Magazine*. The focus of last week's Retreat was exploring what movement activists should be doing in the wake of September 11.

The gathering's unfolding was profoundly affected by what participants had learned from the Detroit tour: that the destruction of the World Trade Center that had taken place in five seconds before the eyes of the whole world on September 11 has been taking place in slow motion over the last fifty years in Detroit, but that in Detroit a new society is rising up from the ashes. As a result, the gathering came to the conclusion, which is depicted on this graphic, that out of the anger, the fears, our new vulnerability, and the elementary need for safety that all Americans are feeling in the wake of September 11, can come the profoundly human questions (who are we? where have we been? where are we going?) that are necessary to inspire the movement to change America that is now urgently needed, a movement that will be led by people of color, and that will require the redefining in theory and practice of all the truths that we have considered self-evident—about Work, Technology, Education, Citizenship, Patriotism. In the course of building this movement, we will begin to think very differently about the relationship between revolution and evolution, between the inner and the outer, between Spirituality and Materiality, and between Freedom and Necessity.

Notes

1. Eric Hobsbawn, *The Age of Extremes: A History of the World, 1914-1991* (New York: Pantheon Books, 1994).

2. Immanuel Wallerstein, *After Liberalism* (New York: The New Press), 214-215.

3. Lenin, *The State and Revolution*, Collected Works, Vol. XXI (New York: International Publishers, 1932).

4. James Boggs, *The American Revolution: Pages from a Negro Worker's Notebook* (New York: Monthly Review Press, 1963).

5. *Ibid.*, 83.

6. Collected in *Racism and the Class Struggle* (New York: Monthly Review Press, 1970).

7. James and Grace Lee Boggs, *Revolution and Evolution in the Twentieth Century* (New York: Monthly Review Press, 1974).

8. Available from www.boggscenter.org.

9. See www.boggscenter.org.

10. "The Greening of Detroit: Planting Visions for a Post-Industrial City," www.boggscenter.org.

11. Gustavo Esteva and Madhu Prakash, *Grassroots Post-Modernism* (New York: Zed Books, 1998).

Tin vendors, Kashgar.
© 2001, Eric Chang

Terrorism as a Way of Life

Vinay Lal

The Geopolitics of Terror: Notes from/on South Asia

It has been a truism in politics that friends and enemies are never stable categories, and the ruthless advocacy of self-interest, which is not calculated to introduce idealism into political relations, is intrinsic to the logic of the nation-state. Great Britain, which wags its tail when the master shouts, and has in consequence become an embarrassment to nations with even a modicum of pride, might appear to be an anomaly: it has long enjoyed a "special relationship" with the United States. In George Bush's joint address to Congress shortly after the terrorist attacks of September 11, Britain was described as America's truest friend. Ironically, the last attack upon the mainland United States was perpetrated by the British during the War of 1812. They sacked Washington and burned most of the city, including the White House and the Capitol, to the ground. In contemporary times, it is with shock that one recalls the *mujahideen* being welcomed to the White House by President Reagan as "freedom fighters" and being compared with the "founding fathers." No one was then thinking of the "Islamic menace"; thought, insofar as there was any, was expended only on the "evil empire." Some years after that signal event, Osama bin Laden was recruited to help the intrepid Afghans dispatch the Soviets to oblivion. The "evil empire" remains; only the "evil-doers," an appellation dear to the gross executioner who now runs the affairs of the United States, are "Islamic fundamentalists" presiding over an empire of terror. Meanwhile, the former invaders of Afghanistan have promised the Northern Alliance, some of whose leaders acquired legendary reputations fighting the Soviets, shipments of guns and tanks.

VINAY LAL is Associate Professor of History at University of California, Los Angeles.

Osama bin Laden has dedicated himself to the fulfillment of the task left unfinished by the British 200 years ago. All this makes one think that the cynicism of early Indian secular texts, such as the *Hitopadesa* and *Pancatantra*, which described friendship as an arrangement of convenience and naked self-interest, was not misplaced.

South Asia is scarcely exempt from the iron-clad rule of nation-state politics and the dogma of "national security," though one wishes that the animosity between Pakistan and India had displayed less constancy since the partition of India in 1947. The transformation of Pakistan into a frontline state in the "war against terrorism," a surreal outcome for most Indians who are habituated to thinking of Pakistan as the sponsor of state terrorism in Kashmir, has brought awareness of South Asia to American audiences. In the aftermath of 9/11, it has been assumed by the American media that there are two constituencies *naturally* positioned to enlighten the public on the atrocities and terrorism, experts in the history, politics and culture of Middle Eastern societies, and American foreign policy experts. The left-wing, in the United States, India, and elsewhere, has assimilated the terrorist attacks into the general category of American foreign policy failures. The other tendency, which necessitates the expertise of specialists in Middle Eastern politics and Islamic history and theology, is to assimilate the terrorist attacks to the pre-existing category of "Islamic fundamentalism."

Though an effort has been made to disassociate Islam from the events of 9/11, everyone presumes to know what is constituted by "Islamic fundamentalism," and no one doubts the wisdom of the category itself: if anything, "Islamic fundamentalism" is at times construed as a redundancy, since Islam is itself fundamentalist. The adherents of this view seldom openly express themselves in this vein, but mainstream commentary should be read for its slippages and betrayals. The editorialists for the *New York Times* weighed in after 9/11 with the assurance that the attacks arose from "religious fanaticism" and from the "the distaste of Western civilization and cultural values" among the perpetrators, but when they added that the attacks represented the "anger [of] those left behind by globalization,"[1] we begin to understand that those implicated are not only the terrorists but nearly all the Muslim masses of the Middle East, Indonesia, South Asia, and Central Asia who have gained nothing, and perhaps lost much, from globalization and the structural adjustment policies imposed purportedly for their benefit by the mandarins at IMF. All these millions of people are potential terrorists. What the *New York Times* is loathe to admit, the militant Hindu embraces openly: thus HinduUnity.Org, a group which espouses the same worldview that one has come to associate with such organizations advocating Hindu hegemony as the Vishwa Hindu Parishad (VHP) and the Rashtriya Swayamsevak Sangh (RSS), in a press release on September 12 declared that "Islamic fundamentalism will forever stay and plague our world as its 'roots' are deeply embedded in Islam itself. The conquests and plunder that have been committed by hordes of Islamic barbarians to continents like North Africa, Europe and India cannot ever be blamed to any type of Islamic Fundamentalism but Islam itself."[2]

The copious commentary on the atrocities of September 11, and on the wider implications of the events of that fateful day, is in itself an extraordinary instance of the imperialism of categories and the alarmingly narrow scope for dissenting perspectives. Within the American academy, with its two-pronged focus on disciplinary formations and area studies, Afghanistan has never had anything of a presence. Specialists in Middle Eastern history and Islamic studies, who are accustomed to thinking of the "Middle East"—which is itself an invention of area studies programs—as the "authentic" home of Islam, have characteristically displayed not the slightest interest in Afghanistan, indeed—with the obvious exception of that very small fraternity of scholars working on Indo-Islamic history—not even in South Asian Islam. There remains more than a lingering feeling among scholars of Islam that the Muslims of South Asia, who number about 400 million, embody an inauthentic, compromised, hybrid, adulterated, even "bastardized" version of Islam. Ernest Gellner's widely acclaimed study, *Muslim Society* (1981),[3] the scope of which is not qualified by any subtitle or the demands of geography, barely mentions India, the home of the second largest Muslim population in the world; and similarly R. Stephen Humphreys' *Islamic History: A Framework for Inquiry* (1991)[4] altogether omits South Asia from its capacious canvas. Close proximity to the idolatrous beliefs of polytheistic Hinduism is supposed to have contaminated the Muslims of South Asia, and since Islam is presumably best studied in its pure form, scholars have turned to Islam's primordial home in the "Middle East." Now that the Taliban have come to the attention of the West, one should not marvel at the recent spate of articles which seek to establish, not without justification, that the Taliban are inspired by that puritanical strand of Islam which goes by the name of Wahhabism, apparently the state religion of Saudi Arabia.[5] Sheikh Mohammed ibn Abdul Wahhab sought, in the eighteenth century, to return the practices of Islam to the pristine state of the seventh century. As Edward Said has argued, the "myth of the arrested development of the Semites" remains critical to the Orientalist worldview[6]; and to study the Taliban is perforce to gain an insight into the origins and early history of Islam. However despised the Taliban might be, they are useful to the scientific and scholarly community in the West as part of the fossil record of humanity.

The social organization of knowledge is such that, for different reasons, Afghanistan has never been part of South Asian area studies programs in the United States. Sandwiched between the Islamic and Indic worlds, Afghanistan has been seen as belonging to neither, and has suffered the fate of those who cannot be accommodated within the known categories.[7] (Pashto, the language of the Pathans, the dominant ethnic group in Afghanistan, is not taught at a single American university.) It matters little to American "experts" that South Asians themselves recognize the longstanding relations between the Indian sub-continent and Afghanistan, and that Afghanistan, Pakistan, and India are seen as sharing an intertwined history. Many Indians might not remember that north India was governed by Afghans for the greater part of the first half of the second millennium, but the tombs of the Lodi kings in Delhi are a palpable reminder of the times when Afghanistan was the source, not of terrorist networks, but of ruling dynasties. Perhaps even fewer will have experienced a sense of recall at hearing the news that the most widely mentioned political resolution of "the Afghanistan problem" entails the restoration from exile of the former monarch, Muhammad Zahir Shah, who is now in his mid-eighties and has been living in Europe for nearly three decades.[8] Nearly 150 years ago, when Hindu and Muslim mutineers took to arms and momentarily threatened to bring British rule in India to a swift conclusion, they marched to the residence of the last monarch of the great Mughal dynasty, Bahadur Shah Zafar, and persuaded him to lead the rebellion against the colonial pretenders. For about the same time as Muhammad Zahir Shah has been living in exile as the deposed King of Afghanistan, Bahadur Shah, also in his eighties, had been confined to the grounds of the Red Fort as the titular King of Delhi. Then, as now, it remains the supposition, even among many colonized subjects, that democracy is not for these countries, and that only the transcendent figure of the monarch, howsoever old or distant from his people, can bring together a fractious people torn apart by ties of religion, ethnicity, and language.

Thus the history of Afghanistan belongs in great measure, and not merely in fragments, to the history of South Asia. When the events of September 11 transpired, in India at least the implications of the terrorist attacks for South Asia, rather than the relations between the terrorists and Islamic fundamentalist groups in the Middle East, became the subject of the most searching commentary. There was a widespread feeling that the United States would now better understand India's own protracted battles with terrorists, and that it would be more attentive to repeated claims by the Indian government that terrorist networks operating in Afghanistan, Pakistan, and Pakistan-occupied Kashmir (POK) had fuelled, and continue to be the lifeblood for, the decade-old insurgency in Kashmir. Did the Americans "finally understand," asked the columnist Vir Sanghvi, "what we've gone through these ten years?"[9] Another writer, writing apropos of Washington's failure to assist India in counter-terrorism measures in Kashmir, complained that "U.S. international policy has been parochial. It concentrated only on terrorist threats that were aimed at its national interests."[10] The editor of the *Indian Defence Review* recalled that the "Jehad Factory run by the Taliban and the Inter Services Intelligence (ISI) of Pakistan" had let loose thousands of "warriors" across Kashmir, Chechnya, Dagestan, Bosnia and Xinjiang [the Muslim-majority provinces of China],"[11] while the respected sociologist, Dipankar Gupta, was candid in expressing the view that though a great gulf separated the superpower from a poor and inefficient nation such as India, the two countries had nonetheless arrived at something of a "parity": "both [had] been hit by identical forces of terror." The Indian "diagnosis of terrorism," Gupta submitted, now stood vindicated: "We have always advocated a full-scale onslaught against terrorism even if that meant giving notice to countries like Pakistan; and now America is saying the same thing." Gupta conjectured that to many Indians it was "deeply satisfying" to consider that the United States would presumably be prepared henceforth to join India in giving the lie to the idea, perpetrated by Pakistan, that there could be such a thing as "just terrorism."[12]

Moreover, as the spotlight began to focus in less than a day following the attacks upon Osama bin Laden and his terrorist training camps in Afghanistan, many middle-class Indians felt pleased that the Pakistani spy agency, Inter Services Intelligence (ISI), would now stand exposed as an avid supporter of the most notorious terrorist groups sworn to indiscriminate use of violence and the expansion of Islamic fundamentalism,[13] and that Pakistan itself would be discredited as the creator of the Taliban.[14] There was much speculation that India could take the opportunity to cross the Line of Control (LOC), which stands as the interim border in Kashmir between India and Pakistan, and wipe out terrorist training camps along the LOC in Pakistan-occupied Kashmir. Indeed, India's former High Commissioner in Pakistan, G. Parthasarthy, penned an opinion piece in the *Hindustan Times* to remind readers that if the Americans could plan on waging strikes against terrorist bases "wherever they exist," did that not serve "as an appropriate international precedent for us to act similarly when our people and our cities are subject to terrorist outrages?"[15] Characterizing the reaction of many Indian commentators, the Indian journalist Harish Khare does not appear to have been amiss in stating that for the first few days following the attacks, "the Indian foreign policy constituency was in a tizzy. The barely disguised gleeful anticipation was that the Americans would now solve the Kashmir problem for us. . . . The more excitable among us believed that the Americans would look the other way should Indian commandos be let loose across the Line of Control in a mission to destroy *jehadi* camps."[16] However, among educated Hindus, the feeling has long persisted that India is a "weak and soft state," and consequently some commentators wondered whether India would have the stomach to recognize that General Pervez Musharraf belonged essentially to the same class of criminals as Osama bin Laden and was deserving of similar treatment. "Will we face the problem the way America will," asked one columnist, "with resolve, determination and firepower? Or will we light candles on the Wagah border and suck up to Musharraf over breakfast?"[17]

Exulting, perhaps, at the dilemma of General Musharraf, caught between the American demand for unstinting cooperation and the large fundamentalist constituency in his own country, even in his own armed forces, little did Indian commentators know that Pakistan would be transformed into America's indispensable partner in the war against terrorism, indeed into a "reliable" friend now apparently intent on persuading the world that it has never been a party to terrorist actions. If in politics it is an axiomatic proposition, in the words of one Russian political analyst, that "even if you do something in your own interest, you must charge a price from your ally,"[18] then it stood to reason that Pakistan would extract from the U.S. a hefty bounty in exchange for its agreement to stand by the U.S., offer it the use of its intelligence services and military facilities, and convey American ultimatums to the Taliban. Before long it became clear that the U.S. had agreed to lift all sanctions against Pakistan, "reschedule" Pakistan's astronomical debt burden ($38 billion), assist Musharraf in his new-found battle against fundamentalism, resume military ties between the two nations, and ignore its previous call for the rapid restoration of democracy in Pakistan. The veteran journalist Prem Shankar Jha, musing over the "dizzyingly rapid rehabilitation of Pakistan from the nether zones of a failing near-terrorist State to a darling of the western alliance in this new 'war' against terrorism," warned that the unpublicized concession Musharraf would squeeze out of the U.S. and its allies would be a promise of indifference towards terrorist activities in Kashmir on the grounds that such activities represented the legitimate aspirations for independence of an oppressed people.[19] Two weeks later, on October 19, Jha declared himself vindicated: Colin Powell had in the interim visited Pakistan and India, and declared, to the grave dissatisfaction of the Indians, that Kashmir represented the "central" issue between the two countries. It is transparent, Jha wrote, that the "U.S. has lost its way in Afghanistan," and that the "clear objectives" with which it began had disintegrated until "all that remains is utter confusion and a growing, self-defeating, dependence on Pakistan."[20]

Among Indian journalists, Jha is known for his hawkish views, but he was scarcely the only one to express bewilderment at Pakistan's "bizarre" elevation into the frontline state waging the war against terrorism. Anil Narendra, the editor of the Hindi daily, *Vir Arjun*, noting that Pakistan was to be rightly viewed as part of the "problem of global terrorism" rather than "part of the solution," scathingly observed that "according to the U.S., an act of terror essentially means an act of terror executed *against Americans and their country*." Nothing else could explain the obliviousness of the U.S. to India's encounter with terrorism in Kashmir over the last twelve years, leading to not less than 30,000 deaths. There is "irrefutable evidence," Narendra wrote, "which shows that terrorism is an integral part of Pakistan's state policy to control Afghanistan, Jammu and Kashmir and to Talibanise parts of Central Asia."[21] To many Indian commentators, the situation in 2001 seemed uncannily similar to what transpired in 1979: then the faltering government of General Zia ul Haq, who came to power in a coup that toppled the democratically elected government of Zulfikar Bhutto in 1977, suddenly found itself being courted by the U.S. The Soviet invasion of Afghanistan provided the pretext for Zia's resuscitation; neither the U.S. nor Pakistan expended an iota of thought on the question of democracy. Two years into his overthrow of the corrupt albeit democratically elected government of Nawaaz Sharif, General Musharraf, presiding over a country which was increasingly being viewed the world over before September 11 as a "failed state," must be marveling at the ways of providence.[22]

Many Indians have, then, thought of Pakistan as a country for which "terrorism is a way of life." Anguishing over Pakistan's newly acquired status as an ally of the world's only superpower, as that vital nodal point in the travel plans of Western heads of state and their emissaries, few Indians have paused to consider the fact that the United States has never in its history shown a predisposition towards permanent bonds of friendship with natives outside the orbit of "Western civilization." With the rest of the world, the United States understands only strategic alliances, and often not even that: the grammar of its conduct includes coercion, bribery, carpet bombing, incineration, starvation by inches, genocidal sanctions, death, and destruction. A senior military official in the Pakistani army is reported to have said, after the defeat of the Soviet Union in Afghanistan and America's subsequent neglect of that region, that the United States had flushed Pakistan down the drain much as a man might dispose of a used condom. The Pakistanis themselves appear to have forgotten that widely circulating story. But perhaps Indians should ruminate further on the notion of "terrorism as a way of life," and ask whether the fullness of thinking about terrorism as a way of life cannot be better understood by extending the scope of their reflections to encompass, as I shall in due course suggest, "the American way of life."

The Politics of Terror:
Notes on the Indian and American Left

The numerous interpretive frameworks brought to bear on the present "crisis" in Afghanistan share this: they presume to "know" the Afghans, and so have failed to ponder how these people came to this pass. It is unnecessary to rehearse here the story of how the Soviets might have been "trapped" into invading Afghanistan,[23] the American desire to turn Afghanistan into Soviet Union's Vietnam, the enlistment of Islam in the battle against communism, the recruitment of Osama bin Laden and other Arabs sworn to defend

Islam against atheists, the birth of the international mujahideen movement with every blessing of Pakistan, the use of Stinger anti-aircraft missiles in bringing down Soviet war planes, the defeat of the Soviet Union, the regression among the Afghans to their supposedly time-honored traditions of fighting each other, and the emergence of the Taliban, between 1994 and 1996, from the chaos, anarchy, and wild bloodshed of the preceding years. The principals are largely agreed on this narrative, but attach different ethical significance to its various parts: thus, to take only one example, the actions of the Americans in the 1980s are thought by some to be well-intentioned, emanating from classical geopolitical thinking; others declare that Americans were typically shortsighted. One encounters a still larger narrative about Afghanistan in the form of a cautionary tale. Americans are warned that Afghanistan has never been conquered in the last millennium, and that it will be their graveyard: the British were unable to subdue the Afghans, the Soviets got quagmired in that hostile terrain, and it is the fate of each superpower to be humbled by the intractable Afghans. If one desired a demonstration of the efficaciousness of iteration in political discourse, one could not have asked for more. Babur, the founder of the Mughal dynasty in India, captured Kabul in 1504; and, in 1738, Nadir Shah, in his customary fashion, savaged the city. Even the nineteenth-century battles with the British were seldom as one-sided as some would like to believe, though the British, who captured Kandahar, suffered much humiliation.[24] Ranjit Singh, the Sikh ruler, nearly extended his empire to Kabul in the 1830s; and the ferocious economic pressure that the Americans placed over the Soviets did as much to drive them out of Afghanistan as the actions of the mujahideen. An unconquerable people?

So, then, how did Afghans come to this pass that they are now the very embodiment of brutality and ruthless violence? The salience of that query acquires all the greater force when we consider that no less a person than Mohandas Gandhi, who insisted upon the most exacting standards of nonviolence, considered the Pathans, the ancestors of the contemporary Taliban, as the most perfect practitioners of nonviolence that he had ever encountered. In the late 1920s, the Pathan leader, Khan Abdul Ghaffar Khan, later nicknamed the "Frontier Gandhi," came to embrace the Gandhian doctrine of *satyagraha*.[25] He forged an army of volunteers and disciplined them into a fighting force of *satyagrahis*: these were no effete rice-eating vegetarians or *banias*, to use the mocking language of some of Gandhi's critics, but towering men. Their reputation for military prowess was legendary. Such was the strength and resolve of the Khudai Khidmatgars, "the Servants of God," that they even paralyzed British administration in Peshawar.[26] Years later, the Pathans, who hold aloft the banner of their faith in Islam with pride, repudiated the two-nation theory on the basis of which Pakistan was carved out of India as a Muslim-majority state and openly declared themselves unhappy with the partition of India. Afghanistan would also be the only country to oppose Pakistan's admission into the United Nations. Where is this history, and what is the politics of this amnesia? Apparently Afghanistan required a Soviet invasion so that it could at least enter into the consciousness of the West and become the slum and marginalia of Western existence. This is the condition of the wretched of the earth: they must perforce be impregnated by Europe, or by ideological movements of Western provenance, before they can be said to have entered into the pages of history. What possibilities of politics were abjured when Abdul Ghaffar Khan and the Pathans were sidelined and browbeaten into submission? What alternative histories might have been generated had the Pathans then received the ear of the world?

That the left in the U.S., as in India, should be oblivious to anything which cannot be comprehended with the conception of an "authentic" left history is no surprise. The nonviolence of Gandhi and his associates has never been attractive to the left, and not only because Gandhi held to certain ideas about the caste system, the relation of religion to politics, industrialism, science, modernity, and the use of violence in the war against capitalism which the left has always found unpalatable.[27] The left is more charmed by the likes of Fanon and Che Guevara; nonviolence has none of the cathartic effects attributed to violence by its theorists, and it is also not very sexy. Thus the left's history of Afghanistan, usually commencing with the Soviet invasion of 1979, is predictable, and similarly its intellectual framework for the attacks of September 11 extends no further than the familiar critique of American state power and the terror of American hegemony, conjoined of course with observations about the ignorance of the complex history of Islam among members of the media and the public, the inability of Americans to think of the Arab people as endowed with distinct histories, traditions, literatures, and identities to which the same dignity should be extended as one might extend to other cultures and traditions, and the American propensity to engage in "double standards." There are numerous variants of these arguments: thus the left points, again with complete justification, to the failure of the United States and the West to enter into a genuine dialogue with Islamic countries, and the abrogation by the U.S. of its own values and standards of ethical conduct. Only those who remain willfully blind need to be reminded of the American support for the most despotic and authoritarian regimes, in and out of the Middle East, the hand of the United States in assisting countries such as Indonesia in their extermination of the intellectual elite and progressive political organizations, and the numerous "special relationships" that the United States has entered into with repressive and ferociously anti-democratic regimes such as that of Saudi Arabia. Everyone has had to live with the American genius for creating Frankenstein monsters—Saddam Hussein, Noriega, bin Laden, the Taliban, while the more theoretically inclined have mused over the course of dialectical reversal in history.

Thus, to follow the voices which have been prominent in their critique of American foreign policy and militarism, it has been the United States which has been conducting *jihad* upon the rest of the world. America's pact with terrorism fills many pages, takes many forms, and knows no bounds: let us say that America is multicultural even in its sponsorship of regimes and oppression of people. It has no special animus against Muslims, Africans, the nations of Central America, or the speakers of strange tongues in Southeast Asia: it is predisposed towards a frightening ecumenism in its objects and strategies of pacification of recalcitrants and in its sentiments of overlordship towards the world. Writing in the pages of the *Guardian* on September 29,[28] Arundhati Roy recalled the long history of America's record of genocidal intent and behavior, but her passionately written denunciation of America's barbarous conduct abroad is just as interesting for its reticence, common to the left-liberal critique of American foreign policy, in entertaining more daring questions about the widespread animus against the U.S. which not unfairly can now be described as a distinct characteristic of "world consciousness." To see where she falters, let us recall that no sooner had the attacks taken place than Bush described them as an assault upon "the American way of life"; four weeks later, as the U.S. began its air war against Afghanistan, Tony Blair was still speaking of the murder of innocents in America as "an attack on our freedom, our way of life . . ."[29] Yet to Roy it is altogether inexplicable that the U.S. government should have represented the attacks as an assault upon the "American Way of Life." It's "an easy notion to peddle" amidst rage and grief, but she urges us to resist the thought, and "wonders why the symbols of America's economic and military dominance—the World Trade Center and the Pentagon—were chosen as the targets of the attack. Why not the Statue of Liberty?"

If the business of America is business, and the military is deeply interwoven into nearly all the political, social, and civil institutions of American society, then Roy is perhaps missing the pulse of America. She has the idea that the voice of the American people remains unheard in the web of military institutions, as though the entrails of the military did not extend into tens of thousands of American communities and homes. She is aware of the yellow ribbons and the display of flags, which come out far more quickly and in embarrassing abundance in America than they do in any other country, but this appears disconnected to her from the meanings generated by the Pentagon. "American people ought to know that it is not them," Roy declaims, "but the government's policies that are so hated," and she points to the acclaim with which the country's many "extraordinary" musicians, writers, actors, and sportsmen are received worldwide. If the disjunction between the government and "the people" is so vast, then American democracy must be dismissed as an entirely farcical exercise—a view that the comedy of last year's presidential race would appear to support, but that neither the U.S. government nor the American people will accept as credible. To imagine that "the American people" have a government wholly at odds with their sensibilities is to suppose that they are entirely gullible and ignorant, and yet wiser than their leaders; it also makes a mockery of the idea of representation, which is the formal mainstay of all democratic polities. Since leaders in the U.S. are elected, one cannot but think that elections must mean something, however obviously inane the exercise may be of choosing between indistinguishable Democrats and Republicans.

Variations of Roy's argument are frequently encountered among those critical of the U.S. government but eager to exculpate, as perhaps the moral imperative must be to do so, "the American people" and civil society. The American people have many spokespersons: certainly in no other country does the government, and similarly its critics, purport to act and speak as frequently in the name of the people. In India, the Prime Minister or President addresses "the nation"; the American President addresses "the American people," the ultimate tribunal of civilized values, humanity, and reasoned opinion. The world is constantly reminded that "the American people" will not tolerate assaults on freedom, democracy, human decency, and civilization, and it is striking that Bush began his address to a special joint session of Congress on September 20 with the observation that "the American people" had already delivered a report on the State of the Union. The people were, in effect, the answer to bin Laden, rebutting his terror-laden acts with scenes of courage and compassion: the Union remained strong. Thus, even as seasoned a political commentator as Noam Chomsky, a relentless chronicler over three decades of American state terrorism, gallantly persists in the belief that if "the American people" *really knew* of their government's widespread complicity in the perpetration of gross abuses of human rights, their outrage would be sufficient to arrest the government in its tracks. (What prevents the people amidst the "information explosion" of our times from shedding their ignorance?) Roy, Chomsky, and many others persuaded about the inherently democratic propensities of American civil society—while persuaded that American state terrorism represents the greatest threat to global society—ignore as well the consistent poll findings showing massive public support for military intervention, whether at the time of the Gulf War or in the aftermath of 9/11. Polls are, doubtless, not innocuous exercises in the calibration of public opinion, but their instrumentality in matters of policy, governance, and opinion-making is widely acknowledged, and the left has just as eagerly embraced poll findings when it has been in their interest to do so.

The Culture of Terror:
Notes on "the American Way of Life"

> The civilized have created the wretched, quite coldly and deliberately, and do not intend to change the status quo; are responsible for their slaughter and enslavement; rain down bombs on defenseless children whenever and wherever they decide that their "vital interests" are menaced, and think nothing of torturing a man to death: these people are not to be taken seriously when they speak of the "sanctity" of human life, or the "conscience" of the civilized world.
>
> —James Baldwin (1976)[30]

The most conventional definition of terrorism adverts to violence that is indiscriminatory, targeting not only soldiers and functionaries of the state but civilians, not only government installations but the pillars of civil society. The distinction between the government and "the American people" is precisely what the terrorist actions of September 11 sought to undermine, and the conservative elements in American society may be much closer to the truth than left commentators in recognizing that an attempt was made to put "the American way of life" under the bomb. Arguably there is no one "American way of life," but the vast bulk of American commentators, as even a cursory examination of the print and visual media suggests, are firmly persuaded that the United States is the eminent custodian of those eternal values of freedom, democracy, and compassion without which a people cannot be viewed as civilized. The U.S., Bush told FBI agents, is "the most free nation in the world," and it has a special "calling" which can be inferred from the fact that it is a "nation built on fundamental values that reject hate, reject violence, reject murderers and reject evil." This has been the daily refrain of Bush's briefings, his radio addresses, his speeches before the CIA and forums of businessmen: the "civilized" world and "freedom" themselves are under attack, America is a "good" and "compassionate" country, its people have "moral values" and place a premium on the "sanctity" of life, and their opponents are "faceless cowards" who are "evildoers" hiding in caves and waging a "new kind of war." To the overwhelming question, "what is it that the terrorists so hate about America," Bush replied in Congress: "They hate our freedoms—our freedom of religion, our freedom of speech, our freedom to vote and assemble and disagree with each other." We might ask why in an elected body with over 430 members, only one Congressperson (Rep. Barbara Lee, D-CA) had the daring to cast a dissenting vote when Congress decided to give the President untrammeled authority to prosecute the war, but American democracy is not habituated to the discussion of subtleties. Chastising postmodernists, relativists, pacifists, and other critics of "modern-day American imperialism," William Bennett assured his readers that "America's support for human rights and democracy is our noblest export to the world," and that "America was not punished because we are bad, but because we are good."[31] Little do Bush, Bennett, and their ilk realize that the very self-righteousness of America, particularly when it is brought into service as the ideological plank of American domination, is read by many people around the world as America's license to commit terror.

Other commentators have attempted more complex readings. Thus, the burden of an editorial by Joyce Appleby, who recently served as the President of the American Historical Association, is that the inheritance of the Enlightenment divides the "modern West" from those determined upon a course of obscurantism and violence. This specialist in the intellectual history of the American revolution says that "Muslim culture is not Western culture 300 years earlier. Its bias against individual autonomy and self-interested economic exchanges runs deep."[32] There is not much work for interpretation here, the message is writ large: the terrorists, and their Muslim brethren, share a profound dislike for the free market and that emblematic figure of the American West, the Lone Ranger. Could they be further removed from "the American way of life"? Orientalist discourse has always insisted that the non-West has no idea of the individual, and that collectivities—organized around religion, caste, tribal loyalties, and the like—alone matter among the less civilized and those without a conception of the free market. If, moreover, anyone should be foolish enough to hazard the speculation that interculturality is a far more promising avenue to the understanding of diverse histories, Appleby has this rejoinder: "Sexual relations, so basic to all social organizations, are ordered along entirely different principles [among Muslims]." The day may not be far away when we will be informed by Western experts that Muslims and "we" moderns in the West have different anatomies. Judging from the attacks upon Sikhs, Hindus, Afghans, Muslims, Pakistanis, Iranians, Arabs, and many others, some Americans, whose premise for action is the formula that "they who look different, are different," are already enacting the street versions of this particular superstition derived from the Enlightenment. This is "the American way of life."

It has been "the American way of life" to assume that one lives without fear, indeed that one is entitled to live with as much security as a multicultural democracy can promise, while being perfectly free to inflict, through one's representatives in government, fear and terror upon others. Who in the U.S. can presume to understand the trauma, what Ernest Jones described in the 1940s as the "mutism and emotional paralysis," followed by "practical cessation of all mental activity and even death," of those who have had to endure night after night of intensive bombing with missiles, cluster bombs, and payloads of 50,000 pounds of explosive?[33] Osama bin Laden has sought to carry the war to the American public and disrupt "the American way of life," and no other reading is suggested by his ardently expressed desire that America should be "full of fear from its north to its south, from its west to its east." It is another matter altogether that his actions will only reinforce "the American way of life," whether witnessed in the immense surge of militarism, the extraordinarily disproportionate use of

Political poster on nuclear testing in the Pacific, part of "Globalize This!: International Graphics of Celebration and Dissent" exhibit organized by Center for the Study of Political Graphics. (Track 16 Gallery, Santa Monica, California, 2001).

© 2001, Mary U. Kao

airpower against a people who have little else but the clothes on their back, the pretense at internationalism, the pathetic airdrops of packages of peanut butter and strawberry jam, or the scarcely veiled threats of death and destruction for those states that are less than willing partners in the coalition against terrorism. Osama bin Laden does not appear to have understood that it is also "the American way of life" to lace terror with a tinge of kindness.

It is demonstrably true that the terrorist acts of September 11 were undertaken with utter deliberation and executed according to a plan perversely admirable in its devotion to detail. The terrorists conjoined this means-end rationality, at the altar of which all great powers have worshipped, to another form of life equally well understood by Americans—namely that captured by the domain of the symbolic. One of the most visible symbols of "the American way of life" in late modernity is the sport utility vehicle (SUV), which now accounts for nearly fifty percent of sales of consumer vehicles. The SUV is likely to be found on the freeways of Southern California, and generally the driver is its only occupant. Elbowing other vehicles off the road, terrorizing other drivers into submission, the SUV is the battle-tank of highways and surface streets. Its track record on safety is acknowledged to be severely wanting. It has almost nothing to do with "sports," and its only utility is to feed the coffers of an automobile industry that has moved to more expansive forms of exploitation of the earth's resources. The SUV is illustrative, even in its mere designation, of the terrorism of hegemony. Even in American parlance, the SUV is a "gas guzzler," a not slight admission in a country where the unhindered supply of cheap gasoline is virtually a constitutional right.

Installed in this vehicle is "the American way of life"—with 4 percent of the world's population, the United States consumes nearly a third of the world's oil and other resources. A profligate consumer, sworn to criminal levels of waste, the United States has succeeded admirably well in exporting the ideology of consumerism to the entire world. Its academics have also made an industry of exporting critiques of consumerism, but this should not surprise us, considering that as by far the largest manufacturer and exporter of arms and military hardware, the United States also describes itself as the greatest force for peace in the world. One is reminded as well of a conversation that transpired between Gandhi and a journalist, who probed the Mahatma on his opposition to industrialization and big science. Gandhi is on record as having said that if a small island like England had to engage in such massive exploitation to attain comfortable standards of living for its people, he shuddered to think what levels of exploitation would be required to give a few hundred million—now a billion—people in India comparable standards of living. Perhaps such arguments might be dismissed as entailing a "romantic" critique of modernity, but if we are unable to understand the linkages between the twin scourges of terrorism and consumerism, between terrorism and unilaterialism—witnessed, for instance, in Bush's rejection of the Kyoto climate accords and the American repudiation of the international conference on racism held in Durban a mere few days before September 11—then terrorism will simply remain an aspect of "evil" perpetrated by a few "fanatics." The trail that leads from the gross energy abusing vehicles known as SUVs to America's huge oil bill, the Middle East, the Gulf War, and now the conflagration in Afghanistan and the untapped petroleum reserves of Central Asia is covered in blood. Oil flows through the veins of George Bush and Osama bin Laden: this is the happy marriage of "the American way of life" and terrorism as a way of life.

Epilogue: On Ways of Life

Somewhere the Scottish poet Robert Burns has written that the greatest gift is the ability to "see ourselves as others see us." The ways of life followed by others seem laden with terror, and the supposition that terrorism has become a way of life among some Muslim men in most Islamic countries runs deep in the Western press and academy. A decade ago, Bernard Lewis, whose shadow over Middle Eastern studies has loomed large in the academic world, spoke incomprehensibly of the "roots of Muslims rage,"[34] which he located in the inability of Muslims to live in the modern world, their antiquated social and political institutions, their loss of power and failure to cope with that loss, and their exclusion from the orbit of world political activity. He was not the first to represent Islam as an obscurantist faith that had clumsily inserted itself into modernity, nor should one think that his style of thinking does not resonate widely among educated and influential Americans. Francis Fukuyama, whose prophetic voice and obsequies to capitalism endear him to Washington, has in the aftermath of 9/11 assured us that "Islam. . .is the only cultural system that seems regularly to produce people like Osama Bin Laden or the Taliban who reject modernity lock, stock and barrel," and of that "of all contemporary cultural systems, the Islamic world has the fewest democracies." While certain that "there are no insuperable cultural barriers" to prevent underdeveloped people "from getting there," that is to the mountain-top occupied by the free-market economies, Fukuyama evidently thinks that Muslims may have to be exempted from the circle of optimism.[35]

This chorus of voices has been joined by brown men. Recalling Lewis's "The Roots of Muslim Rage," the Indian-born editor of *Newsweek International*, Fareed Zakaria, presses forth the view in his article "The Roots of Rage" that Islamic fundamentalism is akin to fascism, Nazism, and even populism in the U.S., having widespread acceptance in Muslim-dominated societies. The anger and despair of unemployed young men, conjoined to the success of fundamentalist organizations in offering various social, cultural and political services that the state is unable to provide, accounts for the success which the "medievalists" have had in recruiting youth to their cause.[36] *Madrassas* in Saudi Arabia, Pakistan, and Afghanistan are said to churn out tens of thousands of pupils steeped in parochial versions of Islamic history and theology and ill-equipped to face up to the modern world. Terrorism can be an attractive way of life when all other options have disappeared.

For Salman Rushdie, even this much analysis is unnecessary. Purporting to speak as a New Yorker, and—one suspects—slyly exploiting his own experience with the terror of Khomeini's *fatwas*, the recently arrived immigrant celebrity deplores "the savaging of America by the left" and finds it heartless that a "country in a state of deep mourning and horrible grief" should have been told that its own policies may have contributed to the culture of terror. To prove the fundamentalist wrong, Rushdie avers, "We must agree on what matters: kissing in public places, bacon sandwiches, disagreement, cutting-edge fashion, literature, generosity. . .movies, music, freedom of thought, beauty, love." For good measure, Rushdie adds "a more equitable distribution of the world's resources" to his list.[37] Rushdie's conviction that Islam to most Muslims means little more than "the sermons delivered by their mullahs of choice; a loathing of modern society in general, riddled as it is with music, godlessness and sex; and a more particularized loathing (and fear) of the prospect that their own immediate surroundings could be taken over—'Westoxicated'—by the liberal Western-style way of life" is underscored by his recent *New York Times* editorial. Here Rushdie affirms that the affair of September 11 has everything to do with Islam, and more particularly with Islam's failure to become modern. "If terrorism is to be defeated," he writes, "the world of Islam must take on board the secularist-humanist principles on which the modern is based, and without which Muslim countries' freedom will remain a distant dream."[38]

The sentiments expressed by Zakaria and Rushdie are shared far more widely across the educated, middle-class, and urban sectors of Indian society. The very culture of others becomes construed as the breeding ground of terror: we have all heard of Islam's purported culture of the sequestration of women, the culture of fanaticism bred by a harsh and unrelenting monotheistic faith born in the inhospitable environment of an unyielding land, the culture of the *madrassas*, and so on. Having said this, let us be certain that the atrocities of September 11 can be known by no other name but terrorism. More than one Indian commentator, writing apropos of Osama bin Laden and the Taliban, has been inclined to think of the United States as "hoist to its own petard."[39] If one had to think of proverbs at this juncture, one should be riveted only to Gandhi's expression that an eye for an eye will end up making the whole world blind. But much of the world has been living with terror for years and decades, and the greater part of terrorism is the fact that the United States, indeed nearly the entire "civilized" West, has never had the courage to admit that it purchased its long night of peace with a long night of terror abroad. If there is to be any "enduring freedom" arising from the terrorist acts of 9/11 and the events in the midst of which we are placed, it must reside both in the acknowledgment that terrorism has been incubating and flourishing in "the American way of life" and "Western civilization"—that thing of which Gandhi said that "it *would* be a good idea"—and in the commitment to ensure that peace shall henceforth not be purchased with terror abroad. In the midst of the brutality of our times, should we not endeavor to remember and live by Kant's injunction that one's own action must be capable of serving as the basis of universal law?

Notes

1. Editorial, "The National Defense," *New York Times* (September 12, 2001), sec. A.

2. HinduUnity.Org, Press Release (New Delhi), "Islamic Terrorism Hits America," September 11, 2001.

3. Ernest Gellner, *Muslim Society* (Cambridge: Cambridge University Press, 1981).

4. R. Stphen Humphrey, *Islamic History: A Framework for Inquiry*, rev. ed. (Princeton: Princeton University Press, 1991).

5. See, for example, Stephen Schwartz, "Terror and Islam," and Tariq Ali, "Questions and Answers," both available on the internet.

6. Edward Said, *Orientalism* (New York: Vintage Books, 1978), 307.

7. Ahmed Rashid, author of the authoritative *Taliban: Militant Islam, Oil and Fundamentalism in Central Asia*, reprint ed. (New Haven: Yale UP, 2001), stated in a recent television interview (MSNBC, October 29) that over the last two decades, the U.S. government has not had a single notable expert on Afghanistan.

8. Aditya Sinha, "Back to the King," *Hindustan Times* (September 30, 2001), 13. All citations from Indian newspapers are from the Delhi edition of the newspaper unless otherwise noted.

9. Vir Sanghvi, "Moral Math: Musharraf vs. bin Laden," *Hindustan Times* (September 16, 2001), 12.

10. Pramit Pal Chaudhuri, "Apocalypse Now," *Hindustan Times* (September 13, 2001), 10.

11. Bharat Verma, "Faceless Enemy," *The Hindu Sunday Magazine* (September 23, 2001), I.

12. Dipankar Gupta, "Bonded by a Threat," *The Hindu Sunday Magazine* (September 23, 2001), I-II.

13. Vishal Thapar, "ISI Chief Paid for 1998 Attack Tip Off to Osama," *Hindustan Times* (October 10, 2001), 13. The ISI has come to the attention of the American media only recently: see James Risen and Judith Miller, "The Spies: Pakistani Intelligence Had Links to Al Qaeda," *New York Times* (October 29, 2001).

14. Pakistan's Interior Minister in 1994, Major-General Nasirullah Babbar, reportedly described himself as the creator of the Taliban,

and Indian commentators have noted that he arranged for the large arsenal of one group, the Hizb-e-Islami, to fall into its hands. See Prem Shankar Jha, "Nightmare begins," *Hindustan Times* (September 21, 2001), 10, Kapil Sibal, "Fundamentalism Breeds Terrorism," *Hindustan Times* (September 16, 2001), 12; and T. Sreedhar, "Pakistan, Taliban and Osama," *The Hindu* (September 17, 2001), 10. As Sreedhar writes, a special representative from the UN even observed the presence of men from the Pakistani armed forces taking part in the Taliban's capture of Kabul (1996) and Mazar-e-Sharif (1998). The literature on Pakistan's links with the Taliban is profuse, but no one has asked how Omar, the head of the Taliban, and an illiterate, came to be a Mullah. One Indian writer states that "Gen. Nasirullah Babar of the ISI took a liking to Omar and as Benazir Bhutto's principal advisor on Afghan affairs, had him declared a 'mullah'." See Mahendra Ved, "Omar: The Man in the Eye of Hindu Kush Storm," *Times of India* (October 3, 2001), 9.

15. G. Parthasarthy, "U.S. Action: A Lesson for India," *Hindustan Times* (September 30, 2001), 15.

16. Harish Khare, "From New York to New Delhi," *The Hindu* (September 19, 2001), 10.

17. Sanghvi, "Moral Math: Musharraf vs. bin Laden," *Hindustan Times* (September 16, 2001), 12. In April 2001, Musharraf visited India at Prime Minister Vajpayee's invitation. At a breakfast meeting with reporters in Agra, Musharraf was asked how, in the name of political self-determination, the bombing of buses and the murder of school girls could be justified. With apparent nonchalance, Musharraf—who had previously distinguished between "terrorists" and genuine "freedom fighters," the latter designation being reserved for militants in Kashmir—was reported as having explained that in any such struggle, innocent people perforce must die.

18. Jocelyn Noveck, "Diplomatic Debts US Has to Pay," *Hindustan Times* (October 10, 2001), 12.

19. Prem Shankar Jha, "Eyes Wide Shut: The West's Amnesia towards Pakistan Defies Belief," *Hindustan Times* (October 5, 2001), 10.

20. Prem Shankar Jha, "At Sea in Afghanistan," *Hindustan Times* (October 19, 2001), 8.

21. Anil Narendra, "Selective Vision," *Hindustan Times* (October 16, 2001), 10.

22. S. Akbar Zaidi, "Pakistan: Legitimising Military Rule," *Economic and Political Weekly* 36:40 (October 6, 2001), 3822.

23. Interview with Zbigniew Brzezinski, *Le Nouvel Observateur* (15-21 January 1998), 76.

24. John Kaye, *History of the War in Afghanistan*, 2 vols. (London: Richard Bentley, 1851).

25. Eknath Easwaran, *A Man to Match His Mountains: Badshah Khan, Nonviolent Soldier of Islam* (Petaluma, California: Nilgiri Press, 1984). Less readable, but more scholarly, is Attar Chand, *India, Pakistan and*

Afghanistan: A Study of Freedom Struggle and Abdul Ghaffar Khan (Delhi: Commonwealth Publishers, 1989).

26. [V. J. Patel, Chairman], *Report with Evidence of the Peshawar Inquiry Committee Appointed by the. . .Indian National Congress* (Allahabad: Allahabad Law Journal Press, 1930). The wider context is furnished by Sayed Wiqar Ali Shah, *Ethnicity, Islam, and Nationalism: Muslim Politics in the North-West Frontier Province 1937-1947* (Karachi: Oxford University Press, 1999), who admits that "the most significant aspect of the whole Civil Disobedience movement was the strict adherence of the Khudai Khidmatgars to non-violence" (37).

27. For further discussion, I would refer the reader to four of my papers: "Gandhi, the Civilizational Crucible, and the Future of Dissent," *Futures* 31 (March 1999): 205-219; "'He Ram': The Politics of Gandhi's Last Words," *Humanscape* 8:1 (January 2001): 34-38; "Now Are We Men, Not Eunuchs?" *Humanscape* 5:7 (July 1998), 6-9; and "Gandhi and the Ecological Vision of Life: Thinking Beyond Deep Ecology," *Environmental Ethics* 22:2 (Summer 2000): 149-68.

28. "The Algebra of Infinite Justice," first published in *Outlook* (New Delhi). In a similar vein, with respect to the scathing critique of American state terrorism, are the commentaries, among others, of Edward S. Herman, Noam Chomsky, Edward Said, John Pilger, Robert Jensen, Michael Albert, Robert Fisk, Praful Bidwai, and Achin Vanaik.

29. Speech of October 7, 2001, as reproduced in the *Los Angeles Times* (October 8, 2001), A8.

30. James Baldwin, "The Devil Finds Work," in *Collected Essays* (New York: The Library of America, 1976), 489.

31. See note 2.

32. Joyce Appleby, "The Bad News Is, We're History," *Los Angeles Times* (October 16, 2001), B19.

33. Ernest Jones, "Psychology and War Conditions," *Papers on Psychoanalysis*, 5th ed. (Boston: Beacon Press, 1948), 187.

34. Bernard Lewis, "The Roots of Muslim Rage," *Atlantic Monthly* (September 2000), 47-60.

35. Francis Fukuyama, "The West Has Won," *Guardian* (October 11, 2001); also published in *Wall Street Journal*.

36. Fareed Zakaria, "The Roots of Rage," *The Sunday Times* (Singapore), Review section (October 21, 2001), 34-35; see also Susan Sachs, "Behind the Extremism: Poverty and Despair," 35 [reproduced from the *New York Times*].

37. Salman Rushdie, "Let's Get Back to Life," *Hindustan Times* (October 9, 2001), 10.

38. Salman Rushdie, "Yes, This is about Islam," *New York Times* (November 2, 2001).

39. For example: Mohit Sen, "Our Own War against Terror," *Hindustan Times* (October 11, 2001), 8.

Civilization and Dissent[1]

David Palumbo-Liu

The events of September 11th and following have been shocking beyond belief. For me, part of the shock has been the almost instantaneous contradiction in public-speak: the simultaneous evocation of the notion that the world has changed, that the war we will fight will be a "new" war, and the rearticulation of only slightly-modified Cold War rhetoric and "civilizational" discourse. Indeed, in his address before Congress on September 20th, George W. Bush declared, "This is civilization's fight." In so doing he evoked, consciously or not, Samuel Huntington's well-known theory about the "clash of civilizations," a theory that has been used to explain why the attacks took place, and also how the U.S. should respond. Huntington's thesis, if taken *in toto*, has dramatic ramifications for minority studies and minority rights.

Today's new civilizational model goes beyond the cultural internationalism of the 1970s and even beyond the language of the nation *per se*. What we find, rather, is the imbrication of nationalist and civilizational thinking, and that makes the case today difficult to disentangle. National interests seem indistinguishable from "a way of life," and national policy synonymous with large, civilizational imperatives. While the convergence of national and civilizational thinking is nothing new, the historical conditions under which this is taking place today bring the civilizational into the national in a potent and dangerous way for minority rights. Thus, added pressure is put upon critical multiculturalism to address the imperatives of the moment and to rebut the particular assumptions of the new civilizational thinking. By "critical multiculturalism" I mean a multiculturalism that focuses on the material histori-

DAVID PALUMBO-LIU is Professor of Comparative Literature and Director of the Program in Modern Thought and Literature at Stanford University.

cal productions of difference, rather than on "culture" as a ready-made thing.

Akira Iriye has documented the tension between international cosmopolitical aspirations and the realities of racial and other difference. After Bandung, as the three worlds came into existence, what Iriye calls Third World "multiculturalism" came to threaten, or at least call into question, the capaciousness of Euroamerican cultural internationalism. This occurs exactly during a period that saw the increased importance of culture as a mediator of difference. As Iriye notes, "What was [. . .] significant [in the 1970s] was the emergence of cultural themes as important keys to international affairs. It was as if the waning of the Cold War and the crisis of the world economy were calling forth cultural agendas with greater vigor than ever before, the more so because these agendas now included what came to be known as multicultural perspectives."[2]

During this period, we find a statement that trenchantly specifies who would be included in such cultural international discussions. In 1967, Anthony Hartley, writes in *Interplay*:

> A mutual concept for responsibility must unite countries with a *high standard of living* where competition for power once divided them. . .if the *civilization* of the late twentieth century fixes itself in rigid patterns of thought, it will break and crumble to dust. But it is the business of the intellectual to provide a remedy for this mental ossification by drawing the attention of his rulers to the existence of new problems and the need for new attitudes of mind facing them. In 1967 the speed of communication and the increasing cosmopolitanism of the intellectual community allow this task to be carried out on a level above old national oppositions and ideological feuds. . .contrary to Marx's celebrated phrase, to understand the world is also to change it.[3]

What we find then in this period is the increased pressure on multilateralism for international economic and cultural relations, which entailed a rearticulation of civilizational thinking along the axis of developed capitalist states. Hartley's brand of new-thinking was multilateral, but distinctly confined to perpetuating a civilization of only certain countries. But as countries like the U.S. were to be made more flexible and adaptive to such multilateral arrangements in order to facilitate the development of multinational capital, there arose the question of the governability of such flux. How would such rearrangements, their effects on national policy, and, crucially, the impact of various already-existing subaltern pressures on national politics, policymaking, and the academy be managed? To address these domestic pressures, we find a resurgence of national character-thinking. Let me stress that it is this dichotomy between an international economic profile which calls for "cultural internationalism," and the deployment of national-identity thinking to undergird order at home against a potential crisis in democracy brought about by strident minority demands which is under question in the present day.

In the U.S., under the Nixon administration, liberal elites worried that there was a growing lack of congruence between "economic and political worlds," the former being characterized by an increasing global integration, the latter persistently fragmented, with political decisions largely made at the level of the nation-state."[4] There was strong opposition to Nixon-Kissinger unilateralism, which was considered outmoded and dangerous for evolving liberal international economic order. (This has certain manifestations on the international cultural front. For instance, Nixon said he "eschewed gushy optimism of any kind," adding, "some Americans think that we can rely on peace by sending a few Fulbright scholars abroad. . .but that doesn't bring peace. We can avoid war if we are realistic and not soft-headed.")[5] In 1973, the Trilateral Commission was convened by David Rockefeller in order to forge "diverse interests for a common *civilizational* purpose."[6] The U.S., Western Europe, and Japan were its constituent states, and Zbigniew Brzezinski its first director. That key word, "civilizational," comes up again, and provides a foreshadowing of one of the most important works by one of the Commission's advisors. But we are not ready for the "clash of civilizations" just yet. Let me first address Huntington's work for the Commission, which focuses on the domestic scene in ways that will be crucial for his later work. Indeed, the Commission specifically asked its resident intellectuals to prognosticate on the current state of democracy.

In the 1975 publication of the Commission, *The Crisis of Democracy: Report on the Governability of Democracies to the Trilateral Commission*, Samuel Huntington remarks: "The essence of the democratic surge of the 1960s was a general challenge to existing systems of authority, public and private. In one form or another, the challenge manifested itself in the family, the university, business, public and private institutions, politics, the government bureaucracy, and the military service. People no longer felt the same obligation to obey those whom they had previously considered superior to themselves in age, rank, status, expertise, character, or talents. . .each group claimed its right to participate equally—in the decision which affected itself."[7] In short, while lauding the active participation of more and more diverse populations on the one hand, Huntington is concerned that there may be too much of a good thing: "The vitality of democracy in the 1960s raised questions about the governability of democracy in the 1970s."[8] This increase in political participation is "primarily the result of the increased salience which citizens perceive politics to have for their own immediate concerns."[9]

So what's wrong with that? Isn't this the picture of a robust democratic society? Not exactly, for this vigor is largely made up of dissident and minority voices and viewpoints demanding attention to their needs. This puts pressure on the political institutions of the state: "In the United States, the strength of democracy poses a problem for the governability of democracy. . .we have come to recognize that there are potentially desirable limits to the indefinite extension of political democracy. Democracy will have a longer life if it has a more balanced existence"[10]—this ominous phrase is indeed his concluding statement. While the Trilateral Commission focused on multilateral, "civilizational" issues, it also instructed its members to keep their respective national houses in order. Ironically, such order would be mobilized against the "excesses" of American character: "The roots of this surge are to be found in the basic American value system and the degree of commitment which groups in society feel toward that system."[11] And I again would stress the contradiction between international "civilizational" thinking and domestic national-identity thinking. We also need to remember that this authoritarian and anti-democratic criticism of minority voices becomes the backbone of Huntington's "civilization" book two decades later.[12]

The activism of the 1970s which Huntington decries created, among other things, the conditions for the emergence of multiculturalism in the 1980s. But just as much as the multiculturalism of the 80s and 90s can be seen to be the result of gains of Civil Rights era, the Third World and anti-war movements, the rise of the New Left, and the burgeoning of the feminist and gay and lesbian movements, it should also be placed within the context of the continuance of development of multilateralism, here taking the shape of economic neoliberalism which accommodated and even celebrated "diversity" for its own purposes. As Secretary of Labor, Elizabeth Dole issued a publication lauding "diversity" in the work force and urging sensitivity to difference. She noted that making a skilled labor force out of "non-traditional" elements was the key to a healthy economy and the maintenance of social security. Similarly, big businesses initiated sensitivity training and special programs to promote diversity. I say this not to reduce multiculturalism to its worse appropriation by the corporate state, but rather to underscore once again the need to grapple with an historical and intense dialectic around negotiating "difference" and "culture," the need to constantly struggle to define multiculturalism's terms and values against such take-overs.[13]

Thus, on the one hand, we have the interests of multinational corporate and state interests urging for "diversity" and reconfiguring multiculturalism to be consonant with the neoliberal agenda. This tendency can perhaps no better be summed up than in Clinton's sublime statement that his favorite novel was *A Hundred Years of Solitude*. On the other hand, we have the insurgent, contestatory demands of a critical and sometimes radical multiculturalism that called for a rethinking of issues of recognition, distribution, and rights. And it is here that we find the deployment of national identity, national character, national values, and national interests to countermand those contestatory movements.[14] It is in the triangulation of multi- and transnational corporatism, nativism, and what I will provisionally call "progressive humanism," that we find ourselves.

In the 1990s, the world became read as a confrontation between the new transnational capitalism and the resurgence of nativist, local, tribal fundamental identities, and people were asked to make a choice between these two (bad) alternatives. It is the reputed collapse of the nation-state that is deemed either the cause or the effect of these moves toward either civilizational or tribal collectivities. Since neither of these identities was desirable for national policy, what was required is the resuscitation of the nation, but along the most simple, conservative, and anti-progressive lines. Nevertheless, although the third term, what I have called "progressive humanism," drops out, it is that term that I will evoke in the conclusion of this essay as central to any critical and progressive multicultural project. This was the period that saw the publication of books such as Joel Kotkin's *Tribes: How Race, Religion and Identity Determine Success in the New Global Economy* (1993); of Robert Kaplan's *The Ends of the Earth*; (1996); of Benjamin Barber's *Jihad vs. McWorld: How Globalism and Tribalism are Reshaping the World* (1995), and Huntington's *The Clash of Civilizations and the Remaking of World Order* (1996). I hasten to add that Kotkin's book emanates from a liberal standpoint that bemoans the decay of a liberal collective identity, and Barber's is distinguished by his insistence on participatory democracy and a liberal civil society. Their books originate from different ideological perspectives than Huntington's. Nevertheless, these books share the sense that the world was now to be read post-nationally and post-ideologically, and in terms of either large "civilizational" or "tribal" tendencies. Each tries to grasp this new global configuration, split between market forces, the end of the Cold War, and reaction to both in intense, sometimes primordial affiliations.

Huntington's *The Clash of Civilizations* subordinates economic concerns to a purely cultural thesis that argues that multiculturalism is the bane of America's existence. His book spends three hundred pages organizing the world according to "civilizations" in order to launch an attack on domestic cultural politics. The thesis of the book is that in the post-Cold War world, the great conflicts will not occur between nations nor through ideological conflict (capitalism vs. socialism), but through "civilizational conflict." If clashes are to be civilizational, the West had better wake up. Huntington describes a world in which "The West" is losing ground universally, while other areas of the world are gaining various sorts of advantages: "The balance of power is shifting: the West is declining in relative influence; Asian civilizations are expanding their economic, military, and political strength; Islam is exploding demographically with destabilizing consequences for Muslim countries and their neighbors; and non-Western countries generally are reaffirming the value of their own cultures."[15]

Crucially, after extracting the benefits of western modernization, these nonwestern civilizations have realized the importance of indigenous traditions. Huntington is not bothered by this (aside from his dismay that these countries have not had the good grace to be thankful)—this return to "native traditions" is exactly what he will instruct the West to do: for Huntington, the West requires a similar "resurgence," a withdrawal from certain global positions and a retrenchment of "fundamental" values.

Turning inwardly, Huntington does not like what he sees. The fear of civilizational clashes is nearly dwarfed by a fear that the West has eroded to such a degree *internally* that it cannot respond to external threats. He claims that "the central issue for the West is whether, *quite apart from any external challenges*, it is capable of stopping and reversing the *internal* processes of decay [emphasis added]."[16] Now, finally, after some three hundred pages, we move to the central argument of the book. We have been prepared for this by Huntington's covert emphasis on religion (via the more neutral idea of "civilization"). Civilization or religion, it all comes down to a belief in the absolutism of national culture and identity. From this perspective, the real enemy is within, made up of those individuals who would deprive the West of that particular fundamental cultural identity to which all civilizations must hold if they are to survive: "Western culture is challenged by groups within Western societies. One such challenge comes from immigrants from other civilizations who reject assimilation and continue to adhere to and propagate the values, customs, and cultures of their home societies."[17] He then proceeds to define what, exactly, the fundamental identity of the West is. The West is, simply, the United States:

> Historically American national identity has been defined culturally by the heritage of Western civilization and politically by the principles of the American Creed on which Americans overwhelmingly agree: liberty, democracy, individualism, equality before the law, constitutionalism, private property. In the late twentieth century both components of American identity have come under concentrated and sustained onslaught from a small but influential number of intellectuals and publicists. In the name of multiculturalism they have attacked the identification of the United States with Western civilization, denied the existence of a common American culture, and promoted racial, ethnic, and other subnational cultural identities and groupings. . .the multicultural trend was. . .manifested in a variety of legislation that followed the civil rights acts of the 1960s, and in the 1990s the Clinton administration made the encouragement of diversity one of its major goals.[18]

He does not mince words: "Rejection of the Creed and of Western civilization means the end of the United States of America as we have known it. It also means effectively the end of Western civilization."[19] If, as he argues, "in this new world, local politics is the politics of ethnicity; global politics is the politics of civilizations,"[20] then the local politics of ethnicity have to be erased so that the U.S. nation (or, as Huntington equates, the West) can compete for survival globally. The consequence of not so doing are catastrophic: "The leaders of other countries have, as we have seen, at times attempted to disavow their cultural heritage and shift the identity of their country from one civilization to another. In no case have they succeeded and they have instead created schizophrenic torn countries."[21] This leads us to revisit the earlier citations regarding the "second generation": these people have done what is only natural and proper—they have rejected the West and returned to their indigenous heritage: if they had not, they would have suffered the consequences of "schizophrenia."

Huntington's study therefore wipes out any legitimacy for multiculturalism. His agenda is clear from the very title of his book—his argument will exhume essentialist (even fundamentalist) notions of "civilization" in order to rally "the West" to reclaim its territory (diminished as it is). Externally, that means strengthening the West against foreign incursions and erosion of international policy (that is, "American interests"); internally, it means wiping out any element that would differ from and thereby challenge Anglo-Saxon hegemony.

Huntington develops this line of reasoning in a later essay published in *Foreign Affairs*, "The Erosion of American Interests" (1997).[22] He claims that one of the factors contributing to this erosion is the absence of a clearly defined enemy against which to consolidate the nation. Following the path laid out in his *Clash of Civilizations* book, he claims the contemporary need to find an "opposing other" in the absence of a Cold War, which readily provided one in the form of the Soviet Union. Why must we find an "other"? Again, to consolidate the Nation against its enemies within: "Given the domestic forces pushing toward heterogeneity, diversity, multiculturalism, and ethnic and racial division, however, the United States. . .may need an opposing other to maintain its unity." Huntington believes the most likely candidate is China, but he notes, with some disappointment, that "China is too problematic and its potential dangers too distant in the future."[23]

Indeed, in 1997, the very "other" needed to consolidate the United States in the face of widening chasms created by ethnic and other minorities turns out to be those ethnic minorities *themselves*, who are more visible and vocal than ever before because of "changes in the scope and sources of immigration and the rise of the cult of multiculturalism."[24] *They* are the others against whom "we" may set our identity politics, for they have taken over the entire set of apparatuses essential to the running of the state: "The institutions and capabilities—political, military, economic, intelligence—created to serve a grand national purpose in the Cold War are now being suborned and redirected to serve narrow subnational, transnational, and even nonnational purposes. Increasingly people are arguing that these are precisely the foreign interests they should serve."[25] In 1997, there is thus a double "erosion" of the national character carried out on one hand by multiculturalists (largely made up of ethnic minorities) who skew America off course and weaken its resolve, and, on the other hand, by newly internalized "others," diasporics who retain allegiance to their homelands and work from within the U.S. to focus its interests in their favor. Indeed, we see that the two groups might be the same—ethnic Americans are now recast as diasporics, un- or non-Americans, in a rehearsal of the logic of the Japanese American internment. This recasting is made explicit here:

> The growing role of ethnic groups in shaping American foreign policy is reinforced by the waves of recent immigration *and by* the arguments for diversity and multiculturalism. In addition, the greater economic wealth of ethnic communities and the dramatic improvements in communications and transportation now make it much easier for ethnic groups to remain in touch with their home countries. As a result, these groups are being transformed from cultural communities within the boundaries of the state into diasporas that transcend these boundaries [emphasis added]."[26]

In sum, "diasporas in the United States support their home governments."[27]

This evocation of American identity is directly in contradiction with both liberal democratic ideology and the version of American identity promulgated in the post-war period, one which, as we remember, championed the notion that the American *ethos* could be adopted by new immigrant groups, who would then become Americanized. Huntington turns the clock back on that notion—he finds such a possibility remote at best, and only if these new immigrant, ethnic, and diasporic groups agree to be politically inactive.

Crucially, in the *present* incarnation of civilizational thinking, the dichotomy between national identity and international civilizational thinking has collapsed, the two positions intermingling and recombining into a potent ideological position, now mobilized by the events of September 11. To the enemy within (ethnic and diasporic populations) is now added a viable enemy without, something Huntington pined for in order to solidify the Nation just a few years before. The enemy will be "civilizational": it will be Islam. In this process of addition, we find a dangerous mathematics, confused and potent. And while our President urges us to remember that Arab Americans are Americans, too, and that this is a war against terrorism, not Islam, the bombing and invasion of

Afghanistan with all its "collateral damage" makes such distinctions hard to maintain.

The influential Defense Policy Board, whose members include Secretary of Defense Donald Rumsfeld, Deputy Defense Secretary Paul Wolfowitz, Henry Kissinger, Newt Gingrich, Dan Quayle, James Schlesinger, and ex-CIA chief James Woolsey, has argued vigorously for extending the war to Iraq. But this movement to continue the Gulf War started nearly four years ago, when in January 1998, a group letter was sent to President Clinton urging him to reorient foreign policy toward eliminating Saddam Hussein. The signatories of that 1998 letter include some of the very most powerful individuals in the current Bush administration, people who are guiding the war against terrorism: Donald Rumsfeld [now Secretary of Defense], Paul Wolfowitz [now Deputy Secretary of Defense], Robert Zoellick [now U.S. Trade Representative], Richard Armitage [now Deputy Secretary of State], John Bolton [now Under Secretary of State], Paula Dobriansky [now Under Secretary of State], Peter Rodman [now Assistant Secretary of Defense], Elliott Abrams [now a senior NSC official], Zalmay Khalilzad [now a senior NSC official], Richard Perle [now a key Bush adviser]. It has been noted that there is a dangerous fissuring of the Bush administration, now split between a hawkish Department of Defense, which is employing civilizational thinking, and the State Department, which is pragmatically trying to hold together the alliance of Arab states, Britain, and the U.S. Without informing the U.S. State Department, Defense sent former CIA chief Woolsey to Britain to find evidence of Iraqi participation in terrorism; and without clearing it with the State department, in his speech announcing the bombing of Afghanistan, Bush added his famous reference to the possible need to extend the war to other organizations and other nations.

Thus, despite the rhetoric that this is not a war against Islam (a move insisted upon by Colin Powell so as to keep the fragile support of Arab states within the "coalition"), there is a dangerous convergence of civilizational thinking on the part of the right-most wing, now provided with an *international* Other to take the place of the Soviet Union—it is Islam, and national identity thinking, which targets ethnics, immigrants, diasporics. Each fuels the other.[28] But it should be stressed that the deployment of civilizational rhetoric on the part of policymaking hawks is done to forward a *national political* agenda, not a cultural civilizational one. They had already staked out national policy goals in 1998 and before. The civilizational ploy is thus used to mobilize support for a war they had planned four years before September 11, 2001.

Let me conclude by emphasizing the danger of exhuming Huntington's *in toto*, with his presumptions fully intact. This is not a remote possibility, but a real one. For as things unfold, we already see the attempts to curtail civil liberties, privacy, freedom of speech and association. We see the attempt to limit student visas, and allow racial profiling. The conditions for a participatory democracy are worsening, as the imperative to protect our *civilization* trumps all other considerations. In this case, the rights and privileges of minorities of all stripes are at risk. The antidemocratic motif laid down in Huntington's 1975 essay is now reinforced by the current crisis.

American national identity has now been blended with civilizational identity, as the U.S. tries to rally its allies against terrorism. The resulting policies have profound national consequences. The inflammatory rhetoric of "civilizations," unfortunately deployed by both extremes, serves only to obscure the real issues at hand, as in both cases the other side of "civilization" can only remain a cipher of irrational violence. That is not to say that every cause of this violence can be rationalized neatly; however, the caution should be against letting our analyses of this crisis rest on theories whose ramifications threaten whatever progress we have made in terms of tolerance, justice, and equality. Furthermore, the evocation of a "civilizational" war masks the inherently unilateral nature of the armed conflict now underway. To stand outside one civilization or another is to render oneself invisible, or labeled sentimentalist or amoral. This should not be the only choice.

The third term which seems to have dropped out is, again, what I have provisionally called progressive humanism. And I think it is to some notion of humanism that we must turn to get away from the assumptions and dangers of narrow civilizational thinking. It would be a humanism that is not mystified or abstract, but realist and historical materialist. To have this, it is essential that multiculturalism be international in scope, widen its boundaries outside that of any particular nation, and even beyond diaspora studies, to an international frame. This will require no small amount of work, but if we could each, when thinking "multiculturally," think of subnational, national, regional cultures beyond our borders and even continents, and how those cultures have been produced historically, ideologically, materially, and in interaction with each other, we will have made some small move away from the mystifications of civilizations, on both sides.

Notes

1. This essay is derived from a talk delivered at the Future of Minority Studies conference at Stanford University, October 2001. I thank the participants of the conference for their comments, especially Satya Mohanty, Paula Moya, Margo Okazawa-Rey, and Dominck LaCapra. A longer version of this essay will be published in *boundary 2* in July 2002. Parts of this study are taken from my book, *Asian/American: Historical Crossings of a Racial Frontier* (Palo Alto: Stanford University Press, 1999), but reframed for the current context.

2. Akira Iriye, *Cultural Internationalism and World Order* (Baltimore: Johns Hopkins University Press, 1997), 165.

3. Emphasis added; quoted in Stephen Gill, *American Hegemony and the Trilateral Commission* (Cambridge: Cambridge University Press, 1990), 139.

4. Gill, 133.

5. Quoted in Iriye, 160.

6. Gill, 123.

7. Huntington, "The United States," in Michel Crozier, Samuel Huntington and Joji Watanuki, eds., *The Crisis of Democracy: Report on the Governability of Democracies to the Trilateral Commission* (New York: New York University Press, 1975), 76f.

8. *Ibid.*, 64.

9. *Ibid.*, 112.

10. *Ibid.*, 115.

11. *Ibid.*, 112.

12. Dominick LaCapra points out that this is a perversion of traditional liberal political thought, which was used to curb the excesses of sovereign states internationally. Here, he argues, Huntington has deployed the same rhetoric of containment to suppress democratic activity *within* the nation-state (personal communication).

13. See the "Critical Introduction" to my edited volume, *The Ethnic Canon: Histories, Institutions, Interventions* (Minnesota: Minnesota University Press, 1995).

14. The fact that these notions were deployed by Patrick Buchanan, who also argued against multilateralism and corporatism, makes clear the opposition of the two trends.

15. Samuel Huntington, *The Clash of Civilizations and the Remaking of World Order* (New York: Simon & Schuster, 1996), 20.

16. *Ibid.*, 303.

17. *Ibid.*, 304.

18. *Ibid.*, 305.

19. *Ibid.*, 307.

20. *Ibid.*, 28.

21. *Ibid.*, 306.

22. Published in *Foreign Affairs* 76:5 (September/October 1997): 28-49.

23. *Ibid.*, 32.

24. *Ibid.*, 32.

25. *Ibid.*, 37.

26. *Ibid.*, 38.

27. *Ibid.*, 38.

28. For an interesting rebuttal to such attempts to show U.S. support for Muslims, especially as they come out in statements by Wolfowitz, see "Wolfowitz's Remarks on Terror Questionable" (October 18, 2001, *Jakarta Post*).

Bellseller, outside of the Bezeklik Thousand Buddha Caves, Flaming Mountains, Turpan.
© 2001, Eric Chang

South Asian Peace Rally, September, 2001, Jackson Heights, Queens.
© 2001, Corky Lee

IV. PEACE

The first atomic bomb dropped at Hiroshima on August 6, 1945, killing 140,000 people.
Image at pegasus.phys.saga-u.ac.jp/peace

Why Does a Pediatrician
Worry about Nuclear Weapons?

James N. Yamazaki

Present War, Past Wars

When my wife, Aki, called me to the television that morning, I first thought it was a scenario of what could happen to the World Trade Center, but the caption read: "live"—the real thing. Suddenly a cascade of memories beginning before World War II began to tumble out and become entangled with the terrible scenes that now confronted us.

Aki and I have warm memories of Lower Manhattan—we were married at Grace Church at Broadway and Tenth Street on April 1, 1944. The *New York Times* took note of the occasion with a photo captioned "Japanese American soldier and his bride, a student at Columbia's Teacher's College." The photo is the only picture we have of the wedding. Aki was able to go directly to New York from the Santa Anita Assembly Center, where she had been ordered to report along with other Japanese Americans after the Japanese attack on Pearl Harbor. She thus avoided going to the Amache Concentration Camp, where her parents were interned. Terri, Aki's sister, was a graduate student at Julliard School of Music, having been awarded a scholarship following a nationwide audition. Aki then left Teacher's College to be with me at Carlisle, Pennsylvania where I was attending the U.S. Army Medical Field Service School at Carlisle Barracks.

The best man at our wedding was Minoru Yamasaki, the husband of Aki's sister—and, later, the architect who designed the

JAMES N. YAMAZAKI is the author of *Children of the Atomic Bomb: An American Physician's Memoir of Nagasaki, Hiroshima, and the Marshall Islands* (Durham and London: Duke University Press, 1995). He is currently a Clinical Professor of Pediatrics at the University of California, Los Angeles.

World Trade Center. When Yamasaki went to New York for the first time after graduation in the mid-1930s, no architectural job was available. He finally found work wrapping dishes in a Japanese import firm, even though he had graduated with the most outstanding architectural credentials at the University of Washington. Such was the lot of Asians in America in those days. Nevertheless, it was the universities, especially the state institutions, that provided the education for our later advancement in society. From the early 1960s to the late 1970s, Yamasaki planned the construction of the World Trade Center. Ironically, he paid considerable attention to safety for the future occupants and the surrounding structures during the building's planning stages.

When President Bush declared that the crushing blow of September 11 was WAR, all the images of the earlier war that had shaped my life came back to me. My adolescent years were filled with anxiety that a war between Japan and America might happen. So when war was declared after Pearl Harbor, my concern was how the wrath of America toward Japan and all things Japanese might be turned onto us. I worried about what would happen to our families who were summarily dispossessed, uprooted, and incarcerated in camps in desolate areas of the western United States. During those dark days, the stark and violent reality of survival and killing was a part of daily life for everyone on both the battlefields and cities of Europe and in the vast Pacific theater of war. It was a world at war for survival! We must not forget that over fifty million members of our family of man were sacrificed in that conflict.

Like many young Japanese American men, I fought in the European theater, where I was imprisoned by the Germans following the Battle of the Bulge. This distanced me from the Pacific War until I returned home. Back in America, at the rehabilitation facility for veteran POWs, I heard the news of the atomic bombing of Japan and of the surrender that followed. We were all relieved that the killing had finally ended.

I became aware of the enormity of the atomic bombing when I was persuaded to join the Atomic Bomb Casualty Commission in the spring of 1948, just as I was completing my pediatric residency. I was sent to Japan to study the effects of nuclear radiation on surviving children in Hiroshima and Nagasaki. Their tragedy has left a lifelong impact on me. When I was in Nagasaki, the Korean War broke out on the Korean Peninsula, June 1950. Separated by only a few minutes by jet from Nagasaki, U.S. soldiers of the First Calvary were shipped out on a day's notice and immediately sent into combat to halt the North Korean Army approaching Pusan. The initial encounter was disastrous for our soldiers.

Years later, my son, Paul, who was five months old when we went to Japan, expressed his intent to go to Viet Nam with his classmates (jocks). I was able to dissuade him from enlisting. He protested at the time, but a year later he was an activist protesting the War—for which he received a jail sentence of six months in solitary.

World War II: With the U.S. Army

In the early summer of 1941, I felt the first chilling winds of war. An embargo on steel followed by an embargo on oil clinched my decision to immediately fill out an Army application posted on the bulletin board at Medical School of Marquette University. I barely received my Reserve Commission, following a careful review of my citizenship status by the U.S. Army, one week before Pearl Harbor. I hoped this would settle the question of "loyalty" of Japanese Americans that we faced at that time.

However, following Pearl Harbor, applications for service in the U.S. Army were initially denied to Japanese Americans. Moreover, we were branded as enemy aliens—without a country, despite being citizens. But before long, Washington inexplicably asked these young Nisei, confined behind barbed wire, to volunteer for combat in the armed forces. Yet, when we made our decisions to serve, the government refused to release our parents from their imprisonment!

Following my internship at the City Hospital in St. Louis, I was the last of the interns to receive my order to report for active duty at the U.S. Army Medical Field Service School at Carlisle Barracks in Pennsylvania. En route to Carlisle, I stopped by to visit Aki, a friend from UCLA, who I last met over a year earlier during a stopover in Chicago on her way to study in New York. A month-and-a-half later we were married in New York.

When I completed the Army Medical Field course at Carlisle, Aki and I went on a brief honeymoon in the Poconos before I began a tour of duties that eventually sent me to the 106th Infantry Division, encamped at Franklin, Indiana, during the period of D-Day in Normandy (I was the only Asian in the Division). The Division was preparing to join the Army in their advance toward Germany. Even before our departure, the Division soon dispatched a large contingent to help replace the casualties of D-Day. The Division departed Camp Attebury, arriving at Camp Myles Standish in Massachusetts. From there, we crossed the Atlantic, arriving in Liverpool. We then crossed the Channel to Le Havre, leaving for the front. Our weapons were examined and casmoline removed on the outskirts of St. Vith in Belgium before we departed to our position at the boundary of Belgium, Luxembourg, and Germany in the Ardennes Forest. Less than a week after our arrival, the Germans unleashed the largest counterattack of the war on a seventy-five-mile front. This was the Battle of the Bulge.

Of the 10,000 soldiers of the 106th engaged in the combat, mostly kids barely out of high school, about 8,000 became casualties: KIA, MIA, POWs. Eventually one million men fought in the snow-covered Ardennes Forest. After nearly a month of fighting, we had 80,987 casualties, including 19,000 killed and 15,000 captured. We treated the wounded—both ours and theirs—in our aid station in a farmer's house on the mountain ridge. In the heat of the battle, I recall Sgt. George Pinna from Rhode Island carrying a stretcher over his shoulders. Others in our medical detachment joined him, responding to the cries of "Medic! Medic!" in the midst of incessant barrage from the Germans. They were firing at us from the mountain side into the valley where the 590th Field Artillery Batallion was located: vehicles, 105mm howitzers, artillery cannon, and men were overwhelmed. Major Irving Tietze, a senior officer of our group, realizing our untenable position, walked by us with a white cloth and surrendered. Germans allowed us to search for the wounded and to treat them for the next six hours, until our captors ordered us to leave the rest of the wounded men behind.

As we were led out of the forest, we marched by a crossroad in the snow. We saw the dismembered bodies of our black soldiers—a massacre seared forever in my memory. The people in the nearby hamlet of Wereth near Manderfield have erected a cross in memory of the massacred American black soldiers, perhaps the same bodies we came upon.

As prisoners of war inside Germany, we felt the onslaught of Allied Air Power coming up from countries below. Thousands of planes approached overhead to unload their bombs. Sometimes a black cloud would suddenly burst in the carpet of planes overhead, and the plume's trail would plummet earthward. Amazingly, some of the airmen survived and would later join our POW group.

A few days after the surrender, from inside a boxcar at the marshaling yard at Hanover, we could hear the cacophony of roaring planes accompanied by the bleating air raid sirens that repeated at shorter intervals as the planes came closer. Meanwhile, the guards locked us into boxcars and ran for the shelters. The thudding of the bombs shook us and levitated the boxcar. When the raid was finally over, only our boxcar was still in one piece. A close call. I have been unable to find out what happened to the other boxcars.

A day or two later we arrived in Falingbostel, our first POW camp, filled with Frenchmen, British paratroopers wearing red berets captured in Arnhem, and Russians. As the prisoners had no access to the progress of the war in recent weeks, they were anxious to learn the latest news at the front. Were the Germans able to hold back the Allied assault from land and air? I exchanged our tales with the Mongolian Russians in their green uniforms. We spoke sufficient elementary German that we were able to converse. At first they wanted me to explain how I had ever been able to don a uniform of the U.S. Army and come so far from home. I replied it seemed they too were a long ways from home.

The barbed wire fences and the guard towers around the Falingbostel camp reminded me of the incarceration of our families back home in the Jerome, Arkansas, where I had visited my father, mother, and sister before I left for the war in Europe.

During our 800-mile trek by foot and by rail we saw the devastation and terror that the air war rained over Germany. The carpet bombing would sometimes last for hours. As we were marching out of Nuremberg one morning, the raid began after dawn and lasted until midafternoon. The tail of our column was still in the city, and one of our buddies in the 590th Field Artillery of the 106th to which I was attached was among those killed in that Nuremberg bombing.

I would be remiss if I didn't relate how a Task Force of Patton's 4th Armored Division came to rescue us, attacking their way for 50 miles ahead of the battlefront to liberate us from the POW Camp at Hammelberg: 450 men were assigned to fifteen tanks and twenty-five half-track carriers led by Capt. Abe Baum that fought their way to our camp to liberate the prisoners. Underestimating the number of prisoners, they were only able to take a small number back with them. I decided to go with the task force while most of the prisoners returned to camp. I was able to get on a tank and then told to jump on one of the armored carriers. Not long after the column began their return we heard tanks in the distance, and soon we could see their cannon barrels on the ridge of an elevation. Knowing the accuracy of their 88mm guns, we immediately fled into the forest. Before the day was over, all of the tanks and carriers of the Task Force were destroyed and many men were killed. The next day we were flushed out of the woods and recaptured. How do you thank those who would risk their lives for you? The rescue expressed the same indomitable courage as the firemen and police at the World Trade Center.

After our failed liberation in March of 1945, during our march toward Nuremberg, we walked into chambers and showered with delousing fluid. We were relieved to see the first group emerge from the building, for, by then, word of the holocaust began to filter down to us. Jews from throughout Europe were herded into hundreds of camps throughout Germany. In Treblika alone it is reported that 900,000 were killed or died. The utter disregard for our fellow human beings reflect the depth of depravity to which we can sink in war. Among the Allied forces that first opened the gates to Dachau were the Japanese American soldiers of the 522d Field Artillery Battalion of the 442 Regimental Combat Team who had volunteered from America's concentration camps. They came face-to-face with the starving and dying inmates of Dachau.

General Patton's tanks liberated us for the second time at Mooseberg near Munich at a camp of over 50,000 POWs in late April. In the early morning of May 7, the train stopped at Rheims where the Germans surrendered to the Allies. By the next day we arrived at Camp Lucky Strike, where tens of thousands of troops awaited their passage home. The convoy had left Le Havre towards the end of May (1945) packed with veteran POWs. An ocean later, we passed the Statue of Liberty as fleets of small vessels came to greet us. We passed by fireboats that saluted us with arches of water bursting from their fire nozzles. Boats were filled with lovely ladies who blew kisses at us and tried to get us to join them singing refrains. But we weren't quite ready yet to sing. On debarking, Red Cross women at phone banks connected us with our families. They found Aki in nearby Mamaronek for me.

Following my discharge from the Army in March of 1946 at Lovell General Hospital in Massachusetts, I was able to continue medical training with residencies in pediatrics at the Childrens Hospitals, first in Philadelphia and then in Cincinnati. During those years, Aki worked and I am grateful to her. Together with supplements from the GI Bill of Rights, I was able to obtain training from exceptionally fine pediatricians for the next three years.

September 11 and Nuclear Weapons

Why does a pediatrician worry about nuclear weapons? Why does he worry about a satellite in space carrying a nuclear passenger eerily headed toward some human target? How do others in distant lands feel and react if they think they may be suddenly targeted someday?

In 1949, I had just completed my third year of a pediatric residency when I arrived in Japan for the first time, hardly speaking the language, with Aki and my five-month old son—to begin my assignment with the Atomic Bomb Casualty Commission (ABCC). The Commission was established by the National Academy of Sciences and the National Research Council. The NAS/NRC was designated by Congress to advise the government on matters of vital national interest. President Truman, appraised of the findings of the Joint Commission of the Medical Effects of the Atomic Bomb in Japan, directed the NAS/NRC to extend the study of long-term consequences of exposure to radiation among the survivors. A major part of the investigation would involve children. I was assigned to look for malformation among the children who were in the wombs of the mother at the time of the bombing. I was also instructed to visit Dr. James Neel, a geneticist at the University of Michigan, who would need pediatricians to examine the infants of the next generation whose parents were exposed. Dr. Neel had developed a study endorsed by leading geneticists which has continued now for over fifty years. Before my departure, Dr. Joseph Warkany, who was at the forefront of studying environmental factors, including radiation, that would result in congenital malformations, instructed me in conducting a field study of a large population. My training, heretofore, had only involved the treatment of a single child.

However, not long after reporting to ABCC, in Hiroshima, I was given an additional assignment which had not even been discussed in Washington. I was to go to Nagasaki to foster a relationship and rapport with the community and the physicians in order to develop a program to complement the studies in Hiroshima. A clinic and laboratory would need to be established. I would be the sole American physician in Nagasaki affiliated with the ABCC.

Meanwhile, Aki and Paul had to remain in Tokyo because available housing for ABCC representatives in Hiroshima—controlled in this sector of Japan by British Occupation Forces—was available only for those of European descent. You would think that Washington would have straightened this out before our departure or at least informed us about this. The last place I expected that segregated housing would continue to plague us after our return from Europe was in Japan. A private home was eventually found for us in the village of Aga, where I also headed the

ABCC program. The village of AGA is several miles from the British compound. Soon we were en route to Nagasaki.

Nagasaki lies on the southwestern shores of Kyushu, the southernmost of the major Japanese Islands. Japan's relationship with Portugal and Spain had begun early in the sixteenth century. In subsequent centuries, it was through Nagasaki that Japan maintained relationships with the West. Most notable was the influence of Christianity, which, despite prohibition for nearly two centuries, reemerged when Japan "opened its doors to the West" under prodding from Commodore Perry's visit in 1853. In Nagasaki, about 20 percent of the citizens were Christians compared to about 1 percent in Japan as a whole. Western medicine was first introduced to Japan in Nagasaki about 1857 by a very enterprising Dutch physician and was the forerunner of the current Nagasaki University Medical School.

The city encircles the head of a long and beautiful bay. On the western side of the bay is Urakami Valley, dominated in the war years by the large Mitsubishi Industries, enterprises engaged in shipbuilding and armaments. The eastern side, separated from the Urakami Valley by a mountain ridge, has the main commercial and residential sections.

The atomic bomb was detonated 500 meters in the sky midway in the Urakami Valley. The mountain ridge served as a shield affording considerable protection to the eastern central section of the city. The atomic attack, incredibly devastating, was over in a flash. Eight hundred meters from ground zero, the concrete walls of the University Hospital building partially shielded the effects of the bomb. Forty percent of the staff survived, whereas those in wooden structures and those in the surrounding township all perished. The doctors who survived were as close as people could be to an atomic bomb explosion. They became my mentors and disclosed without being killed what they had personally experienced.

I wore the nominal Captain's hat of the U.S. Atomic Bomb Team, and I thought my relationship with the community was forthright. However, it soon became clear that the Japanese believed that the ABCC had come to Nagasaki to obtain information that would better prepare America in the event the U.S. was attacked by an atomic bomb. Yet, the doctors of the city, the practitioners as well as the Medical School faculty, wanted to know what would happen to atomic bomb survivors in the future. A joint collaborative undertaking with the ABCC was thus initiated in good faith. This collaborative investigation is still ongoing over fifty years later. Yet there has been a considerable delay in telling the American public the real human toll of Hiroshima and Nagasaki.

When our government first issued its official report on the making of the bomb, published in August 1945, the author of the report, Princeton physicist Henry DeWolf Smyth, who contributed prominently in the Manhattan Project, wrote:

> A weapon has been developed that is potentially destructive beyond the wildest nightmare of imagination; a weapon so ideally suited to sudden announced attack that a country's major city might be destroyed overnight. . .
>
> The people of the country must be informed if they are to discharge their responsibilities wisely—in a free country like ours such questions should be debated by the people. . .[1]

Yet the Joint Commission Report on the Medical Effects of the Atomic Bomb in Japan by physicians of the Manhattan Project, U.S. Armed Forces, and the Japanese Government conducted from October to December of 1945 was classified "Secret" and was not available even to our staff at ABCC. Their report was eventually published for the Manhattan Project's National Nuclear Energy Series in 1956, but did not receive a wide public distribution. So, eleven years after the bombing, the American public remained virtually uninformed about the only human beings who can tell their story of surviving nuclear weapons. In Japan, soon after the occupation of Japan began, a press code was established that in effect prohibited the dissemination of information about the bomb by the media, including some of our own scientific studies. So in Japan, except for the initial bulletin from Hiroshima and Nagasaki, the conditions of the survivors in the aftermath were disclosed only after the end of the occupation in 1951.

A commemorative exhibit of the atomic bombing fifty years later at the Smithsonian Institute that initially was to include serious treatment of the effects of the bombs on the people of Hiroshima and Nagasaki aroused strong objections from a veterans' group, Congress and the press. They felt that the exhibit highlighted the plight of the victims, rather than honoring the valor of U.S. servicemen. Many of my classmates at Marquette University Medical School were assigned to serve in the final phases of the assault in the Pacific War: George Collentine landed on the beach on the first wave at Iwo Jima; John Conway was on a destroyer hit by a *kamikaze*; Ed Lau and Ed Turic were on ships treating casualties evacuated from Iwo and Okinawa; and Bob Fox in the Philippines was assigned to prepare general hospitals to treat casualties from the anticipated invasion of Japan. Of course, they all felt that the atomic bomb ended the war and spared them from the invasion of Japan that might well have cost them their lives. But by canceling the exhibit, one that eventually millions of citizens would see, the public remained uninformed about the effects of the atomic bomb upon human beings.

After September 11, I have often wondered, what if the terrorists had carried an atomic bomb on their plane? I thought about Trinity at Alamogordo, New Mexico, where the first atomic bomb was tested; about Hiroshima and Nagasaki; about the underwater burst at Bikini Island in 1946, and radioactive fallout from the fifteen megaton hydrogen bomb that was tested in the Marshall Islands in 1954. I thought about the horrendous Chernobyl reactor meltdown in the Soviet Union in 1986.

Had the World Trade Center been ground zero in a nuclear attack, an expanding 400-foot red fireball would cover the top floors of the towers. A brilliant-hued flash of light would illuminate all of lower Manhattan, and reach the city's center. The fireball temperature would be like a giant heat lamp with a temperature of the interior of the sun (millions of degrees), in contrast to the several thousand degrees when the planes' fuel burst into flame on September 11. An atomic explosion would emit thermal radiation at the speed of light, together with penetrating gamma radiation and neutrons, perhaps one hundred times the amount of radiation required to kill. Such heat could penetrate concrete floors and walls, followed by a roaring blast that, in an instant, would crush the supporting frame of both building towers, as well as the three satellite buildings. Debris of concrete, steel, and glass would be flying like missiles. At ground zero there would be no survivors. Then the crumbled debris would be violently stirred, forming a massive dust cloud that would eclipse the sun, plunging lower Manhattan into darkness. All of lower Manhattan would be covered with radioactive dust, and at the same time the intense heat would suck up the mixture to form a mushroom cloud, the unmistakable insignia of an atomic explosion. Fires would be ignited as far out as a mile-and-a-half. Within a radius of 800 meters, the streets would be lined with bodies burned black and felled by the blast wind and penetrating nuclear radiation. The spreading cloud of radioactive dust would cover all of lower Manhattan and the prevailing southeast wind would drift toward Brooklyn.

The first atomic bomb test took place at Alamogordo, New

Mexico. A bomb whose blast was equivalent to 20 kilotons of TNT, identical to the Nagasaki bomb, perched on a one-hundred-foot tower, was detonated on July 16, 1945. Radioactive fallout was traced to the Chapudera Mesa fifty to sixty miles from ground zero, where the fallout was deposited on the skin of grazing cattle. The beta radiation of the fallout particles caused hair loss and discoloration and thickening of the skin; later, skin cancer developed in these animals.

In 1946, a year after the bombing of Hiroshima and Nagasaki, naval vessels of every category from aircraft carriers to submarines were anchored in a lagoon of Bikini Atoll twenty-five miles long to assess the tactical use of nuclear weapons in naval warfare. A twenty kiloton bomb, identical to the Nagasaki bomb, was detonated underwater with a massive eruption of the sea water forming a three-mile wide lethal radioactive foamy umbrella that developed into a thick cloud drifting downwind for several miles. It released a downpour lasting for an hour. The radioactivity in the lagoon became so high that one could not approach the vessels for several hours, and then for only brief forays.

Dr. Stafford Warren, head of Health and Safety in the Manhattan Project and later the first Dean of the UCLA School of Medicine, observed:

> The tests give far clearer warnings of the insidious nature of radioactive agent which makes it such an ideal weapon for use on a civil population. An entirely new danger of atomic war has so saturated every crevice of target ships that scientists and service personnel could visit the vessels on only hurried forays. Were a Bikini-type bomb dropped in New York Harbor under favorable meteorological condition maximum distribution radioactive particles, two million people would die.[2]

In Nagasaki, on August 9, 1945, Dr. Raisuke Shirabe, a professor of surgery, dug himself out of the debris that covered him. When he thought of returning to his office to retrieve some valuables, the smoke and fire was already billowing out of the windows. He was unable to reenter the building. He saw bodies entangled in the window frames. He could hear the roaring fire that already engulfed the neighborhood surrounding the hospital.

Dr. Nishimori, then a student, was sitting at a desk with other students at a seminar when the blast threw him to the floor, senseless. When he regained consciousness, the others at the desk were stacked in the corner lifeless, apparently hurled into this position by the vortex of the blast wind. The hospital ground was littered with bodies, dead and dying, traumatized by the injury, burns, and radiation. When Dr. Stafford Warren arrived at the gutted hospital three weeks later, he saw a mound of skeletal remains, apparently cremated, three feet deep in a circle fifty feet in diameter.

Instantaneous and subsequent death for those without burns or trauma revealed the presence of a puzzling disease that subsequently was called "atomic disease." Different parts of the body respond differently in their reaction to nuclear radiation. Immediate death follows when the brain is overwhelmed with the absorption of massive amounts of radiation. The gastrointestinal tract regularly responds with nausea, vomiting, and extreme thirst. Epilation is a sensitive and early indicator of radiation injury. The blood forming system is among the most sensitive parts of the body that results in hemorrhage in all tissues. Immunity is impaired so that severe infection develops even following minor trauma. In Japan, the majority of the deaths occurred within the first two weeks after the bombing, caused by the synergistic effect of burns, radiation and trauma, although burns were believed to be the major cause of death.

In Nagasaki's Urakami Valley, only a mile wide and three miles long, enclosed by a mountainous spur that shielded central Nagasaki, 70,000 people perished in the ten days that followed. In Hiroshima, situated in a flat delta, 120,000 died, even though the Hiroshima bomb was less powerful than the one that fell on Nagasaki.

I became increasingly aware of the enormity of nuclear destruction beginning in 1950, when our clinic in Nagasaki was completed. We could examine children who survived the Nagasaki bomb, checking for the first time for effects of radiation exposure during pregnancy. This was just the beginning of an involvement that would extend through the rest of my life. My earlier observation of pregnant mothers who received pelvic X-Ray radiation treatment complimented by experimental studies by others, had demonstrated the sensitivity of the developing brain to radiation. Even so, I was seeing for the first time the terrible effect of the atomic bomb on the unborn: mentally retarded stunted children with small, malformed heads. These mothers also had a high incidence of miscarriages, still births, and neonatal deaths. Later, other children who had been in the womb when the bomb was dropped developed seizures and learning disorders.

Cancer is the major late effect of radiation among the survivors of the atomic bomb, but in children, leukemia developed during the first ten years after exposure with a considerably high incidence. In adults, the leukemia appeared years later and with a lower incidence compared to the children.

What would happen to the coming generations of children, offspring of parents exposed to the atomic bomb radiation, was of considerable concern both in United States and in Japan. If the studies revealed that there was a definite increase in miscarriages, stillbirths, and congenital malformations, this might be attributable to the atomic bomb. Thus, every pregnant woman in the two cities was registered and their outcome recorded. In a five-year period in both Hiroshima and Nagasaki, each newborn was examined in the home. Over a five-year period 70,000 pregnancies were evaluated, coupled with requests for autopsies for stillbirths and neonatal deaths. However, statistical evidence of genetic injury has not been demonstrated so far. In subsequent years, new methods to detect radiation injury were utilized in the genetic study. Today, DNA technology is being applied as radiation-induced mutation and links to cancer and immune disease are revealed. To insure continuance of this program, blood samples of the most heavily exposed parents, their children and a control group are being preserved to be made available as new developments in genome research occur.

So far, however, convincing evidence of genetic injury has not been found in the continuing epidemiological investigation that is now reviewed by international experts. At the outset of the studies, it was recognized that the surviving population received relatively low amounts of radiation compared to those who were killed by the bombs. The deaths of the latter victims reduced the likelihood of demonstrating a genetic effect.

Still, for fifty years children of the survivors have been haunted by fears that their progeny, the third generation, might perhaps be tainted by the bomb. Significant advances have been made in understanding the mechanisms by which radiation induces cancer and genetic disorders when DNA is damaged by radiation.

Increasing the power of nuclear weapons a thousandfold with the fifteen megaton hydrogen bomb revealed that thousands of square miles could be contaminated by radioactive fallout; that the fallout can be lethal 120 miles from ground zero; and that radioactive iodine is the principal biological hazard that is ingested and concentrates in the thyroid, leading to thyroid tumors and cancer, especially among the young. This consequence has been repeated in the nuclear reactor meltdown at Chernobyl, where the fallout at considerable distance resulted in increased incidence of thyroid cancer in children, again revealing their particular vulnerability.

Miniaturization of nuclear weapons now allows several one-megaton weapons to be placed in the warhead of a single missile. It has been calculated that a one megaton nuclear weapon can ignite fires ten miles from ground zero and ignite an enormous firestorm to consume a population already immobilized by the effects of irradiation and the powerful hurricane blast waves. Weapons have been developed now that can be put into a backpack.

Just one year into the Atomic Era in 1946, Dr. Stafford Warren observed the human consequences in Hiroshima, Nagasaki, and at Crossroads and noted:

> It would seem that little imagination is required to accept the fact that nuclear weapons can be the ultimate destructive weapons for all mankind, and that the way to peace, unclear and difficult to obtain though it be, must somehow be attained by the people of the world.[3]

When he designed the World Trade Center, "with its location facing the entry of New York Harbor," Minoru Yamasaki expressed hope that his great creation "could symbolize the importance of world trade to this country and its major metropolis and become a physical expression of the universal effort of man to seek and achieve world peace." On September 11, that vision was shattered. But, Minoru, the strong advocate for peace that he was, may have created another vision in its place.

We have reached a critical junction in man's history for survival on this planet that requires our combined intellect, resources, and compassion for our fellow man to prevent another atomic holocaust. Neutralizing the threat of nuclear weapons and other weapons of mass destruction must be the primary objective of all people. We must recognize and struggle for the right of all people of the world and of future generations to live in peace.

Notes

1. Henry DeWolf Smyth, *Atomic Energy for Military Purposes: The Official Report of the Development of the Atomic Bomb under the Auspices of the United States Government, 1940-1945* (Stanford: Stanford University Press), 223, 226. Originally published in 1945 by the United States Government.

2. Stafford L. Warren, "The Role of Radiology in the Development of the Atomic Bomb," in *Radiology World War II* (Washington D.C.: Surgeon General's Office, 1966), 916.

3. Stafford L. Warren, "What Science Learned at Bikini," *Life*, August 11, 1947.

The Hip-Hop Generation
Can Call For Peace

Jeff Chang

As we mourned the countless victims of 9/11 and built with each other in passionate conversations on what to do next, President George W. Bush finally and unequivocally declared war.

He ordered a call-up of 50,000 reservists—the first step towards reinstituting the draft—while preparing Americans for a long, ground war that could leave many innocent Afghanis dead or displaced. He warned that there may be no foreseeable end to this war.

This does not bode well for the Hip-Hop Generation. As STORM, the Bay Area hip-hop activist organization, says, "Increasingly, safety at home will require justice abroad." Bush's open-ended war could leave us increasingly insecure, subject to more terror not less, with less justice for all in the world.

Because of its history, the global hip-hop generation can play a crucial moral role in the call for peace—peace on the streets where we live, and a global peace free from terror.

At one time, others dissed our generation by saying that we were privileged, that we had never been tested by war. [This was before Bush's father opened the Persian Gulf War.] The fact is that hip-hop was born under the conditions of war. It grew and spread as a global alternative to war.

Before hip-hop, during the early 1970s, Jamaica's bloody tribal wars fostered a music and culture of defiance in roots, dancehall and dub reggae. This music and culture—a safe space from the

JEFF CHANG is author of *Can't Stop, Won't Stop: A Political and Cultural History of the Hip-Hop Generation* (St. Martin's Press, forthcoming). He is a 1995 graduate of the Asian American Studies M.A. program at University of California, Los Angeles.

bloody gang runnings on the street—immigrated to the Bronx—a space so devastated by deindustrialization and governmental neglect that when Ronald Reagan visited in 1980, he declared that it looked like London after World War II. In the Bronx, the Universal Zulu Nation, hip-hop's first institution and organization, literally emerged from a peace forged between racially divided, warring gangs.

As Reagan took office, immigration was rapidly browning the face of America. The "culture war" was declared—a way to contain the nation's growing diversity. Culture warriors went after youth in their schools; they fought multiculturalism, ethnic studies, and affirmative action. In Congress, they sought limits on movie and music content.

Hip-hop turned out to be everything they detested—it was real, truth-telling, unapologetic, and, worst of all, their kids loved it. Imagine how they felt when Chuck D enlistened millions into the opposition by rhyming, "They'll never care for the brothers and sisters cause the country has us up for a war."

In one sense, hip-hop won the culture war. By the end of the 80s, Public Enemy and Spike Lee, John Singleton and N.W.A., and other brothers and sisters had crashed the lily-white pop culture mainstream. Hip-hop became the single most potent global youth force in a generation.

But the culture war had serious political consequences, too. Right-wingers manufactured the conditions—moving drugs and guns into the ghetto via the wars in Central America—for a resurgence of gang warfare. And they succeeded in stigmatizing inner-city gangs—whose ranks, of course, were swollen with young, poor people of color—as mindlessly, irredeemably violent and evil.

Hip-hop reveled in the young generation's diversity. The culture warriors taught other generations to be afraid of it. When the 90s came, they warned of a coming wave of juvenile crime, one that would crest with the darkening demographic surge.

Their apocalyptic predictions helped initiate a dramatic shift in juvenile justice, away from rehabilitation towards incarceration. Forty-eight states made their juvenile crime statutes more punitive. Dozens of cities instituted curfews, anti-cruising laws, and sweep ordinances (which were ruled unconstitutional by the Supreme Court but have reappeared in many cities).

Especially after the 1992 Los Angeles riots, as urgent gang truce work forged peaces across the country, the new laws were implemented at a feverish clip and enforced with a heavy hand. Juvenile arrests and detention populations skyrocketed, even as juvenile violent crime rates plummeted.

Local police, the FBI, and private companies began compiling gang databases. Every young boy or girl of color who fit the profile—sagging, baggy jeans, athletic shoes, hip-hop swagger—became fodder for the gang databases. In Cook County, Illinois, the gang database was two-thirds black. In Orange County, California, 92 percent of those listed in the gang database were of color (young Asian Americans later successfully sued the county). Angry Black, Chicano and Latino parents in Denver, Colorado, learned that eight of every ten young people of color in the entire city were listed.

Post-modern racial profiling was invented for the Hip-Hop Generation, the most catalogued and surveillanced in history. Along with the "war on drugs"—the only result of which has been racist sentencing and the largest prison population in world history—what hip-hop activists called the "war on youth" left a generation staring into a tense present and an insecure future.

These are the reasons why thousands of hip-hop activists came out to protest at the Republican and Democratic Conventions last year. They took courageous stands against the massive profiling and imprisoning of a generation; against the death penalty; for better education; and for stopping gang violence. They linked these issues to global struggles for economic and racial justice.

Now that President Bush has declared an open-ended war, the global, multiracial, polycultural hip-hop generation can elevate beyond the chant of "No justice, no peace"—a cry that, in truth, sounds much different when uttered by Bush.

If we can understand the history of wars from Israel to Afghanistan the way that we understand our own generation's history, we can link what is happening on our streets with what is happening in our world.

We can call for peace on our streets—to be free from profiling and imprisoning, to be free from the cycle of violence that causes us to kill each other needlessly.

And we can call for peace in our world—to be free from the kind of terror that strikes our bodies and our hearts, to be free from the cycles of violence driven by geopolitical posturing and economic greed that cause us to kill each other needlessly.

Everyone deserves a better, safer future. Hip-hop has already survived many wars. Time and again, we have learned how to react to crisis by forging a principled peace. As we stand on the brink of the biggest war we have ever faced, let us come together to find the most powerful, lasting peace yet.

[The following is by STORM (Standing Together to Organize a Revolutionary Movement), a Bay Area activist group with deep hip-hop roots.]

9-11 Attacks: STORM'S Four Main Points in Response to the Bombings of the World Trade Center and the U.S. Pentagon

1. Oppose terrorism, and build people's power: We mourn the loss of life and the great pain endured by those who have suffered as a result of these attacks. Those of us who desire a world free from exploitation and oppression must rely on the consciousness, capacity and confidence of working class and oppressed people to carry out our own liberation. There are no shortcuts in this process. Acts of terrorism against civilian targets do not advance this process, but retard it. We oppose the use of terror tactics—especially such tactics against civilian populations—as destructive to the fundamental aims of the liberation movement. We must organize our people to liberate themselves with the clarity of their own minds, the courage of their own hearts and the work of their own hands.

2. Oppose the narrowing or elimination of the people's democratic rights: The U.S. government must stop using the suffering of the victims of these attacks as an excuse to narrow and eliminate the people's democratic rights. We oppose any and all efforts to increase the funding and authority of U.S. police and intelligence agencies as a "solution" to this crisis. We are disgusted by the present attempts by the U.S. security and surveillance establishment to use this tragedy to orchestrate a cynical power grab and to cash in on the pain of the victims. We oppose any efforts to wipe out the people's fragile and precious privacy rights; we oppose any efforts to curtail the people's basic First Amendment rights to assemble, speak, publish, protest and organize free from government harassment and surveillance. We must now be extraordinarily vigilant against

threats directed against the people—not from underground cells, but from the highest levels of government.

3. Rely on global justice to deter future attacks: The system, in the United States and worldwide, has continually denied peaceful, "legitimate" attempts by those seeking justice and freedom. Through its own reckless, violent and oppressive actions against poor people and people of color, the United States government has fueled frustration, grief and outrage here and across the globe. Just as we mourn the pain and the loss of life stemming from these recent attacks on U.S. soil, we continue to mourn the pain and the loss of life that U.S. military and economic domination inflicts on people worldwide. Suffering under this oppression, people throughout the world are becoming more and more desperate. Neither police repression at home nor U.S. bombs abroad will ease this fundamental despair; to the contrary, such actions will only continue this vicious cycle of frustration and violence. Ordinary people in the United States can best deter future attacks by insisting that the U.S. government abandon its oppressive role of keeping down workers and dominating poor nations around the world. Increasingly, safety at home will require justice abroad. Intensified police crackdowns at home and military savagery abroad are not the answer; the answer is justice. We must not allow the United States to respond with bombs for Third World people and continued support for repressive dictatorships and rapacious corporations. Instead, we demand that the U.S. respond to this crisis with efforts to meet the legitimate demands of the majority of the human family.

4. Oppose racist, anti-Arab bigotry: The media is already feeding the frenzy of anti-Arab hysteria. We cannot allow U.S. racism to blind our minds or cloud our hearts. Stereotypes and scapegoating will not lead us out of this crisis. Solidarity and compassion will. All people—and especially African-Americans, Asian/Pacific-Americans, Latinas/os and Native Americans—must stand in solidarity with our Arab and Muslim sisters and brothers.

For more information, call STORM/Standing Together to Organize a Revolutionary Movement, (510) 496-6094.

Silent peace rally by South Asians in Jackson Heights, Queens.
© 2001, Corky Lee

A Merciful End:
A Call to Humanity

Angela E. Oh

The risk in writing these words is the wrath of those who still feel the rage of the massacre that took place on September 11. The benefit in writing these words is a piece of truth that should be noted.

First, words are not adequate to express the feelings of gratitude and respect for members of the emergency rescue teams and fire service who responded to the tragedy visited upon the World Trade Center, the Pentagon, and the fields of Pennsylvania. The sights they encountered in the search for survivors and evidence that might shed light on the reason for the suicide missions will probably never be shared with the public. The terror, the pain, and the suffering of all those who perished must surely have been absorbed into the souls of those who helped with the rescue and clean-up operation.

Now the difficult message. Those among us who were fortunate enough not to be on any of the aircraft that were hijacked are watching many horrible things unfold. As we come out of the shock of the successful mission of the suicide team, the dominant voices are calling for retaliatory hits, expansion of the military and intelligence budget of the nation, restrictions on civil liberties and civil rights of Americans, greater investments in domestic law enforcement budgets, and more. We, as a nation, are "mad as hell, and don't want to take it anymore."

There certainly needs to be an effective move by the United States. But what is happening now—the deployment of warships, the threats of violence against unknown targets, and the cavalier

ANGELA E. OH is an attorney, member of the Los Angeles City Human Relations Commission, and a Zen Buddhist priest, Rinzai Sect.

acknowledgment that innocent people may well die in the response that the United States pursues simply does not inspire confidence that terrorism and further violence will come to an end.

In all of this furor and activity over creating an effective strategy to stem the tide of terrorism and violence, the message sent by this collective sacrifice of lives has been ignored. That message is that we have lost sight of our humanity. The spiritual void felt by people all around the world—those who are buried in the most abject poverty, repressed by governments which cannot and do tolerate the human need to worship something greater than anything that can be manufactured or synthesized, and so desperate that suicide and the taking of innocent lives becomes a viable option—has taken its toll.

In some very incomprehensible way, every human being who lost his or her life on September 11, 2001—whether the suicide hijackers, the innocent passengers on the United and American Airlines flights, or the employees, guests and visitors at the Pentagon and World Trade Center—shared something extraordinary in the end. Their deaths were a cry for help for all of humanity. And the taking of their lives was, in some strange way, merciful. No one had a chance to agonize over the fact that death was coming and yet we all know it is inevitable for each and every one of us. No one had to suffer through experimental treatments, mis-diagnosed illnesses, and the angst of feeling helplessness in trying to find a treatment for a loved one facing death. Yes, the opportunity to say goodbye was stolen. Thankfully, there is prayer, reflection, and something about the human spirit that allows for this kind of grief and sorrow to be embraced.

The destruction of the world as we know it is well within the realm of possibilities, with any number of nations who have nuclear, biological, chemical and technology warfare capacities. The divisions—most recently manifest in the divides over racial, ethnic, religious lines—have already delivered the genocides of many tens of thousands of people throughout the world. The leadership that can deliver a world from the realm of ignorance toward enlightenment still needs to be demonstrated by someone, somewhere. Will the United States, that place on earth that holds the promise of democracy, peace, and dignity for all—no matter what race, nationality, or religion—be that leader? I, for one, truly hope so.

Stop the Bombing,
Stop the War

Michael F. Yamamoto

I know that we public defenders have many more immediate
problems here, in the trenches of the criminal courts, than the military campaign which is being waged in Afghanistan. Our government's initial response to the attack on the World Trade Center
towers was to increase racial, religious and ethnic profiling; expand
the power of police departments and intelligence agencies to
conduct national-security wiretaps in criminal prosecutions; and
place further restrictions on the rights of immigrants. Profiling
of Muslims and persons of Middle Eastern appearance has already
served to effectively exclude these communities wholesale from
the call for national unity, as well as targeting them for hate crimes
and other forms of discrimination. Passage of the U.S. Act to Provide Appropriate Tools Required to Intercept and Obstruct Terrorism (or PATRIOT) now allows pen register/trap-and-trace orders for routing and addressing information for Internet communications, expands the government's wiretapping powers under
the Foreign Intelligence Surveillance Act, and creates a new "rov-
ing wiretap" provision which applies to a target regardless of the
telephone or computer used. Increased power to the military and
law enforcement, less judicial oversight and probable cause standards in the conduct of criminal investigations, with no meaningful limits on the subsequent use of this information, all add
up to more challenges for the defense. So far, over 1,000 persons
have been detained and investigated by or for the INS, visas for
Muslim and Arab students have been delayed for heightened scrutiny and already-diminishing immigrant rights are under further

MICHAEL F. YAMAMOTO is a Los Angeles criminal defense attorney, musi-
cian, and community activist.

siege. Moreover, the recently-published, newly-enacted Department of Justice rule which allows prosecutors to eavesdrop on phone calls between defense attorneys and clients could be the most outrageous Constitutional violation of all.

Though we have more than enough to deal with on the home front, we have to look beyond our cases and our courts to see how much harm this war is inflicting on innocent Afghan civilians as well as on us. This bombing campaign is indefensible. We have already witnessed bombing mistakes which have destroyed Red Cross relief centers, residential homes and other non-military targets. It would be bad enough, in light of the innocent people already killed without any necessity or reason, but this bombing campaign has curtailed the vital food supplies which had been flowing from international relief sources, including the United States and the Red Cross, into Afghanistan, following years of drought and impending famine, from long before the September attack. Our bombs are endangering the lives of those millions of people who are facing exposure and starvation this winter. This threat is imminent and needs to be dealt with now. We have to stop the bombing in order to allow humanitarian relief to get to those who need it or we will be responsible for an enormous and entirely preventable atrocity. Whatever goal was intended by this campaign, it does not justify the harm that has been done so far and, because we can so clearly foresee the masses of innocent victims ahead, we have to stop it now.

I know that most people believe that this military action is the only practical means of apprehending the perpetrators of this terrible crime and the only way we can bring them to justice. I acknowledge how difficult it is to stop a violent aggressor with anything short of violence and that it has certainly been our habit to bomb those countries, governments and individuals with whom we disagree. Still, that doesn't mean we can't find and choose to employ nonviolent alternatives in the diplomatic, economic and political realms, in order to achieve our goals, before prematurely and reflexively resorting to military aggression as a first option. This nation is internationally known to be powerful enough to pursue nonviolent alternatives without appearing to capitulate. Everybody already knows how much damage we can do. They can see how much damage we've done. We are strong enough and secure enough to stop this war. If we could demonstrate the forbearance and compassion of a truly evolved civilization, we are influential enough to inspire a real international consensus against terror as an instrument of politics, one that could eventually isolate those who would commit crimes against humanity and subject them to the investigations, prosecutions and judgments of a legitimate tribunal. We might gain even more international credibility in this quest if we choose to stop the violence now.

Since I am writing this article on Veterans' Day, I want to mention that I have seen firsthand who dies in war, and it is the children, theirs and ours. We send our teenagers to kill theirs and, though most don't include them among the "innocent victims" of war, it is hard for me to see it any other way. My experience with the "official enemy body count" is a pile of kids, too young to comprehend the political forces that have sacrificed their lives and too fully indoctrinated to turn back, wounded and dead before they can finish growing up.

This "War on Terrorism" already looks as misguided and self-destructive as our "War on Drugs," which, by focusing on supply, neglecting causes and eroding our legal protections, left our society worse off for having waged it and unable to find an end to it. This new war threatens even worse damage to our national interests abroad and our constitutional protections at home. What we are now facing in the criminal courts of California is just another aspect of the same indiscriminate and brutal response which endangers the lives of so many people a half a world away. Though we defenders are besieged by these ongoing attacks on our legal rights, we can't ignore the plight of those innocent victims whose lives might be saved if we join the call to stop this bombing and to stop this war.

Blessed are the Peacemakers.

Community teach-in and youth speakout on hate crimes post-9/11 attack on World Trade Center, New York University, September 22, 2001. Sign in Korean is translation of "Hate Crime is another Terror."
© 2001, Corky Lee

Asian Americans
and the Peace Imperative

Mari J. Matsuda

This time, march to save your own life. I call on Asian Americans to join the new peace movement. I start this peace message from a place of grief called September 11. The masters of terror have taken parents from children, children from parents, peace from the hearts of a nation of mourners. We have not enough tears nor enough rage to respond to this chasm of loss. I condemn terrorism, and I call it murder.

I start this peace message from a place of pain because it does no good to turn first to love when that is not what is in your heart. My first love is for my family and the neighbors I know and look in the eye, and that is the reality of how human love forms. The masters of terror have taken people from our cities who wanted nothing more than to wake up in the morning, kiss their children, go to work, come home, and prepare to do the same thing all over again the next day. Many Asian Americans are among the dead, and many, many more are among the displaced and newly jobless: thousands of garment workers, restaurant workers, and laborers in New York Chinatown alone; thousands of hotel workers in every major city; thousands of airline, airport, and security workers. Asian Americans are disproportionately represented among the economic casualties of September 11 because we are a significant segment of the service worker and low-wage worker strata, particularly in the major urban areas most affected by this disaster. While we are not the face the editors choose for their pictorials, I

MARI J. MATSUDA is a member of DC Asians for Justice and Peace. She is author of *Where Is Your Body: And Other Essays on Race, Gender, and the Law* (Beacon Press, 1996) and *We Won't Go Back: Making the Case for Affirmative Action* (Houghton Mifflin, 1997). She is a professor at Georgetown Law School.

know from reading the Asian American press and from talking to Asian American community organizers that we were in those towers at every job level, from undocumented busboy to bond trader. We, with our Asian faces, stand in the great American community of mourners.

And I choose peace. Not the idealized peace of the summer of love. No lilacs in my hand this time. This is a cold, calculating peace activist. Someone out there wants to kill me, and I have to figure out how to save my own life out of the history I know and the tools I have.

What do Asian Americans know? I know of a war fought to stop fascism. My father was there. He is the only survivor of a machine gun squad sent in to rescue the Lost Battalion.[1] I know that war was hell to those who fought it. Freezing-rain, suicide-mission, screaming-pain hell. My father described his surprise at seeing his company after one campaign. "It's supposed to be lots of guys," he said, "when we marched you were supposed to see rows and rows," but when they marched out, "it was so few, just a few guys walking. I couldn't believe that was all we had left."

I know that when the Nisei soldiers liberated little towns in France and Italy, they were greeted with cheers. The best wine came out of the cellar, the fattest chickens went into the pot. The Americans have come! Even today, school children in Bruyeres, France, will tell you it was Japanese Americans who saved their city.[2] I know we fought a hard war with clear purpose, and we were welcomed as liberators.

Asian Americans know of mistakes made in the name of war. My grandmother waited behind barbed wire for her son to come home from World War II. Military necessity is never an excuse I can accept without question. I am a Japanese American. My birthright is to question military necessity. Heart Mountain is the return address I give when I send forth my questions.[3]

And Hiroshima.[4] My Lai.[5] No Gun Ri.[6] No bombs are smart enough to ask what we must ask: If you take these lives in our name, what is the purpose? Is your end clear and is it just? Can we trust you to have to good map (Where is the Chinese embassy?[7]) and a moral compass? And most important, is this the only way?

I am satisfied that my father did have to go to war to stop fascism. I am not satisfied that the military incursions of the next war, the cold war, were justified. Nor am I satisfied that everything we did in World War II was just and wise. Mistakes were made, including, I believe, some of the decisions to send the Nisei soldiers on those suicide missions—too many lives lost for too little gain. If we cannot raise these questions, we are not supporting our military.

Asian Americans serve in the current war. Soldiers cannot ask questions. That is the ethic of war and military discipline. Do not question the play once it is called, or the whole effort collapses. Because the soldiers whose lives we risk cannot question, we, citizens of a democracy, must question for them. Is this the right path, will it bring us what we want, are we risking lives—whether American soldiers or Afghan children—without good reason?

We in the peace movement must necessarily act on incomplete information, just as the warmakers do. We do not have all the answers, but I do know this: No one in my government has offered a clear objective for the bombing, nor any definition of victory that is attainable through bombing. If victory is stopping terrorism, they have not shown how bombing will do that. If victory is getting bin Laden and his followers, they have not shown how bombing will do that. If victory is simply dropping bombs in retaliation, to show that they will bomb someone, somewhere, when the United States is attacked, then they should come clean and admit that illegal goal. I listen carefully to every word of justification offered by the United States of America. The president promises his aim is peace. His spokespeople say there are "not a lot of high value targets"[8] and they offer no reason for their actions because their reasons are classified. They say they are targeting training camps and military installations, but we know where the terrorists planned and trained: Hamburg, New Jersey, Florida, American flight schools.[9] The president's men now admit they have hit villages and hospitals and Red Cross warehouses holding a winter's worth of food supplies for the starving, and they respond that this is war, there will be collateral damage.[10]

I do not want to become my enemy, the people who treat the loss of innocent lives as null value given their higher cause. Every civilian life that we Americans take, we should scrutinize precisely because we are Americans. We are not heartless terrorists. We are part of a democracy in which the government works for us and not the other way around. Whether a Chinese embassy, a Sudanese factory, an Italian ski lift, or a village in Afghanistan, we must know the facts.[11] Were civilians killed? How many? Was our equipment defective? Were the pilots ill-trained or misinformed? Did our intelligence let us down yet again? How can we prevent such errors? And the question I find the American press particularly deficient in asking: Who were these people we killed? What were their names, their families, their interests, their foibles, their aspirations? What was the stuff of their daily lives that might begin to make them human beings and not just places where a misplaced bomb fell?

Listen carefully. Our government is offering no plan for stability in Afghanistan. There is no plan for a replacement government that is democratic, committed to human rights, or any less likely to produce the next generation of terrorists. Our government has not told us how wiping out the "low value" military installations in Afghanistan has anything to do with wiping out terrorist cells that meet in Las Vegas motels. Our government has not told us how the Taliban supporters who defect and change uniform are any more reliable allies this time than they were when they first joined the Taliban, with U.S. support.

We need allies. In the Arab world and in Pakistan broadcasts of civilian victims of this war go on all day. Unlike Americans, our global neighbors see the faces and learn the names of the children orphaned by errant bombs.[12] The people we need on our side to stop terrorism—the people who know the language and culture and worldview of the suicide bombers—are turning against us. We need to know where the terrorist cells are and what they are planning next. I am no naïve peacenik in this. I support full, aggressive law enforcement[13] to stop terrorism—whether the threat is from homegrown militias or international organized gangs. As an Asian American, I also know this: People of color have had to sue to get jobs in law enforcement.[14] The call for native speakers of Arabic went out *after* September 11 and not before, even though we had reams of evidence documenting and predicting terrorist activities going unread because no one in law enforcement knew Arabic.[15] There are good people all over the Islamic world who, though they have reason to resent the United States, remain morally opposed to the tactics of the September 11 murderers. We need them willing to take chances to provide us with information and tactics for fighting terror. We are losing support with each bomb that falls on the home of an innocent family in Afghanistan.

I will march for peace, first, because this war will not bring peace and will only bring more terror. I will march for peace, second, because militarism is wrong. The choice of the bigger bomb; of shooting before thinking, arguing, debating, and talking; of silencing dissent in the name of defense is the most dangerous choice we can make in the nuclear age. Listen, my friends, to the sound of nuclear testing in Pakistan,[16] and put it together with anti-American chanting in the streets of Karachi.[17] What standard of dispute resolution do we want for this well-armed world? The Taliban had someone we wanted. We dropped a bomb. Many Americans responded with glee: "They made a big mistake messing with us and we showed them."

When we teach this definition of supremacy—hit first, hit hard, have more bombs—I don't see how we make ourselves safer, given that we are not the only ones with The Bomb.

The only safety lies in choosing the hardest way: Legal means to address disputes, international fora, and legitimacy gained through diplomacy and generosity, not coercion. If the United States were bringing democracy and running water and electricity and food and schools and roads and houses to the world's poorest villages, we would hear cheering in the streets, as did the Nisei soldiers in Italy and France. Our global neighbors would see us as the good and generous people we are, and the bin Ladens of the world would lose the ranks from which they recruit. They would truly have nowhere to hide. You may say that I'm a dreamer, but I am really a stone-cold realist with a strong self-preservation instinct. If we could have made the world safe through superior military strength, it would be safe already. No one can touch us in military capability, and our military is useless against someone hiding in the suburbs with a small cache of anthrax. The way to peace is the harder way, but it is our only fighting chance. From whence came this morass of bitter hatred, global instability, absence of democracy, armed teenagers, and chemical weapons in the hands of despots and cranks? Think about our need for friends and allies everywhere, people who will call in a tip to the international terrorist hotline because, after weighing their need for self-preservation against all they know about the United States and its enemies, they decide that helping us is the better choice.

Those on the left who have suggested that American economic exploitation and militarism have turned legions against us are accused of giving comfort to the enemy, but it was the left that previously demanded accountability instead of blind support for the Taliban.[18] Throughout the cold war and since, the U.S. has supported human rights violators in the name of expediency, treating democracy as a luxury that the third world does not deserve. This is what gave aid and comfort to the enemy.

We are a good nation of good people. I believe this in spite of every piece of evidence you can show me of American inhumanity at home and abroad. My people came to this country with hope, and even as they went off to the internment camps, they had neighbors, teachers, and friends who were sad to see them go. The witnesses felt helpless to make it otherwise, but they did not all cheer, those white and Latino and African American neighbors who watched as the Japanese Americans were loaded onto trains and carried off to the horse stalls. The good heart of the one who will bring a casserole when someone dies, who will help an immigrant child with unfamiliar homework, who will pull over when they see a car in distress at the side of the road, exists in every American community I have lived in. These good people could not easily watch an Iraqi child dying from lack of simple medicines or an Afghan child crying in the street, searching for a dead parent. I have known the generous American heart all my life even as I have fought my own battles against racism and sexism. I was not surprised, even as I wept, by the stories of magnificent bravery that emerged from September 11. I have been blessed to know fellow citizens who would, indeed, enter a burning building to help another. There is so much courage and care in America the Beautiful. It is a crime against us that bombs fall in our name, teaching the lie that we have no heart.

The citizens of this planet created the United Nations after World War II because war was too real then. No one was untouched by the fear and hardship. We didn't need the atom bomb to convince us—mustard gas was enough, for anyone who had seen it in World War I, to push the international consensus toward a new way of resolving disputes. Okinawa, my grandfather's *furusato*,[19] lost nearly one third of its civilian population in the war. One out of three: farmers, fisherman, school children.[20] The Okinawans are all pacifists now. It is very late in the history of humankind for state-sponsored violence to remain a considered choice. Why weren't the 70,000 who died in one second at Hiroshima enough to let us decide forever? They are gone, leaving us the gift of their memory. We do not need to learn it over and over and over, each time with new bodies. There is enough pain, already, to pierce deep inside, to teach us that the hard road of peace is the only one for us, we humans, with our vulnerable human bodies and heartbreaking human need to tuck our children safe in bed each night.

Asian Americans come from places savaged by war. We know that war is hell for the winners and the losers and that winning counts for little if we have to live this way: keeping that stash of jade in case we have to leave quickly in the night, teaching our children—as my *Uchinanchu*[21] elders taught me—that you can boil the center pith of the Sago Palm and eat it in starvation time, or, for that matter, keeping a rifle behind the counter of your convenience store, as a survivor of the urban war called *Sa-ee-gu*.[22] Waiting for the next plane to fall out of the sky, with gut clenched even as we wash the dishes and scan the channels for news, is no way to live. Violence brings violence and justice brings peace. I distrust the military path my government has chosen. I don't have to prove my loyalty or my love for this country as I proclaim my distrust. My father's Purple Heart Battalion[23] earned for me the right to stand tall in protest, criticizing the mighty if conscience so compels. In a democracy, it is the citizen's job to ask hard questions in difficult times. Asian Americans, take up your places at the patriot's table and ask the questions that will lead us to sweet dreams, to justice, and to peace.

Notes

Thanks to the following for research, editorial, and analytical contributions. (The position taken in this piece is mine alone.) Tracy Bridgman, John Cheng, Mark Chien, Joshua Goldstein, Chris Iijima, Annalisa Jabaily, Charles R. Lawrence III, Jinsook Lee, Don Matsuda, David Meyer, Tony Nguyen, John Showalter, Dawn Veltman, and Leti Volpp.

1. In 1944, the Texas "Lost Battalion" was trapped behind German lines for seven days, the wounded dying without medical care, and the "able" surviving on rain water caught in tent canvas. "We were tired, hungry, and cold and in all probability would not be able to hold more than 36 hours longer..." Major Charles Roscoe recalled. Nisei soldiers who broke through to rescue the Lost Battalion suffered more than 800 causalities to rescue the 211 trapped survivors of the Lost Battalion. Lyn Crost, *Honor By Fire* (Novato, California: Presidio Press, 1994), 196-198; Thomas Murphy, *Ambassadors In Arms*, (Honolulu, Hawaii: University of Hawaii Press, 1954).

2. In October 1944, the Nisei soldiers liberated the town of Bruyeres, France. The 7th Army report said, "Bruyeres will long be remembered, for it was one of the most viciously fought-for towns we had encountered in our long march against the German. The enemy defended it house by house, giving up only a yard when it became so untenable they could no longer hope to hold it." Quoted in Bill Hosokawa, *Nisei: The Quiet Americans* (New York: W. Morrow, 1969), 405.

    > [W]herever they had been in Europe they had left, among civilians, indelible memories of their kindness, generosity, and thoughtfulness. They were to become a legend in a corner of France: the little town of Bruyeres. Busloads of Japanese-American families come to Bruyeres, including grandchildren who never had a chance to know their Nisei grandfathers who fought or died there. They come

to see the monument that the townspeople erected in honor of the Combat Team as evidence of their gratitude and lasting devotion to the men who freed them from the terrors of Nazi occupation. It had been a moment in life when love for fellow humans transcended race and creed.... And children of Bruyeres still sing the Hawaiian song loved by many of their liberators, 'Aloha Oe' (Farewell to Thee), as well as they sing the 'Marseillaise'." Crost, 308.

3.   My father was incarcerated at Heart Mountain, Wyoming, where he volunteered for combat duty in World War II. In 1980 Congress formed a bipartisan Commission on Wartime Relocation and Internment of Civilians. After extensive investigation, the Commission found that the internment of 120,000 Japanese Americans during World War II "was not justified by military necessity.... The broad historical causes that shaped these decisions were race prejudice, war hysteria and a failure of political leadership. Widespread ignorance about Americans of Japanese descent contributed to a policy conceived in haste and executed in an atmosphere of fear and anger at Japan. A grave personal injustice was done to the American citizens and resident aliens of Japanese ancestry who, without individual review or any probative evidence against them, were excluded, removed and detained by the United States...."

4.   70,000 instant deaths from the Hiroshima bombing is the figure cited in Ronald Takaki, *Hiroshima: Why America Dropped the Atom Bomb* (Back Bay Books, 1995). John Dower suspects that the official U.S. estimate of 70,000 to 80,000 is probably one-half of the actual count. John W. Dower, "The Bombed: Hiroshimas and Nagasakis in Japanese Memory," *Diplomatic History* 19:2 (1996), 275. Many more died after the actual bombing from injury and illness caused by the bomb, and many Hibàkusha (survivors) continue to suffer from their injuries.

5 .   I have discovered that most of my students are not familiar with the My Lai massacre, the most publicized atrocity of the Vietnam War. In March, 1968, U.S. soldiers entered a civilian village and beat, tortured, stabbed, raped, burned, and shot hundreds of unarmed villagers, including many elderly and children. Lt. William Calley, a responsible officer, was charged with 122 deaths, and was sentenced to life in prison, but intervention by President Nixon and others resulted in minimal punishment.

The U.S. Government's Peers Commission Report stated that the number of Vietnamese civilians killed in the My Lai incident was "at least 175 and may exceed 400." Joseph Goldstein, *The My Lai Massacre and It's Cover-Up: Beyond the Reach of Law?: Peers Commission Report*, (U.S. Department of the Army, 1976).

6.   Korean survivors report that civilian refugees during the Korean War were herded under a bridge at No Gun Ri and fired upon, leaving 300 dead. In 1999, individual U.S. veterans confirmed these allegations. Sang-Hun Choe, Charles J. Hanley, and Martha Mendoza, "War's Hidden Chapter: Ex-GIs tell of Killing Korean Refugees," *The Associated Press*, September 29, 1999; Sang-Hun Choe, Charles J. Hanley, and Martha Mendoza of the Associated Press, "G.I's Tell of

a U.S. Massacre in Korean War," *New York Times*, September 30, 1999. The official U.S. government investigation concluded that civilians were, indeed, killed by U.S. soldiers at No Gun Ri, but that the number is uncertain. "Koreans reported to the Office of Yong Dong County an unverified number of 248 Korean civilians killed, injured or missing while the testimony of U.S. veterans supports lower numbers." "Statement of Mutual Understanding Between the United States and the Republic of Korea on the No Gun Ri Investigations," U.S. Department of Defense, 2001.

7.   On May 7, 1999, NATO forces bombed the Chinese Embassy in Belgrade, killing three Chinese nationals and wounding approximately twenty others. Sean D. Murphy, "Contemporary Practice Of The United States Relating to International Law," *American Journal of International Law* 94 (2000), 102, 127. The Director of the Central Intelligence Agency stated to Congress: "The attack was a mistake. There were three basic failures. First, the technique used to locate the intended target. . .was severely flawed. Second, none of the military or intelligence databases used to validate targets contained the correct location of the Chinese Embassy. Third, nowhere in the target review process was either of the first two mistakes detected. The unintended attack happened because a number of systems and procedures that are used to identify and verify potential targets did not work." DCI Statement on The Belgrade Chinese Embassy Bombing, House Permanent Select Committee on Intelligence Open Hearing, July 22, 1999.

8.   Secretary of Defense Donald Rumsfeld Briefing on Enduring Freedom, Sunday, October 7, 2001, News Transcript from U.S. Department of Defense.

9.   See Joel Achenbach, "'You Never Imagine' A Hijacker Next Door," *Washington Post*, September 16, 2001, (describing movements of terrorist bombers through Europe and the United States).

10.   Q: General Myers, could you explain how it was that U.S. aircraft hit that Red Cross warehouse complex a second time, after there had been quite extensive communication with the Red Cross about its location?

Myers: Obviously, that's quite disturbing. And we do not have an explanation at this point. It is something that General Franks at Central Command is investigating very thoroughly. It should not have happened. And —

Q: Can you say it was human error? What does the term "human error" mean now?

Myers: Well, we don't know yet on why that target complex was not wiped off any target list after the last strike. So —

Rumsfeld: Apparently, it is a warehouse complex, and apparently no one was killed, although it is correct that it was hit a second time, and there may have been some Red Cross material still in that warehouse.

Secretary of Defense Donald H. Rumsfeld and General Myers, Department of Defense News Briefing (October 29, 2001) (transcript available at Federal News Service, Inc.); White House Chief of Staff Andrew Card stated that civilian casualties are regrettable but are not a reason to shift the administration's war plans. "Collateral damage is something that the United States tries to avoid," Card said on NBC's "Meet the Press." Bob Kemper, "War on track, U.S. insists." *LA Times* from *Chicago Tribune*, October 29, 2001.

11. See note 7 for Chinese Embassy bombing errors; in August 1998 the United States military initiated air strikes against an alleged chemical weapons factory in Sudan. According to a December 3, 2000, *Washington Post* analysis, "the missile attack on the El Shifa pharmaceutical plant in Khartoum, Sudan's capital, appears to have been a mistake. U.S. officials have backed away from claims that its owner is linked to bin Laden. They now concede that the plant produced medicines and may not have been involved in making chemical weapons, as they had originally alleged." Vernon Loeb, "U.S. Considers Array of Actions against Bin Laden," *Washington Post*, December 3, 2000, A03. On February 3, 1998, a U.S. Marine jet engaged in a low-level training flight in the northern Italian Alps severed a cable-car line at a ski resort in Cavalese, killing twenty people. President Clinton and Secretary of Defense Cohen issued an apology. Statement by Secretary of Defense William S. Cohen regarding Tragedy at Cavalese, Department of Defense News Release, March 10, 1999. The pilot stated the accident could have been prevented by "making sure everybody knows the rules for flying in a foreign country." He was flying at 350 feet, while Italian rules for that area prohibit jets below 2000 feet. Steve Vogel, "After Pilot's Acquittal, Blame Hard to Assign," *Washington Post*, March 6, 1999.

12. See Kevin Sullivan, "War Support Ebbs Worldwide, September 11 Doesn't Justify Bombing, Many Say", *Washington Post*, November 7, 2001. (reporting declining support for U.S. military action as reports of civilian casualties are broadcast in other countries).

13. I believe that acting within the constraints of the Bill of Rights and International Law there is much we can do to investigate and prosecute terrorists, and that the rapid move to war obscures the need for old-fashioned, gumshoe interdiction. Consider, for example, the fact that the FBI did not follow up on pre-September 11 reports of suspicious flight school students with terrorist connections. See Steve Fainaru and James V. Grimaldi "FBI Knew Terrorists Were Using Flight Schools," *Washington Post*, September 23, 2001; Stephen Braun *etal.*, "Haunted By Years of Missed Warnings; as terrorists traveled the US over a decade, signs pointing to their plans went unheeded. . ." *Los Angeles Times*, October 14, 2001.

14. For discussion of the effects of discrimination in law enforcement employment practices see Mari Matsuda "Crime and Affirmative Action," *The Journal of Gender, Race and Justice* 1:2 (1998), 309; see also "FBI Agents Ordeal: Meanness that Never Let Up," *New York Times*, January 25, 1988; Michael Isikoff, "FBI Settles Black Agents' Discrimination Charge" *Washington Post*, January 27, 1993.

15. Claire Berlinski, "English Only Spoken Here: There's a Desperate Shortage of Foreign Language Speakers at Our Intelligence Agencies," *The Weekly Standard* 7:12:3 (2001), 22.

16. Pakistan announced its nuclear weapons capability in 1998. See Associated Press "Pakistan Explodes Nuclear Devices," *New York Times*, May 28, 1998.

17. In the months following September 11, violent anti-American demonstrations filled the streets in Pakistan's cities. See Pamela Constable, "Pakistani Mobs Destroy KFC Outlet and U.S. Flags," *Washington Post*, October 13, 2001; and Pamela Constable, "Anti-U.S. Sentiment Spreading In Pakistan Growing Street Protests Precede Visit by Powell," *Washington Post*, October 15, 2001.

18. The Feminist Majority Foundation, for example, demanded non-recognition of the Taliban and the listing of the Taliban as a terrorist organization in 1999. It opposed UNOCAL's support of the Taliban in conjunction with a U.S.-backed oil pipeline agreement, which would have generated up to $100 million dollars a year for the Taliban. The Feminist Majority Foundation, Campaign To Stop Gender Apartheid in Afghanistan, released in 1999.

19. *Furusato* is Japanese for place of origin; homeland

20. 150,000 civilian casualties out of a population of 450,000 is one conventional estimate, although undercounting is probable given the massive "typhoon of bombs", which killed more civilians than combatants. Feifer "The Rape of Okinawa," *World Policy Journal* XVII (2000), 3.

21. *Uchinanchu* is how Okinawans refer to themselves.

22. *Sa-ee-gu* is the Los Angeles riot/uprising of 1992, in which Korean merchants were forced to take up arms to defend their stores. See K. W. Lee, "Legacy of Sa-ee-gu: Goodbye Hahn, Good Morning Community Conscience," *Amerasia Journal* 25:2 (Los Angeles: Asian American Studies Center, 1999), 42-64.

23. The 100th Battalion was awarded 1,703 Purple Hearts. My father, like so many Nisei vets, carries these notations in his military record: BS (bronze star); CIB (combat infantry badge); DUB (distinguished unit badge); and PH (purple heart). Murphy, 316, 329.

Shepherd. On the highway to the Pamir Mountains.
© 2001, Eric Chang

A Chronology of the "War on Terror" and Domestic Hate Crimes

Stephen Lee

"Worthy" and "Unworthy" Americans?

In their seminal work, *Manufacturing Consent: The Political Economy of the Mass Media*, Edward S. Herman and Noam Chomsky examine the ways U.S. mass media acts as a propaganda device in justifying governmental policies and actions both at home and abroad. They argue that the quantity and quality of news coverage for stories of abuse inflicted by the state is proportional to the degree to which such stories challenge U.S. hegemonic rule:

> While the coverage of the worthy victim was generous with gory details and quoted expressions of outrage and demands for justice, the coverage of the unworthy victims was low-keyed, designed to keep the lid on emotions and evoking regretful and philosophical generalities on the omnipresence of violence and the inherent tragedy of human life.[1]

Today, as President Bush wages his "War on Terror," this model of "worthy" and "unworthy" victims is a useful tool for understanding how mass media information (and disinformation) operates on a selective basis. News networks no longer strive for journalistic objectivity; rather, zealous patriotism overshadows any attempts to present a balanced view. As Fox News Network executives put it, to be unequivocally fair and balanced is to participate in the worst kind of cultural relativism.[2] In light of this "U.S.A. Fever," it is no wonder that for all the generous coverage President Bush receives on his many calls for racial tolerance,

STEPHEN LEE is Publications Assistant for *Amerasia Journal*. He received his M.A. in Asian American Studies, University of California, Los Angeles.

there is remarkably little in print on the nearly 2,000 people who have been detained by Attorney General John Ashcroft since September 11th, the vast majority of whom are of South Asian and Middle Eastern descent. The murmured consensus around the nation seems to be "you're either with us, or against us."

The overtly patriotic and imbalanced media coverage on the one hand supports Herman and Chomsky's claim of media as propaganda device, but on the other, it also reveals the still-deeply rooted strains of racism in America. More than defining who *is* American, this sentiment serves the purpose of defining who *is not* American. Douglas Kellner writes: "It is as if U.S. popular and political culture needs evil demons to assure its sense of its own goodness."[3] On September 11th, news networks and political leaders immediately proclaimed a war of "good vs. evil," but as public suspicion of the Middle East turned into military mobilization *against* the Middle East, in the public mind, there became no difference between "the enemy" and those who "looked like the enemy." On September 11th, Sikh cab drivers, Egyptian store owners, Lebanese doctors, and any other American who struck a Middle Eastern appearance became a suspect in the hunt for terrorists.

Reminiscent of Japanese American community victimization during World War II, Middle Eastern, Arab, and South Asian communities all over the U.S. are bearing the brunt of fervent xenophobia. Harassment, assault, murder: from Beverly Hills to Dayton, Ohio, the number of hate crimes are on the rise against Arab, Middle Eastern, and Asian Americans and, ironically, they are being committed in the name of patriotism. "I stand for America all the way!" decried Frank Roque upon being arrested for the murder of Balbir Singh, a Sikh gas station owner. What does danger look like? What does the face of America look like? Once again, Asian Americans are among those being asked to prove themselves as citizens or else face the consequences. Herman and Chomsky's contentious question of who are "worthy" and "unworthy" victims is now giving way to a new question, one that asks who are "worthy" and "unworthy" Americans.

To this end, we offer you a two-part chronology.[4] The first part documents the major events and turning points of the current "War on Terror" providing a basic historical record of the events that transpired on and since September 11th. Despite the unilateral rhetoric that paints the war as a struggle between 'the West' and 'Islam', as the chronology demonstrates, the war has been of the utmost concern to many nations and has left no corner of the globe untouched. Here at home, meanwhile, in response to the skyrocketing number of reported hate crimes, many South Asian, Arab, Middle Eastern, and Japanese American groups have organized themselves to better serve their communities. In Washington D.C., young Sikh American professionals gathered regularly at George Washington University to discuss hate crime protest strategy; in Glendale, California the Armenian National Committee Western Region has established a hate crime hotline so their community could have "a resource where people can speak their own language"[5]; and in San Francisco, Nosei, a local Japanese American group, organized a peace gathering in Japantown Peace Plaza as a show of solidarity and a denouncement of violence.

The second part of the chronology is a listing of domestic hate crimes. It is both a challenge to the biased media coverage of the war and a wake-up call to our communities. Whereas one C.I.A. operative lost in the line of fire justified front page spreads all over the country, the dozens of lives lost to hate crimes here at home have gone largely unnoticed. The loss of innocent lives at home at the hands of hate, hysteria, and racism are as much a part of the reality of war as those lost "on the battlefield," and therefore cannot be discounted in assessing the scale of war as a human tragedy. Moreover, hate crimes are not singular acts of aggression, but symptomatic outbursts of the deeper problems of racism, xenophobia, and economic decline. They affect all of us and are popping up all over the country—from crowded urban centers to dusty country roads—and claiming the lives of anyone who "looks like a terrorist."

Notes

1. Edward S. Herman and Noam Chomsky, *Manufacturing Consent: The Political Economy of the Mass Media* (New York: Pantheon Books, 1988), 39.

2. Jim Rutenberg, "Fox Portrays a War of Good and Evil, and Many Applaud," *The New York Times*, December 3, 2001.

3. Douglas Kellner, *Media Culture: Cultural Studies, Identity and Politics between the Modern and the Post Modern*, (New York: Routledge, 1995), 208.

4. For a protracted version of this chronology, see Stephen Lee, "U.S. Intervention in the Middle East, the 'War on Terror,' and Domestic Hate Crimes: An *Amerasia Journal* Chronology," *Amerasia Journal* 27:3/28:1, 2001-2002, 295-318.

5. Karen S. Kim, "Armenian Group Sets Up Hate Crime Hotline," *Los Angeles Times*, October 2, 2001.

The second day of Tibetan Buddhist prayer and candlelight vigil at Union Square Park, New York City. The vigil lasted 49 days, taking place in a different location each night.
© 2001, Corky Lee

Part I.

Chronology of the "War on Terror"

September 11, 2001

American Airlines flight 11, carrying 92 people from Boston to Los Angeles, crashes into the north tower of the World Trade Center.

United Airlines flight 175, carrying 65 people from Boston to Los Angeles, crashes into south tower of the World Trade Center.

American Airlines flight 77, carrying 64 people from Washington to Los Angeles, crashes into the west side of the Pentagon.

United Airlines flight 93, departing from Newark to San Francisco, crashes in rural Pennsylvania.

Transportation Secretary Norman Mineta approves first shutdown of U.S. airspace in history.

Wall Street closes.

September 14, 2001

President Bush visits the remains of the World Trade Center towers.

Congress approves the use-of-force resolution by a margin of 420-1. It authorizes the president "to use all necessary and appropriate force against those nations,

organizations, or persons he determines planned, authorized, committed, or aided the terrorist attacks that occurred on September 11, 2001." The lone dissenting voice is registered by Representative Barbara Lee, D-California.

September 17, 2001

Wall Street reopens

President Bush visits Islamic Center of Washington, pleas for tolerance towards Arab Americans.

September 18, 2001

Megawati Sukarnoputri, president of Indonesia, visits the White House.

September 20, 2001

President Bush announces ultimatum to Taliban demanding that they deliver all leaders of Al Qaeda. "The Taliban must act and act immediately. They will hand over the terrorists, or they will share in their fate."

President creates Office of Homeland Security. Pennsylvania Governor Tom Ridge, a republican, is named the first head of the new office.

Nosei, a San Francisco-based Japanese American group, organizes a peace gathering in Japantown's Peace Plaza.

September 21, 2001

Taliban responds to President Bush's ultimatum to hand over Osama bin Laden. Taliban will not comply unless there is evidence linking bin Laden and his Al Qaeda organization to the attacks.

September 22, 2001

350 protestors gather around Federal Building in West Los Angeles, California to protest the Bush administration's planned military response.

September 25, 2001

Kingdom of Saudi Arabia cuts all ties with Taliban government, joins United Arab Emirates in move to isolate the Afghani regime.

September 28, 2001

Nikkei for Civil Rights and Redress sponsors a candlelight vigil in Los Angeles' Little Tokyo.

October 1, 2001

United Nations General Assembly kicks off week-long discussion on counter-terrorism. New York Mayor Rudolph Giuliani kicks off forum with speech claiming "You're either with civilization or with terrorists."

October 5, 2001

First victim of anthrax is confirmed. Sun photo editor Bob Stevens dies of inhalation anthrax in Boca Raton, Florida.

October 7, 2001

U.S. begins bombing Afghanistan.

October 13, 2001

Reports come through that an aide to NBC anchorman Tom Brokaw has contracted anthrax and though there is no evidence linking it to the 9/11 attacks, it is treated as a criminal investigation. This comes on the heels of three Florida cases.

October 14, 2001

Demonstrations in Jacobabad, Pakistan against U.S. military actions lead to the death of one protestor and twelve injured. A Pakistani police officer states: "I beseech America to stop the bombings. These will tear our country apart."

Taliban proposes a discussion on the handing over of Osama bin Laden. Requests third country intervention and proof of bin Laden's involvement in the World Trade Center attacks. President Bush refuses request, continues bombing.

October 15, 2001

Three more cases of anthrax are reported in New York City over the weekend. The Bush administration

officially dubs the anthrax phenom-
enon a case of bioterrorism.

October 16, 2001

Capital Hill office of Senate Majority
Leader Tom Daschle (D-S.D.)
receives a letter testing positive for
anthrax. Authorities close an entire
wing of the Senate Office Building.

October 18, 2001

A federal judge sentences four
followers of Osama bin Laden to life
in prison in the bombing of two U.S.
embassies in East Africa that killed
224 people in 1998.

October 21, 2001

Annual APEC (Asia-Pacific
Economic Cooperation) meeting
comes to an end, this year held in
Shanghai, China. China and
Russia pledge support in "War on
Terror" but urge quick end to
strikes.

October 22, 2001

Two Washington D.C. postal
workers become second and third
victims of anthrax.

October 26, 2001

President Bush signs anti-terrorism
bill. It is dubbed the "Uniting and
Strengthening America Act by
Providing Appropriate Tools
Required to Intercept and Obstruct
Terrorism (USA PATRIOT) Act of
2001."

Transportation Secretary, Norman
Mineta, meets with leaders of the

Arab and Islamic communities to
discuss security, safety, and profiling issues.

Taliban captures and executes
Opposition leader, Abdul Haq.

October 31, 2001

Kathy T. Nguyen, a New York City
hospital worker, becomes fourth
victim of anthrax.

Justice Department introduces
tighter measures to crack down on
foreigners who 'endorse' terrorism,
extending their powers to visa
denial and immigrant deportation.

November 1, 2001

Governor Gray Davis warns of a
"credible" terrorist threat against
major bridges in California,
including the Golden Gate Bridge
and the Vincent Thomas Bridge in
San Pedro.

November 2, 2001

President declares that the U.S. will
not slow offensive during the
Muslim fasting month of Ramadan.

November 7, 2001

U.S. freezes the assets of sixty-two
organizations and individuals
suspected of raising money for
Osama bin Laden.

November 9, 2001

Afghan opposition forces seize
northern Afghan city of Mazar-i-
Sharif.

November 10, 2001

Pakistani Journalist Hamid Mir, the pro-Taliban editor of the Urdu-language newspaper Ausaf, claims that in an interview, bin Laden claimed to have chemical and nuclear weapons capability.

President Bush addresses the U.N. General Assembly and reiterates that: "For every regime that sponsors terror, there is a price to be paid and it will be paid"; furthermore, nations that disregard such a claim "are equally guilty of murder and equally accountable to justice."

Pakistani President Pervez Musharraf arrives in the United States to meet with American leaders. President Bush promises an aid package of $900 million.

November 13, 2001

Afghan opposition forces enter capital city of Kabul, taking it without a fight as Taliban forces flee or defect.

President Bush issues an order allowing for the use of special military courts to try suspected terrorists. Those designated as terrorists may not seek the aid of "any court of the United States," nor "any court of any foreign nation or any international tribunal."

November 15, 2001

President Bush and Vladimir Putin conclude a three-day meeting in Washington and at President Bush's central Texas ranch.

Among the things discussed are: a U.S. national missile defense, the reduction of arms, the war in Afghanistan, and a post-Taliban government.

Eight humanitarian aid workers are freed by Afghan opposition forces from Taliban control.

November 19, 2001

President Bush signs into law the Aviation Security Bill, a measure that will make airport baggage checkers federal employees. The bill also calls for more secure airplane cockpit doorways and an increased number of armed Federal Marshals on flights.

November 21, 2001

Elderly Connecticut woman dies of inhalation anthrax. Becomes fifth confirmed victim of anthrax.

November 24, 2001

Northern Alliance troops move into Kunduz, the Taliban's last northern stronghold.

November 25, 2001

Hundreds of U.S. Marines land in Kandahar, a southern Taliban stronghold; marks the first major step of an American troop build-up in Afghanistan.

A prison riot erupts at a fortress in Qala-I-Jangy, 10 miles west of Mazar-i-Sharif, involving Pakistani, Arab and Chechen fighters who had surrendered following a two-week siege of Kunduz. Hundreds of prisoners lose their lives as U.S. warplanes and special troops respond.

November 26, 2001

President Bush demands that Saddam Hussein allow for international weapons inspections. When asked what would happen if he failed to comply, President Bush responds with, "He'll find out."

November 27, 2001

The prison riot in Qala-I-Jangy finally ends as Northern Alliance forces crush a building where Taliban prisoners were holed up.

November 28, 2001

U.S. confirms first U.S. combat death in Afghanistan. The victim, Michael "Mike" Spann, 32, was working for the C.I.A. Directorate of Operations, the part of the agency responsible for covert operations.

December 1, 2001

Two suicide bombers kill 10 people in Jerusalem.

Over 80 Taliban soldiers surrender to Northern Alliance forces, among whom is Abdul Hamid (a.k.a. John Philip Walker Lindh), a twenty-year-old white American convert to Islam who hails from Marin County, California.

December 2, 2001

Approximately twelve hours after the first pair of suicide bombers in Jerusalem, Israel, another bomber kills 16 and injures 35 in Haifa.

December 3, 2001

Israel F-16 fighter jets attack civil police headquarters and the Offices of Palestinian Authority president, Yasser Arafat, leaving at least 15 wounded.

December 5, 2001

In Koenigswinter, Germany Hamid Karzai, a Pushtun, is chosen as prime minister for interim government in post-Taliban Afghanistan.

Three U.S. Green Berets and Five Afghans are killed by a "friendly fire" bomb dropped by an American bomber during the fight to take Kandahar.

December 6, 2001

Mullah Mohammed Omar, Taliban leader, tentatively agrees to surrender Kandahar. Remaining Taliban fighters to return arms.

December 7, 2001

Mullah Mohammed Omar reneges on offer to disarm and opts to flee Kandahar with remaining members of the Taliban.

December 11, 2001

A federal grand jury indicts Zacarias Moussaoui, a French man of Moroccan descent. Moussaoui is the first person charged in the United States for the September 11th attacks.

December 12, 2001

In San Diego, 10 foreign students are arrested for overstaying their visas, the first government crackdown since the September 11th attacks. The students were sought primarily because they were from countries deemed to have terrorists links: Iran, Sudan, Syria, Pakistan, Libya, Saudi Arabia, Afghanistan and Yemen.

December 13, 2001

U.S. government releases video tape of Osama bin Laden speaking of the September 11th attacks. The tape is dated November 9 and allegedly recorded in Kandahar, Afghanistan; it was confiscated in a private residence in Jalalabad.

President Bush announces that the U.S. will be withdrawing from the 1972 Anti-Ballistic Missile (ABM) Treaty, beginning a phase-out period of six months. This clears the way for President Bush to proceed with his much-debated and yet-to-be-proven-effective Missile Defense system.

A suicide bomber attacks India's Parliament in New Delhi leaving 14 dead.

December 16, 2001

In Tora Bora, Afghanistan, Militiamen overrun the Taliban's last bastion. Though Secretary of Defense Donald Rumsfield remains skeptical, Secretary of State Colin Powell states: ""We've destroyed Al Qaeda in Afghanistan, and we have ended the role of Afghanistan as a haven for terrorist activity." The whereabouts of Osama bin Laden are still unknown.

December 18, 2001

Officials report that U.S. intelligence agencies have expanded the hunt for bin Laden into Pakistan.

December 19, 2001

Al Qaeda prisoners escape in a revolt while being transferred by bus to another prison in Pakistan. At least 13 are dead and more than 40 prisoners have escaped.

December 20, 2001

The Federal Government will offer an average of $1.6 million in tax-free aid to the families of September 11th victims, the program administrator announced today.

December 22, 2001

A man aboard an American Airlines flight from Paris outbound to Miami is wrestled and subdued after apparently trying to ignite his shoe, later to be found with explosive materials. It is not clear if his actions are connected to the Al Qaeda network. The flight is escorted by two military F-15 fighter jets and lands at Logan International Airport in Boston, Massachusetts.

In Kabul, Afghanistan, Hamid Karzai is sworn in as prime minister for the post-Taliban interim government. He states: "I promise you that I will fulfill my mission to bring peace to Afghanistan."

January 2, 2002

Zacarias Moussaoui, the first person charged as an accomplice in the September 11th attacks, enters a plea of not-guilty before U.S. District Judge Leonie Brinkema in Alexandria, VA.

January 4, 2002

U.S. airstrike hits suspected Taliban camp in eastern Afghanistan for the second day in a row. A U.S. military member is lost in gunfire in Eastern Afghanistan, the first U.S. combat death in the War on Terror.

January 5, 2002

A 15-year-old boy crashes a Cessna plane into a Tampa, Florida highrise. The recovered suicide note claimed sympathies to Osama bin Laden. There were no reported injuries or deaths.

January 9, 2002

A U.S. military refueling plane crashes into a mountain in Pakistan killing all 7 marines aboard.

January 11, 2002

First batch of captured Al Qaeda suspects arrive in Guantanamo Bay Naval Base in Cuba from Afghanistan.

January 20, 2002

A marine helicopter crashes in Afghanistan killing two marines and injuring five.

January 29, 2002

President Bush, in his State of the Union Address, states that "a terrorist underworld . . .operates in remote jungles and deserts, and hides in the centers of large cities," and if other governments "do not act, America will." He also lists North Korea, Iran, and Iraq as members of an "axis of evil."

February 22, 2002

President Bush concludes a six-day trip to Asia. Highlights include praise for Japanese Prime Minister Junichiro Koizumi and Japan's effort in the War on Terror, a speech on the 30th anniversary of President Nixon's groundbreaking visit to China at Tsinghua University, and demonstrators in Seoul, Korea, decrying Bush's "axis of evil" remarks.

March 9, 2002

The *Los Angeles Times* obtains copy of a Pentagon-drafted Nuclear Posture Report. The classified report lists seven nations—China, Russia, Iraq, North Korea, Iran, Libya and Syria—as possible targets in contingencies for possible nuclear attack.

Stephen Lee

215

Jeffrey and Susan Hor stop at World Trade Center memorial at
Chatham Square, Chinatown, September 22, 2001.
©2001, Corky Lee

Part II.

Chronology of Domestic
Hate Crimes and Responses

September 11, 2001

Palos Heights, IL: A man attacks a Moroccan gas station attendant with the blunt end of a machete. Police take Robert J. Shereikis into custody, charge him with hate crime, aggravated battery and aggravated unlawful use of a weapon. Shereikis admits that he believed the victim was Arab and attacked him because he was upset with the attacks in New York City and Washington D.C.

Manhattan, NY: Amrik Singh Chawla, a South Asian American (Sikh), is chased by a group of four men yelling "terrorist." They chase him for four blocks. He is un-harmed, but deeply shaken by the entire incident.

Richmond Hills, NY: A gurdwara is fired upon with rubber bullets. An arrest is made when the individual returns the following morning.

Richmond Hills, NY: Attar Singh Bhatia is severely injured and hospitalized when he is attacked with a baseball bat.

Richmond Hills, NY: Two Sikh Americans are attacked with a paint ball gun. The police arrest two men.

Newport Beach, CA: A Newport Beach woman receives harassing and threatening phone calls all morning. "I have an Arabic-sounding last name and I'm in the phone-book, that's the only explanation I can think of," she states.

San Jose, CA: Maha El Genaidi, executive director of the Islamic Network Group in San Jose, receives two threats to her organ-ization and personally fields more than seven threatening calls and e-mails. "One of them threatened my life and the lives of all Muslims. And others were saying, 'Get the hell out of the country. You ruined the country, and you will all die,'" El Genaidi says.

Stockton, CA: Amarjit Singh Dadwal, a Sikh, is shouted at and called an "Iraqi" by four or five white teens and adults in a van.

Tulsa, OK: According to local police, a Pakistani native is beaten by three men in a hate crime. By Thursday, the victim is in a fair condition at a hospital.

Washington, D.C.: As a South Asian American (Sikh) exits work, he is accosted by pedestrians on the street who begin to yell verbal expletives at him, and threaten to "get" him and bomb him in retaliation for the terrorist acts earlier in the day. Although he was able to escape the crowd, he was deeply upset by the incident.

September 12, 2001

Providence, RI: Sher J.B. Singh is pulled from an Amtrak train and arrested for possession of a concealed weapon. Mr. Singh was carrying a three-inch kirpan. National press wrongly claims that Mr. Singh is one of the terrorists being sought by the FBI.

Cleveland, OH: Guru Gobind Singh Sikh Temple is attacked with lit bottles of gasoline.

Bridgeview, IL: Police turn back 300 marchers—some waving American flags and shouting "USA! USA!"—as they try to march on a mosque in the Chicago suburb. Three demonstrators are arrested. There are no injuries and demonstrators are kept blocks from the closed Muslim house of worship. "I'm proud to be American and I hate Arabs and I always have," said 19-year-old Colin Zaremba who marched with the group from Oak Lawn.

Chicago, IL: A firebomb is tossed at an Arab American community center.

Gary, IN: A man in a ski mask fires an assault rifle at a gas station where a Yemen-born U.S. citizen is working.

Washington D.C.: Tamara Alfson, an American working at the Kuwait Embassy, counsels frightened Kuwaiti students attending schools across the United States. "Some of them have already been harassed. People have been quite awful to them," said Alfson, an academic adviser to about 150 students.

Boston, MA: Meera Kumar is racially profiled and harassed by police on a Boston-NY train, along with other South Asians and Arabs.

Collingswood, NJ: Vandals attack two Indian-owned businesses, spray-painting, "leave town."

Brooklyn Heights, NY: A man drives past a small group of men and boys gathered at a Mosque for afternoon prayers and yells, "Murderers!"

Huntington, NY: A 75-year-old man who is drunk tries to run over a Pakistani woman in the parking lot of a shopping mall. The man then follows the woman into a store and threatens to kill her for "destroying my country," the police report.

Long Island, NY: A man is arrested on suspicion of waving a pellet gun and shouting obscenities at a South Asian gas station worker in Ronkonkoma.

Carrollton, Denton, and Irving, TX: Mosques in all three cities are attacked in what authorities believe could be reaction to the terrorist attacks. Shots are fired into the Carrollton and Irving mosques, and a firebomb is thrown into the mosque in Denton.

Napa, CA: Dale Singh, manager of a fast-food restaurant finds his car's finish and windows scratched and scraped.

September 13, 2001

Colorado Springs, CO: Buggie and Pinky Bajwa, Sikh Americans, awake Thursday morning, to find the word "Terrorists" sprayed in red paint across their family's driveway and "Terrorist on board" written on their white car.

Los Angeles, CA: Sign in the elevator at the Hall of Records says, "Kill all towel heads."

Brooklyn, NY: An Arab grocery storeowner is threatened with violence by his supplier.

Denton, TX: Early Thursday, a Molotov cocktail is thrown against the side of the Islamic Society, causing an estimated $2,500 in damage, says Kiersten Dieterle, a spokeswoman for the Dallas suburb. The building was empty, and there are no injuries.

Salt Lake City, UT: James Herrick, 32, tries to set fire to a Pakistani American family's business.

Seattle, WA: Shots are fired at worshippers at a mosque and attempts were made to set the building on fire. Police have charged Patrick Cunningham, 53.

September 14, 2001

Los Angeles, CA: A young Persian woman is eating lunch with a friend who jokingly calls her an Arab. A young woman sitting next to them follows them out of the restaurant, asks the woman if she is Arab, and punches her in the eye.

Long Beach, CA: Anti-Israeli graffiti is found on a home at Woodruff Avenue & Conant Street. Local newspaper accounts that day indicate there have been 12 incidents in Long Beach since September 11th, the same amount reported in all of last year.

Tempe, AZ: A 19-year-old Muslim Arizona State University student is pushed to the ground in a parking lot and hit with eggs by two men while they shout, "Die, Muslim, die!" That same night, a 31-year-old student of Pakistani descent is also attacked.

September 15, 2001

Ceres, CA: Surjit Singh Samra, 69, leaves for his daily walk Sunday morning, but never returns to the family's home in Ceres, which is just outside Modesto, California. His body is found in a canal September 18th. Police are currently investigating to determine whether the man was murdered or died of natural causes.

San Francisco, CA: Sean Fernandes, a 26-year-old Indian Catholic is attacked while walking with a white Australian friend in the early

Stephen Lee

219

morning. An unidentified man approaches the pair, calls Fernandes a "dirty Arab," and punches him and the friend. The attacker also allegedly directs an ethnic slur at Clarke and told him, "Your friend is Arab, and we kill Arabs." Fernandes' friend is stabbed in the ensuing brawl and remains hospitalized in critical condition.

San Gabriel, CA: Adel Karas, a 48-year-old storeowner of Egyptian descent, is gunned down in his import shop.

Tulsa, OK: Kimberly Lowe, a 21-year-old full-blood Creek Native American, is killed when she and several Native friends are followed and harassed by a vehicle of white males. The males throws items at the car and yells "Go back to your own country!" Lowe, the driver, stops the car and gets out to confront the males, at which point the attackers drive and pin her against another vehicle, then back up and run over her again.

Mesa, AZ: First-degree murder charge is filed in shooting of Mesa Sikh, Balbir Singh Sodhi, 49. Forty-two-year-old Frank Roque is charged with first degree murder and is also charged with attempted murder in the two other attacks and three counts of drive-by shooting. Saad Saad, a 35-year-old male of Lebanese descent, is the owner of the Mobil station in Scottsdale where the second shooting occurred. It is reported that Roque shouted, "I stand for America all the way," as he was handcuffed Saturday night.

Dallas, TX: A Pakistani grocer, Waqar Hasan, is found shot to death in his grocery store.

September 16, 2001

Eugene, OR: A 54-year-old California woman is arrested for trying to pull the turban off the head of a Sikh man at a highway rest stop.

San Diego, CA: On Sunday evening, an explosion from what was apparently a cherry bomb on the sidewalk outside the Islamic Center of San Diego forces worshippers to evacuate the building during a prayer service.

Stony Brook, NY: Shots are fired at the home of an Indo-American, a graduate of Stanford University. No injuries are reported.

September 17, 2001

Beverly Hills, CA: A women at a bagel shop wearing a Koranic charm on her neck sits down with a friend and is openly disparaged by another woman. The perpetrator accusingly yells, "Look what you people have done to my people" and lunges at the victim, but held back by one of the men with her. The victim calls police, and the woman continues to make derogatory comments. No one comes to her aid, and when it is all over, the owner goes over to the perpetrators and offers to pack their lunch and apologizes for any inconvenience.

Encino, CA: An Afghan Restaurant is set on fire at about 1:40 A.M., causing $30,000 in damages. It is unclear as of yet whether the case of arson can be categorized as a hate crime.

Fremont, CA: Afghan restaurant in Fremont is attacked with bottles and rocks.

Los Angeles, CA: A sign on the freeway reads "Kill all Arabs."

Oxnard, CA: A Sikh employee at an Oxnard convenience store is thrown to the ground and beaten by four men during a robbery. The case is being investigated as a possible hate crime.

Palmdale, CA: Reports of shots fired into a convenience store.

Quartz Hill, CA: Murhaf Maida's store on Avenue L is hit by four shots. This is the second attack on his store in three days.

Sacramento, CA: Sikh temple in West Sacramento is vandalized.

San Gabriel, CA: A woman wearing Muslim clothing is shopping at the Albertson's on Garey and Foothill when a Caucasian woman begins attacking her and yells, "America is only for white people." The victim is taken to emergency.

San Antonio, TX: Ashraf Khan, 32, is asked to leave his first-class seat on a Delta Airlines flight set for Dallas. According to Khan, the pilot said, "I'm not going to take you.

Myself and my crew are not safe flying with you. They don't feel safe."

Parma, OH: A man rams his car into the Islamic Center of Cleveland in the early hours of morning. No one is injured.

September 18, 2001

Berkeley, CA: More than 100 protestors clog the lobby of UC Berkeley's student publication, *The Daily Californian*, demanding an apology for an editorial cartoon that one student claims as "a vile form of ethnic characterization." `

Palmdale, CA: A note is posted at a public high school saying that the World Trade Center attacks would be avenged with a school massacre. The anonymous note lists the names of several Muslim students.

September 19, 2001

Washington D.C.: Satpreet Singh, a 21-year-old web designer, is shot at by a man in a blue pickup truck on U.S. Interstate 15.

September 20, 2001

Rio Arriba, NM: A Sikh community in the northern New Mexico county, Rio Arriba, reports numerous cases of harassment.

Wiggins, MS: Hasnain Javed, a student of Pakistani descent, is detained by authorities for immigration violations. Placed in a large jail dormitory, he is beaten by inmates throughout the night as they yell

221

derogatory remarks. He is eventually transferred and released.

Tacoma, WA: An arson attempt is made on the city's only synagogue. Sunday's attempt is the third apparent hate crime since the 9/11 attacks. A week earlier, the message "Zionism plus U.S. equals 5,000 dead," was found spray-painted on the synagogue's parking lot.

September 24, 2001

Huntington Beach, CA: An elderly Iranian receives a verbal assault while out for a walk on Monday morning. In the assault, a white male drove past the couple, made an abrupt U-turn, parked the car in a side street and approached the couple on foot while threatening them and demanding to know where they were from. Steven James McManus, 43, is indicted as a suspect.

September 25, 2001

Tempe, AZ: A 19-year-old student of Indian descent at Arizona State University is pushed to the ground, punched and kicked in a parking lot near University Drive and McAllister Avenue at around 1 A.M. During the assault, the attackers makes anti-Muslim remarks.

Also in Arizona, 42-year-old, Frank Silva Roque, the man suspected of killing Balbir Singh Sodhi, is indicted on nine charges, including first-degree murder, drive-by shooting, and endangerment.

September 28, 2001

Lancaster, CA: Two men in a white truck follow a Latino man— apparently mistaken as of Middle Eastern descent—to his home and beat him in his house. Mark Martin, 20, and Timothy Martin, 35, have been indicted on suspicion of assault and burglary against Gerald Pimental, 47.

San Francisco, CA: The Iranian American-owned City Blend Café has its windows smashed in. The owner is an outspoken critic of hate crimes and was the focus of a *San Francisco Chronicle* profile a week earlier.

September 29, 2001

Reedley, CA: A Yemeni grocer Abdo Ali Ahmed, 51, is killed at his convenience store after having received a death threat and a series of racial slurs.

September 30, 2001

San Diego, CA: Swaran Kaur Bhullar, a Sikh woman, was stopped at red light in her car on Miramar Road when two men on a motorcycle pulled up and attacked her. She is subsequently yanked from her car and stabbed twice in the head. She is rushed to the emer-gency room and released later in the day.

October 1, 2001

Ontario, CA: An unidentified man throws a molotov cocktail at a hotel window. The room was occupied by a man of Middle Eastern descent.

October 5, 2001

Greensboro, NC: Yasir Hassan, a Pakistani student on a student visa at the University of North Carolina at Greensboro, is attacked along with his friend in the front yard of his house by two truck and two carloads of men. He is punched and hit by a beer bottle in the head.

October 21, 2001

Anaheim, CA: A Diamond Bar man of South Asian descent is attacked outside of a bar by a group of Asian men. The victim, a physical therapist at USC University hospital, suffers a shattered jaw and is released from the hospital Monday.

November 18, 2001

San Diego, CA: Horatio Plascencia, 30, attacks a Middle Eastern service clerk with a screwdriver.

Palermo, NY: The Sikh Temple, Gobind Sadan USA, is severely damaged by an arson fire.

December 25, 2001

Washington D.C.: An Arab American Secret Service Agent en route to Texas to protect President Bush is asked to de-board an American Airlines flight.

December 29, 2002

Columbus, OH: The Islamic Center of Columbus suffers over $100,000 in damage after vandals drilled holes in the floor, desecrated copies of the Koran, and pulled water pipes from the walls flooding and saturating the mosque.

January 8, 2002

San Diego, CA: Horatio Plascencia, 40, pleaded guilty to battery during a hate crime in his November 18 attack on a Middle Eastern service station clerk. He is sentenced to six years in prison.

Salt Lake City, UT: James Herrick, 32, who attempted to set fire to a Pakistani American family's business, is sentenced to more than four years of prison.

List of Sources:

Asian Pacific American Legal Center (www.apalc.org): Compilation of Hate Crimes *Arizona Republic* (www.arizonarepublic.com): 09/26/01, 09/7/01

Associated Press (wire.ap.org): 09/18/01

CNN Online Reporting (www.cnn.com): 09/15/01, 09/20/01

Contra Costa Times (www.contracostatimes.com): 09/19/01

The Council on American Islamic Relations (www.cair-net.org)

Stephen Lee

223

The Daily Californian (www.dailycal.org): 09/19/01

Dallas Morning News (www.dallasnews.com): 09/17/01

Detroit Free Press (www.freep.com)

The Guardian (www.guardian.co.uk)

Indian American Center for Political Awareness (www.iacfpa.org): Emails dated 09/11/01, 09/17/01, 09/18/01

Institute of Global Communications (www.igc.org)

James and Grace Lee Boggs Center to Nurture Community Leadership (www.boggscenter.org)

The London Globe (www.londonobserver.com)

Los Angeles Commission on Human Relations (www.ci.la.ca.us/hra/)

The Los Angeles Times (www.latimes.com): 9/12/01, 09/18/01, 9/24/01, 10/02/01, 10/03/01, 10/09/01, 10/12/01, 10/15/01, 10/23/01

The Nation (www.thenation.com)

New California Media (www.ncmonline.com)

New Left Review (www.newleftreview.net)

The New York Times (www.nytimes.com): 09/13/01, 09/18/01, 09/22/01

Newsday Online Reporting (www.newsday.com): 09/13/01

Nichi Bei Times (www.nichibeitimes.com)

Office of Cook County State Attorney Richard A. Devine (www.statesattorney.org): Press Release

Philippines News Link (www.philnews.com/content.htm)

The Record: 09/14/01

Pacific News Service (www.pacificnews.org)

Sacramento Bee (www.sacbee.com): 09/18/01

San Francisco Chronicle (www.sfgate.com/chronicle): 09/13/01

San Diego Tribune (www.uniontrib.com): 10/05/01

San Jose Mercury News (www.bayarea.com): 09/18/01, 09/19/01

The Village Voice (www.villagevoice.com)

The Washington Post (www.washingtonpost.com): 09/24/01, 11/28/01

www.sikh.org

Yahoo! News (www.yahoo.com): 09/20/01

UCLA Asian American Studies Center
3230 Campbell Hall, 405 Hilgard Avenue
Los Angeles, California 90095-1546

Tel. (310) 825-2974/Fax (310) 206-9844
website www.sscnet.ucla.edu/aasc
Director: Don T. Nakanishi /dtn@ucla.edu

UCLA Asian American Studies

Asian American Studies addresses a rapidly changing global society, one that is marked by cultural, political, and demographic shifts and trends within, across, and outside California and the United States. Interdisciplinary in nature, Asian American Studies is changing, bridging, and infusing the classic concerns of racial and ethnic relations, immigration and labor studies, literature and cultural studies, women, gender, and sexuality studies, and the visual and media arts with new ideas, new images, and new social applications.

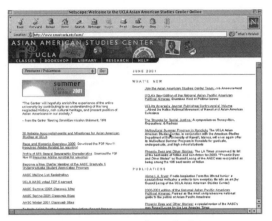

www.sscnet.ucla.edu/aasc

Since 1969, the UCLA Asian American Studies Center has "sought to enrich the experience of the entire university by contributing to an understanding of the long neglected history, rich cultural heritage, and present position of Asian Americans in our society," (Steering Committee to establish the UCLA Asian American Studies Center). Thirty years later, Asian American Studies and the Center at UCLA are making important educational and intellectual contributions to American higher education in terms of pedagogy, research, and strengthening campus and community linkages nationally.

Teaching and Degree Programs

UCLA has one of the largest teaching programs in Asian American Studies in the nation, and has been one of two major sites for the training of Asian American Studies scholars for the past three decades. The Center annually offers 60-70 classes that enroll over three thousand students. It also has an undergraduate specialization/minor, and a Bachelor of Arts and a Master of Arts degree program. The M.A. program, established in 1972, held its 25th anniversary in 2002. In addition, the M.A. program has diversified to offer joint degrees with the Department of Community Health Sciences amd with the School of Social Welfare. UCLA produces more doctoral dissertations on Asian American Studies topics than any other university, and trains future scholars through its many departments that have permanent Asian American faculty.

Faculty

The program's teaching faculty and faculty advisory committee are nationally, internationally and professionally recognized for their achievements in scholarship, teaching, and community service in the areas of: Anthropology, Law, Library and Information Science, Ethnomusicology, Geography, Medicine, Education, Psychiatry, Political Science, East Asian Languages and Culture, Economics, Asian American Literature, English and Creative Writing, History, Psychology, Public Health, Social Welfare, Urban Planning, Film and Television, Sociology, Nursing, and Management (see listing of Faculty Advisory Committee).

Research

Since its founding in 1969, the UCLA Asian American Studies Center has attempted to document, analyze, and forecast the contemporary, historical, and future experiences and concerns of peoples of Asian and Pacific Islander heritage in the United States through scholarly, policy-oriented, applied, and creative forms of inquiry. Research includes: sponsored research and collaborative projects; affiliated research institutes; support for individual faculty members; collaborative creative projects with campus and community organizations including museums, historical societies, and civic and professional leaders; publications and multimedia projects, archival and data-collection activities, and the training of new scholars, policy analysts, and creative artists.

UCLA affiliated institutes include: Center for EthnoCommunications; UCLA/VA/ RAND MedTep Center for Asian Pacific American Medical Outcomes Research; and the Joint Public Policy Research Institute of the Asian American Studies Center and Leadership Education for Asian Pacifics (LEAP). The Asian American Studies Center was officially designated as one of 60 new national Census Information Centers.

UCLA Asian American Studies Center Press

UCLA has the only academic press that publishes works on Asian and Pacific Americans. The Press views Asian and Pacific Americans as "active participants" in the making and interpreting of their history. During the past ten years, the Center's Press produced over 100 publications, including 30 issues of the *Amerasia Journal*, 30 books, 13 directories and reports, 12 bibliographies and archival collection guides, and 20 issues of CrossCurrents. New areas of scholarship published by *Amerasia* include theory and practice in Asian American Studies; race and Asian Americans; sexuality; religion; and special issues on Pacific Islanders, Filipinos, and Asian Indians, and forthcoming issues on Latin America, on Korean American history, and on Asian American literature.

The Center, in conjunction with the University of Hawaii Press, also produces a entitled series "Intersections: Asian and Pacific American Transcultural Studies."

The Center's Press also works with other organizations including the Simon Wiesenthal Museum of Tolerance, the Smithsonian Institute, the Chinese Historical Society, and Visual Communications to produce books on topics ranging from American garment workers to independent Asian and Pacific American film and video.

Amerasia Journal Subscriptions

Amerasia Journal is the foremost, most comprehensive and leading interdisciplinary journal on Asian Americans for thirty years, published three times annually. 200+ pages per issue, with illustrations. $35.00 annually for individuals, $55.00 for libraries.

Articles and books for review should be submitted directly to: The Editor, *Amerasia Journal* at the Center's address; orders should be addressed to Publication Orders. For a listing of available back issues from 1971-2001, please see the centers website: www.sscnet.ucla.edu/aasc.

UCLA Asian American Studies Reading Room

The Reading Room Library houses the most extensive archive on Asian and Pacific Islanders in the nation. Its holdings include 5,000 books and monographs, 30 Asian Pacific ethnic and regional newspapers, over 300 community and campus newsletters, and 5,000 pamphlets. The Reading Room also develops indexed bibliographies, electronic reference aids and guides.

In collaboration with UCLA's University Research Library, the Center has established The Asian American Movement Collection, Japanese American Research Project, the Chinese American Archives, the Korean American Research Project, and others. The Reading Room welcomes community users and is open during the academic year from 10:00 AM to 3:00 PM.

Student/Community Projects (S/CP)

Student Community Projects serves as academic advisors for the Bachelor of Arts and Minor in Asian American Studies. S/CP also serves as a liaison between Asian and Pacific Islander Communities and the Center by coordinating student internships and field studies projects to enhance academic study and to foster practical experiences on community issues and organizations. Student empowerment and activism have been intrinsic to the Center's development since its inception. S/CP sponsors student organizations including the Asian Pacific Coalition, a coalition of more than twenty API student organizations at UCLA. S/CP also serves in an advisory capacity, especially on issues of student leadership, programming support, and organizational development. With other campus and community organizations, S/CP coordinates the annual Community Research Roundtable, bringing together scholars, researchers, students and community leaders.

Asian Americans on War and Peace is the first book to respond to the events of September 11, 2001 from Asian American perspectives, from the vantage point of those whose lives and communities in America have been forged both by war and by peace. Twenty-four scholars, writers, activists, and legal scholars have written for this collection. Together, their voices reveal how Asians, Asian Americans, South Asians, Arabs, and others view the future of the planet in relation to the events of both yesterday and today. We join others who continue to question both the ongoing crisis of the American presence in the Middle East, and the concurrent crisis of civil liberties and democracy in the United States.

Since 1971, the UCLA Asian American Studies Center through its faculty and students, and teaching, research, and publications, has shaped the scholarly and public dialogue around Asians in the Americas.

Russell C. Leong is the editor of *Amerasia Journal* and Adjunct Professor of English at UCLA.

Don T. Nakanishi is Director of the UCLA Asian American Studies Center and Professor of Education and Asian American Studies.

Book Design: Mary Uyematsu Kao

www.sscnet.ucla.edu/aasc

© Moustafa Bayoun
© Grace Lee Bogg
© Jeff Chan
© Frank Chi
© Arif Dirli
© Jessica Hagedor
© Jerry Kan
© Amitava Kuma
© Vinay L
© Stephen Le
© Russell C. Leon
© Mari J. Matsuc
© Janice Mirikitar
© Don T. Nakanish
© Ifti Nasir
© Angela E. O
© David Palumbo-Li
© Vijay Prasha
© Roshni Rustomji-Kerr
© Susan Kiyomi Serran
© Eric K. Yamamot
© Michael F. Yamamot
© James N. Yamazal
© Helen Z